GUILTY at GUNPOINT

GUILTY at GUNPOINT

How the Government Framed Me

Crime & Corruption in the Department of Justice, FDA, and Big Pharma

Paul Singh

SCIENCE LITERARY BOOKS
A Singh Global Initiative
Menlo Park / San Francisco

Published by:
Science Literacy Books
Menlo Park San Francisco

To contact the publisher, please email
Paul@ScienceLiteracyBooks.com

Or write to: Singh Global Initiatives/Science Literacy Books
P.O. Box 7716
Menlo Park, CA-94026

Science Literacy Books website address:
www.ScienceLiteracyBooks.com

Manufactured in the United States and printed on acid free paper.

Paperback Edition ISBN 978-0-9970541-8-7
ePub3 eBook ISBN: 978-1-949454-10-9
Kindle eBook ISBN: 978-1-949454-11-6

Library of congress has catalogued the paperback Edition as follows:
Library of Congress Control Number: 2018908684
Includes Bibliographical references and Index

I dedicate this book to all those who have fought and continue to fight for truth, equality, peace and Justice and stood their ground against insurmountable odds.

—From my Prison Cell - Author

Author's Note

This is a book of non-fiction and is based on my own personal experience, the research and investigation that I conducted, legal analysis of evidence based on statutory and criminal case law, court records, and media reports. It is a book of reporting and commentary on an issue of urgent and enduring public interest – the crisis in our courts and our criminal justice system.

Individuals who worked in law enforcement, government agencies, the courts, and other public employees and officials, and some people directly involved in my case are identified by their real names. Individuals who are private citizens are identified only by a fictional name where indicated in the text. Any resemblance between these fictional names and any real person is strictly coincidental.

I am a physician, and my own case arose from the birth control devices I prescribed in good faith to my clients. I learned a great deal about the law while I was involved in the investigation of my case, the court proceedings that followed, and the prison sentence that I was compelled to serve. However, this is not a book of legal advice, and it does not take the place of consultation with an appropriate professional about legal issues that the reader may be facing.

CONTENTS

1. **My Opening Statement Before the People's Court** **13**
   - Case Background 13
   - Government Corruption, Prosecutorial and Judicial Misconduct 17
2. **The Story Leading up to My Conviction** **27**
   - The FDA and Big Pharma's Incestuous Relationship 27
   - Medical Board Investigation and Decision 41
   - March 28, 2012 - FDA Raids My Office 49
   - Facing the Wrath of My Patients 72
   - FDA Urges Medical Board to Reopen the Case 83
     - Medical Board Files Charges 83
     - Review of FDA's Discovery Documents 85
     - August, 2014: Medical Board Hearing 100
     - September 5, 2014: Accepting Medical Board's Decision 108
3. **Guilty at Gunpoint** **115**
   - Mounting Threats of Arrest and Indictment 115
   - My Conference Call with a Former Prosecutor 137
   - Federal Government – A Story of Sodom and Gomorrah 154
   - My Inner Turmoil Leading up to the Court Date 172
   - August 24, 2015: Pleading Guilty Under the Gun 176

4. Moving Forward – Into the Sink of Debauchery 189

Fraudulent Alteration of My "Personal Statement" 189

The Probation Department's Showbiz - Cut-and-Paste Reports 194

Defense's Pretenses Personified – Complicity with Government Crimes 197

Defense Attorney's Pre-Sentence Report 201

March 7, 2016: Prison Sentence 212

Two Sets of Rules 220

Final Thoughts 227

5. Applicable Law - Government's Criminal Misconduct **229**

Brady Violations: Withholding Exculpatory Evidence 230

Omissions & Concealments: Mishandling, Mistreating, and Destroying Evidence 237

Criminal Conspiracy, Collusion, False Statements, and Cover-ups 239

Fabrication of Evidence, Perjury, Forgery, and Fraud 242

Misrepresentation: Fraudulent Inducement of Patients and Witnesses 247

Fraud on the Court 251

Probation Department's Dereliction of Duty 260

Prosecutorial and Judicial Misconduct 263

Witness Tampering: Obstruction of Justice 273

The Due Process of Law: American-Style "Justice" 277

The Burden of Proof: The "Evidence" 283

False Statements to the Media to Arouse Public Indignation 287

Fraudulently Induced "Restitution" and Civil Suits 294

"Mail Fraud Statute": Archaic Laws Vaguely and Corruptly Employed 304
Violations of U.N. Charter, International Conventions, Human Rights and the International Court of Justice 308
Acknowledgements **317**
Resource List **319**

When Government wants to commit a crime, it must enlist people, and whenever you enlist more than one person, there is always the risk that the other person will spill the beans.

—Howard Zinn, my friend and the author of *A People's History of the United States*

CHAPTER 1

MY OPENING STATEMENT BEFORE THE PEOPLES COURT

Case Background

I CONDUCTED SCIENTIFIC RESEARCH AND WROTE ON MANY subject matters in my life, but I never once thought that I would be writing a book about the U.S. government, a government that has now become a full-time servant of corporations. But here I am in my prison cell writing about the inconceivable.

After working hard for four decades, devoting thirty years to science education and research, advocating for the rights of the poor, and financially helping indigent patients, everything was taken away from me in a heartbeat. I lost my license to practice medicine, and my financial, physical, family, and spiritual health were destroyed. All of this happened because an FDA agent told me that it was okay to continue using a brand of IUD that he later stated I shouldn't have used and built his entire case against me on that point. In other words, I was set up and framed. All of this was done to support Big Pharma and a company that was selling a birth control device at a price that was marked up a million percent. And this is a conservative estimate.

This publicly traded, profit-driven pharmaceutical giant is Teva, which is one of five drug makers allegedly responsible for our opioid crisis and the deaths of 111,000 people in this country in 2015 and 2016. There were also thousands of class-action lawsuits pending with hundreds already settled by Teva for billions of dollars during the same years — 2010-2015 — the years of the FDA's criminal investigation of me. (A crime is defined as an act that the law makes punishable per Black's Law Dictionary.) The lawuits against Teva were filed for predatory price fixing; price collusion; bribing government officials, doctors, pharmacists, and those in sales; and illegally selling their products in the United States and around the world (Exhibit 8.)* It is hard to find a country where Teva has not bribed government officials. Its full financial relationship with the U.S. FDA is yet to be unravelled.

Between 2010 and 2015, TEVA engaged in unlawful agreements to allocate customers, use unapproved off-label opioid painkillers, downplay risks while exaggerating benefits, and use false advertising and deceptive and fraudulent marketing schemes contributing to our national epidemic of opioid addiction, while concealing scientific evidence of the dangers of these drugs (Exhibit 8). It is ironic that

*Exhibit numbers in this book refer to exhibits in the companion book, *The Death of the Rule of Law: A Companion Guide to Guilty at Gunpoint,* which focuses on the end of the rule of law, as it relates to the story in this book.

during the same years the FDA was busy building a fake case against me for not using the IUD made by Teva, which I did not use because my patients couldn't afford it, Teva was engaged in criminal activity to help it eliminate competition for its birthcontrol device, T Cu-380A, in collusion with the FDA (Exhibits 1 and 11). Teva's brand of copper IUD called the ParaGard was sold at price-tags deemed nothing short of financially criminal in the People's Court of America. Teva is an Israel-based drug company whose claim to fame is being the good guy and the most prominent manufacturer of, and advocate for, more affordable generic products. At the end of the day, what matters to our federal government, a nanny state for Big Pharma, is one thing: profit over people, no matter how grievous the economic consequences for the rest of us – the 99 percent of the population that is struggling every day to survive.

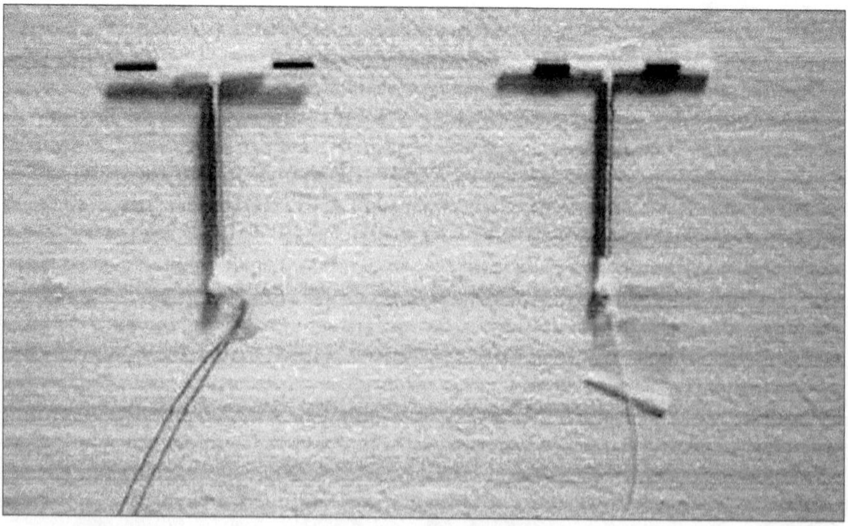

Exhibit 1*: Photos of the CU-380A IUDs discussed throughout this book. Left: German-made CU-380A IUD, T-Safe. Right: U.S.-made CU-380A IUD, ParaGard.

T-Safe Cu-380A IUD is the number one Copper IUD brand used by women in Western Europe, an IUD with fewer side effects compared to other brands of the same drug. 170 million women worldwide use T-Safe and other brands, sold at a fraction of the price of ParaGard. T-Safe is approved by the German FDA (Federal Ministry of Health: The Federal Institute for Drugs and Medical Devices [Bundesninstitute fur Arznemittel und Mediziproduckte, BfArM]). ParaGard sold in the United States is used by only 0.001 percent of women using Copper IUDs worldwide.

Source U.S. Data 2002 and European Data 2006: Guttmacher Policy Institute Policy Review. University of Hawaii Data 2010.

*This picture and caption are taken from Exhibit 1 in the companion book, *The Death of the Rule of Law*

Bernie Sanders called it "the Establishment," I prefer to call it the revolving-door establishment. This refers to those inside the protective bubble allowing the criminal behavior of politicians, bankers, Wall Street, the three branches of the government, the military-industrial complex, and the media all of whom work together to protect the interests of the oligarchs. Even our universities, law schools, business schools, medical schools and scientific institutions are now on board with the Establishment in exchange for cash and to influence what is taught. The rest of us have no advocates and are so brain-washed that many cannot acknowledge the reasons we are getting poorer and struggling more every day.

Government Corruption, Prosecutorial and Judicial Misconduct

My personal story is not about justice. Justice is a farfetched idea, and no one knows for sure what justice is, but we can certainly sense when there is an injustice. This book is about the law and the assumed principle that no one is above the law. At least they shouldn't be. The reality is, with most laws written by lobbyists and corporate lawyers, it's easy to see how a conflict of interest contributes to corruption and the protection of corporate profits. How can we expect politicians to argue with the same people whose money got them elected in the first place?

My experience proves that prosecutors and government agents, indirectly and sometimes directly engaged in working for large corporations, are above the law and have absolute immunity from prosecution for commission of any crime of their choosing against anyone, anytime, anywhere. Such behavior by government agents can be conceivable only under tyrannical governments. It is also important to understand that tyranny is not giving government power, tyranny is giving government power that is not regulated and controlled. Charles Montesquieu, one of the influences on the founding of our nation once said, "There is no crueler tyranny than that which is perpetuated under the shield of the law and in the name of justice." One of the biggest problems we face in America today is the unhindered and unlimited power granted to government agents and Department of Justice (DOJ) prosecutors. One hundred years after Montesquieu, Lord Acton said that "power corrupts, and absolute power corrupts absolutely," a sentiment that few among us can dispute today.

As I take you on this journey, you'll see an outcome that wasn't just an inadvertent miscarriage of justice, but a carefully crafted plan on the part of the DOJ and the FDA to make an example of one doctor so all Ob/Gyns would get the message. And it took concealment of evidence, fabrication, conspiracy and collusion, cover-ups, perjury, obstruction of justice, violation of due process of the law, fraudulent inducement of patients, intimidation of witnesses, and fraud on the court, to get the job done.

I immigrated to the United States from India nearly four decades ago to avoid persecution for exercising my inborn right to free speech and opinion. Our family was always poor because we stood for what was right. Fighting corruption and defending the rights of the poor is not a recipe for riches, it only invites a more difficult life. So, I decided to leave the struggle of fighting it behind, and moved to the United States, never thinking that I would be going from the frying pan into the fire.

When I visited India in 1992, my siblings wanted to hear all about my life here. One of my brothers, six years older and wiser asked me, "What about corruption in America?" (The word corrupt is defined in

Black's Law Dictionary as something done by a person that is "unlawful and has depraved motive"). It was a legitimate question coming from someone who lived in one of the most corrupt third-world countries on the planet at that time. I responded, "No, I don't think there is corruption." He burst out laughing. In retrospect, I guess he was trying to tell me that it exists everywhere in varying degrees, but I was in denial, or perhaps not mature enough yet to understand human nature to the extent I do today. As the great American lawyer, Gerry Spence stated in his book, *With Justice for None: Destroying an American Myth*, the difference between corruption in a third-world country and the United States is "one of form not of substance."

I am embarrassed to tell you that it took me so long to understand that the same corruption existed in the United States that I saw back home, only worse in many unfathomable ways. I was not well informed in that sense. I was one in the bewildered herd and a victim of an "engineered consent" (a phrase of Edward Bernays) or "manufactured consent" (a phrase of Walter Lippman) like the rest of the American population and did not know how the system worked. It was harder for me to tell the difference, because the corruption in the United States was much subtler and executed through a vast propaganda machine, not to be easily detected by you and me. It was not the blatant corruption that I saw in India. Here in the United States, it was covert corruption, done behind the scenes, privy to only the most elite and involved a false narrative from our government and support of those lies on the part of the media. Indoctrination is subtle but present. I naively viewed corruption using the model I had left behind in India; a cop taking cash in exchange for turning a blind eye on something he'd seen, for example. The possibility of more sobering corruption, masterminded by the ruling class, never entered my mind.

I pled guilty on August 24, 2015 with a knife pointed to my jugular vein, (an apt metaphor for someone like me pinned against the wall by a bully a million times my size, backed by the full faith and unlimited almighty power of the government of the United States). I was sentenced on March 7 of 2016 for two and a half years: six months to be served in federal prison followed by one year under house arrest, with my ankle hooked up with monitoring devices, and then followed by an additional year of supervisory release. (Exhibit 23.) The only other option given to me by my defense lawyers was to come up with $750,000, more or less my entire net worth, if I made a choice to plead not guilty, with no clear answer as to how many millions it would cost to reveal the truth about the government, or whether I would even be allowed to disclose the truth. I had only one month of emergency funds remaining in my bank account and three months of emergency funds in my IRA retirement account. I learned of other cases during this process in which the government had managed to conceal information although millions had been poured into defense to get that information out. Odds were high that the government would continue to conceal facts even if I had millions to put toward fighting them. This simplified my defense to one sentence, "Yes, I am guilty."

I don't expect you to believe me when I say I was totally innocent, but I am confident you will believe everything by the time you finish reading the story in this book and reviewing the evidence in its Companion book, *The Death of the Rule of Law.* The former CIA whistleblower, Kevin Shipp has repeatedly said, it is extremely difficult for the American people to cross that psychological barrier to believe that our government is capable of wholesale violations of our domestic laws and our constitution, the supreme law of our land. I name real names and provide all the evidence you could want (barring tons of additional evidence that the government is still hiding). It is a no-brainer that I cannot give you that part of the evidence that the government refuses to make public. But I have enough to convince you of my claims.

Glenn Greenwald, the famous American journalist, and Constitutional and Civil Liberties Lawyer, writes about a two-tiered legal system (one for the rich and one for the poor) in his book, *With Liberty and Justice for Some: How the Law is Used to Destroy Equality and Protect the Powerful.* My case would have been a fitting example for him as Greenwald describes in detail how the system of corruption and crime works in our "land of the free" and the home of the brave.

Sidney Powell, a renowned criminal defense attorney, wrote in her book, *Licensed to Lie: Exposing Corruption in the Department of Justice*, that "When anyone other than a prosecutor hides evidence or makes false statements in court or to a government agent, it is a federal crime or crimes, perjury, obstruction of justice, false statements to a federal agent, subornation of perjury, witness tampering and so on" (*Licensed to Lie*, pg. 397 line 4 — 7.) But what about the federal prosecutors and federal agents? Do the same laws bind them? The answer is they can lie, commit perjury, fabricate evidence, and not be held accountable for any wrongdoing because they are exempt from those laws of the land.

Powell refers to these corrupt prosecutors as "misguided, ignorant, overzealous, ambitious, narcissistic, and dishonest prosecutors, some of whom destroyed innocent people while they deliberately withheld evidence they knew contradicted their case, who are making daily decisions that affect all of our lives and the very future of our country." "Their conduct," she says, "stands in sharp contrast to the oath by which they swore to 'uphold and defend the Constitution of the United States of America" (*Licensed to Lie*, pg. 413.). And I like to remind my readers that the Constitution of the United States is the supreme law of the land, it is the law of all laws, it supersedes all federal statutes and regulations, and laws enacted by Congress or decisions made by the President of the United States. Therefore, to violate the fundamental constitutional rights of a U.S. citizen by any government official under the color of law is a felony. Although it is true that the Constitution is subject to interpretation from time to time, it is also true that certain fundamental provisions in the bill of rights and civil rights are carved in stone and not subject to interpretation. That is why we have such language in the Constitution as "Congress shall make no law…" etc.

Almost everyone Powell names in *Licensed to Lie* who committed criminal acts of hiding information were promoted to more powerful positions in the Obama administration, an administration that has been among the least transparent of all administrations since the founding of our nation in 1776. Sidney Powell wrote in her book, "Corrupt prosecutors had extraordinary ascension to the top of the Criminal Division of the Department of Justice and promotions to the White House during the Obama administration." Referring to this cabal of prosecutors, she states that they have been promoted by Obama to postions of enormous power and influence despite their legacy of injustice. (pg 408)

I would be remiss if I failed to express my gratitude to Sidney Powell for showing tremendous courage and fearlessness in naming people in the DOJ for the first time in the history of the United States. She speaks fearlessly. I believe she had gone before me and paved the dangerous path for me to tread on.

I will be adding many more names to Powell's list in this book, all potential future promotions within the government for hiding exculpatory evidence and falsifying documents in my case. Given that many prosecutors are honest — and they must be for the system to function at least minimally, there are hundreds out there who are corrupt to the core. And corruption is now the criteria for seeking promotions in our judicial system. Those who do their job honestly in enforcing law, order, and justice are never rewarded or promoted. According to the Ninth Circuit Appellate Court Chief Justice, Judge Alex Kozinski, this is a problem for the honest prosecutors working in our government who want to uphold the Constitution and our laws by always doing what is right.

The Department of Justice has set up what is called, "the Center for Prosecutorial Integrity," to address issues of corruption in the Department of Justice. The Center for Prosecutorial Integrity is ironically part of this "Department of Justice." Thankfully, the DOJ at the very least acknowledges the following as some of the gravest types of prosecutorial misconduct that exists within the Department of Justice:

1. Withholding or delaying the release of exculpatory evidence.
2. Deliberately mishandling, mistreating or destroying evidence.
3. Allowing witnesses, they know or should know are not truthful to testify.
4. Pressuring defense witnesses not to testify.
5. Making false statements to the media that are designed to arouse public indignation.
6. Making improper or misleading statements to the jury.

Steve Weinberg incorporated additional categories of prosecutorial misconduct published on the Center for Public Integrity website of the Department of Justice on June 26, 2003:

7. Courtroom misconduct (making inappropriate or inflammatory comments; introducing or attempting to introduce inadmissible, inappropriate or inflammatory evidence; mischaracterizing the evidence or facts of the case to the court.
8. Hiding, destroying or tampering with evidence, case files or court records.
9. Using false or misleading evidence.
10. Harassing, displaying bias toward, or having a vendetta against the defendant or defendants counsel (including selective and vindictive prosecution).

In my case, the prosecutorial misconduct consisted of withholding exculpatory evidence that contradicted the DOJ's so-called evidence and proved my innocence. They broke the law in a number of ways: by destroying evidence, strong-arming a defense witness, lying to the media to incite public indignation, falsifying information, and engaging in a good number of other criminal activities inclusive of, but not limited to, all the concerns listed on DOJ's Integrity site in terms of the prosecutorial misconduct.

I challenge the government of the United States as a self-proclaimed nation under one God for "life, liberty, and justice for all" to open an independent investigation of my case. Let the independent investigators be the same as those in former U.S. Senator' Ted Stevens case. I'd like to see the outcome if an American hero, Judge, Emmet G. Sullivan, appointed Henry F. Schuelke III (the

United States vs. Theodore Stevens 2009) as an independent special prosecutor to investigate the Department of Justice attorneys, Patrick Delahunty, Kirk Sherriff, FDA agent Richard Pueschel, and others involved in my case. I would be remiss in suggesting my being framed was an unusual occurrence. I'd like to know what else these people have done. It can happen to anyone at any level.

I think you will find that the most disturbing part in all of this is the knowledge that it could happen to anyone, including you. You will believe me more as you delve deeper into this story. We should not take personal freedom for granted. Truth doesn't always win. Justice does not always prevail. Our freedom and civil liberties are being held hostage by large corporations and corrupt government agencies and branches.

In telling of my experience, I hope to tell the story of countless others who have suffered in silence. The time is long overdue for someone to reveal to the public the corruption in the United States government. Sidney Powell has taken the lead, and I follow with the hope that from now on, those who are insiders and know the truth will start speaking up until the public has a rude awakening of this formidable problem that *we the people* are facing together as a nation.

CHAPTER 2

THE STORY LEADING UP TO MY CONVICTION

FDA and Big Pharma's Incestuous Relationship

ON THE AFTERNOON OF AUGUST 17, 2010, TWO FOOD AND Drug Administration agents, an Asian American female, (whose identity has been concealed by the government throughout the investigation, before, during and after) and a white male, both in their forties, visited my Obstetrics/Gynecology office in Tehachapi, California.

The male agent, Richard Pueschel, will be a name you hear throughout this story because he was one of the leading architects and masterminds of the plan to find someone they could frame and use as an example, a plan that ended my career and devastated my family and me. Some of the things that happened are so outrageous you may wonder if I'm making any of it up. I assure you, this is the truth, not fiction. I did not know exactly what was going on until late in the game, which was far too late for me to do anything about it. In a book of fiction, we often see endings where justice wins out, and perpetrators are held responsible for their nefarious deeds. In my story, the bad guys are too powerful for anyone to fight, and justice isn't possible. I always believed that "we the people" ordained a Declaration of Independence in 1776, followed by a Constitution in 1787 with ten Amendments that gave us all an equality before the law until I went through my nightmare which changed my understanding of how things work in this "land of the free."

The two FDA agents identified themselves to my receptionist and asked if they could speak with the physician. My medical assistant, Sandra Johnson (pseudonym used to protect identity), brought them back into my office. I asked them how I could help. Both agents asked me if I could educate them about the IUDs that I prescribed and used in my office for my patients. (IUD stands for "Intra-Uterine Device," which is a device used for long-term birth control in women of fertile age, see Exhibit 1). I said I would be happy to explain. They did not say what brought them to my office. When I asked them the purpose of the visit, they said the FDA had just learned that physicians were using imported IUDs and that the FDA wanted to learn about these devices. I had no reason to question them further and was happy to oblige.

I went to one of my exam rooms and brought back the different kinds of IUDs I had been using. I informed them that there were two kinds of IUDs: those that were hormone-based and those that were hormone-free. The hormone-free IUDs were copper IUDs, because they were made from a copper coil, and were the ones I most frequently used in my medical practice. I told them that I rarely used the hormone-based IUD called Mirena.

"What specifically would you like to know about these IUDs?" I asked them as I placed the IUD drug packages in front of them. "Is there a problem with using these IUDs?"

They replied in unison that they did not know. Agent Pueschel stated that the FDA did not know much about them and wanted to learn more. He commented that it was all new to the FDA and they were trying to gather information. Agent Pueschel asked me to describe everything about the IUDs - what they were, how they worked, etc., including where I bought them from and how much I paid for them.

I educated both agents by telling them everything about IUDs that a gynecologist could teach people who don't have a relevant medical background. I informed them that I bought these copper IUDs from a Canadian distributor. I received weekly faxes from this distributor advertising the sale of these IUDs. I decided to buy copper IUDs after I verified that these IUDs were manufactured in Germany and Cu-380A IUD was CDC- recommended (Exhibit 2). I pulled the Copper IUDs and the package inserts out for the German-made Copper IUD, Cu-380A, manufactured by EurimPharm (trade name 'T-safe'), as well as the U.S. ParaGard, Cu-380A (trade name 'ParaGard'), manufactured by the U.S. company Teva, to show that they were the same product manufactured by two different pharmaceutical companies (Exhibit 1). I informed the agents that I primarily used the German-made Cu-380A copper IUD for most of my patients because it was so much cheaper but had also used the U.S. brand of Cu-380A, called the ParaGard from time to time. I informed them that I believed that the German generic that I bought from the Canadian distributor was of equal or superior quality to the U.S. brand ParaGard because my patients demonstrated fewer side effects from these IUDs and better outcomes overall. Then I showed them another copper IUD Cu-375, also made in Germany, endorsed by the World Health Organization but used only in Europe, not America, that I had occasionally used for patients who needed reliable birth control for no more than three years. I told them about the difference between the two German copper IUDs, explaining that the Cu-380A was good for ten years while the Cu-375 was good only for three years due to less copper coil, of only 375 square millimeters of copper as opposed to 380 square millimeters of copper in Cu-380A, as the names suggest. I informed them that I stopped using Mirena (the hormonal IUD) because, in my experience, Mirena had dangerous side effects. There were way too many class action lawsuits pending against Bayer, the maker of Mirena. I also explained how the hormonal IUD Mirena worked as opposed to the non-hormonal copper IUD.

As I got deeper into the discussion, my impatience with Big Pharma got the better of me. Everything I said from this point on could only be interpreted to be an indictment against the FDA's involvement with the U.S. manufacturer of the ParaGard, who I felt was fleecing patients by selling IUDs at predatory prices no average American woman could afford and no insurance company was willing to reimburse. "It really is all about money, isn't it?" I questioned the agents sarcastically. They remained silent and gently nodded their heads, giving me the impression that they agreed with me. I was on a roll and my medical assistant, who had heard some of it, said at the end of the day, "You were going at them about *something,* weren't you?"

I spoke my mind and said what I could while trying my best not to use harsh language or point fingers. I understood they were just employees of the FDA. I had known for a long time that the primary function of the FDA was to promote the interests of the food and drug industry and not so much to protect the health of the American consumer against dangerous foods and drugs, or against price gouging by Big Pharma. This was 2010, and I had already been a harsh critic of the FDA for several years. In fact, there is a video of me on YouTube speaking about FDA corruption that were posted by my fans in the audience.

I held the German and U.S. brands of copper IUD-380A, trade names, T-Safe and ParaGard in my hands and explained to the agents that they looked the same, worked by the same mechanism of action and had the same indications, uses, side effects and contraindications, and were the same drugs as described by their package drug Inserts that I laid in front of them. I educated the FDA agents as to how these IUDs were implanted, how they worked, and how the patient selection was made for suitability for a birth control method. I also told them that these IUDs that I most commonly used were effective for up to 10 years and were used as long-term contraception by women who wanted to avoid pregnancy for a very long time, but not to exceed 10 years. I informed them that the generic copper IUD Cu-380A I routinely used was the gold standard in all developed countries, and was CDC recommended. I went on with my rant, the whole purpose of which was to criticize the fact that the FDA was in bed with the U.S. drug cartel that compelled American women to buy the U.S. brand, ParaGard, at outrageous prices that few could afford. Both agents listened to me like two kindergarten students and did not say a word. I told them I saw no reason why patients had to buy these

IUDs from the U.S. at obscene prices when the same high-quality German made drug was available from Canada at a price they could afford. They listened to me very carefully and did not say a word. It was surreal. I was shaking inside, but I was not going to stop, I was going to speak my mind. *Someone had to do it*, I told myself.

It seemed like the agents paid close attention, sometimes only gently nodding in agreement. At least that was the impression they gave me through good eye contact. Their gentle demeanor further encouraged me to continue to speak my mind even though it was becoming somewhat strange to see them not say a word in response but seemingly continue to pay close attention to what I was saying.

The agents asked me if they could bring these samples of copper IUDs I used in my office back to the FDA's office for inspection. I readily gave them the samples I was holding in my hand. They asked me not to use these IUDs that I bought from Canada until they got back to me with the FDA verdict in terms of whether I was allowed to use IUDs that I purchased from the Canadian distributor. I promised that I would put the use of all IUDs on hold until the agents got back to me with the FDA's decision. Pueschel wanted to know the purchase price of the copper IUD and the name of the Canadian Pharmacy/distributor that I bought the IUDs from. I had trouble recalling the name of the Canadian pharmacy/distributor or the exact price of the IUD, because I had not placed an order for IUDs for a very long time, so I told him that I would look for an Invoice in my files and fax it to him as soon as I find one. The agents said they would be in touch with me, and they left my office. I found a copy of a facsimile that I had received from GetCanadianDrugs, that had the price of the drug and the name of the distributor and faxed it over to Pueschel, Attention to his name, the very next morning on August 18, 2010.

I instructed my medical assistant, Sandra Johnson, and receptionist, Mary Young (pseudonyms), to temporarily put on hold any IUD implantation appointments that were on the calendar until I got further instructions from the FDA. I also instructed my staff to explain to patients that we were waiting to get information from the FDA about the German T-Safes. Fortunately, we had only two patients scheduled for Cu-380A IUD insertions in the following two months, as verified by the appointment book. I was relieved to learn that, since the fewer patients we would have to inconvenience, the better.

One of the patients scheduled for implantation changed her mind and decided to go on a different birth control method after we temporarily postponed her IUD implantation appointment pending the FDA's verdict, while the other patient said she would rather wait for the FDA decision because she really wanted the copper IUD. We rescheduled a tentative appointment for her, subject to news from the FDA, but it had to be postponed three times because the FDA took so long to get back to me with their research and final verdict. I called the FDA about five weeks later to see if the agents had an answer. There was some phone tag between the male agent, Pueschel, and I. When I finally reached him, he said he was still working on it and did not yet have an answer from his superiors. He promised to call me back when I told him that we had to reschedule a patient a couple of times already.

Agent Pueschel went silent for a while, and just as I was beginning to worry about being kept in the dark, on October 12 of 2010, two months (fifty-six days to be precise) after the two agents' visit to my office, agent Pueschel called. He informed me that the Cu-375 IUD that I bought from Canada was not FDA approved. "What about the

Cu-380A?" I asked. He informed me that Cu-380A was approved but he emphasized that I must Fed-ex him my inventory of the Cu-375 because it was NOT approved by the FDA.

I expected him to say this because it was consistent with what I already knew. Cu-375, the 3-year-use copper IUD, was only used in Europe, Canada and the rest of the world, while the Cu-380A IUD was the only copper IUD that was FDA approved and most commonly used in the United States. Frankly, I felt a bit embarrassed by the negative thoughts I had about the FDA. Perhaps the FDA was not as corrupt as I thought. I admitted to myself that I was wrong and had been unnecessarily and excessively critical toward the FDA, and decided to tone it down from that point on.

I gathered all the Cu-375s I could from the exam rooms and immediately shipped them to the attention of FDA agent Richard Pueschel via certified mail, with his signature requested on the returned receipt. I did this on October 12, 2010, the same day within hours of receiving the phone call from Pueschel. I received the green acknowledgment card signed by agent Pueschel eight days later, on October 20 (Exhibit 7.)

It did upset me to have to return them since I was one of many physicians in the country researching the efficacy of the Cu-375 IUD compared to the Cu-380A. There was already published literature by U.S. researchers, but more was needed. In medicine, research must be conducted on a widespread basis to see if the same outcomes can be reproduced. Many doctors throughout the U.S. were conducting such research, and it was also being done in highly regarded institutions, such as Harvard and the University of Southern California. I wondered if other researchers knew that they could not use the Cu-375 and pondered whether they had sought special approval from the FDA to conduct research. The Cu-375 had been approved in Europe for decades, and their researchers found it very safe and highly effective for contraceptive use for up to three years.

I didn't dwell on it since it was a moot point now that I was forbidden from using the Cu-375. A year later, I found more Cu-375s when I was searching for some other medical supplies in the upstairs storage room in my office. I realized that I had ordered these Cu-375s three years prior, in May 2008. It had been so long that I had forgotten that I had so many of them. I decided to return the rest of the Cu-375 IUDs still in my possession to the Canadian distributor to get a refund, but those attempts proved unsuccessful. The supervisor at the distributor, Michael, stated that the timeline for the return of inventory had long passed. I argued that the IUDs still had years of shelf-life left and were years away from becoming expired. I also argued that the U.S. FDA did not allow their use in the U.S., therefore they were useless to me, but I did not win that argument. I had never had a problem returning inventory to any vendor previously. I could have sent these remaining IUDs to the FDA, but more than a year had gone by since my encounter with the FDA agents, and I had stopped using these IUDs. I did not think there was any point in sending the remaining IUDs to the FDA at that point. The important thing was that I immediately stopped using them, when the FDA instructed me to, on October 12, 2010.

After getting the green light to use the Cu-380A from FDA agent Pueschel, my medical assistant called the patient who had been rescheduled three times and set up an appointment for the implant. Prior to that, while awaiting the FDA's verdict between August 17, 2010, and October 12, 2010, I aggressively researched the FDA's interest in German - or European-made IUDs by doing Internet searches. The fact that the agents had pled ignorance about the FDA Discovery that these imported IUDs were being used by U.S. physicians sparked my own interest in finding out more.

I was able to access a lot of relevant information from the FDA website and other sources, which confirmed that the agents were truthful about the FDA recently becoming aware of the IUD issues because just weeks before their visit to my office, in July 2010. Teva, had complained to the FDA about physicians obtaining "counterfeit" ParaGard IUDs from the "Internet-based pharmacies." Teva also supposedly wrote and sent a letter to all "healthcare professionals" in July 2010, in which it complained about the counterfeit IUDs (with absolutely no reference made to equivalent legitimate European brands of Cu-380A IUDs). Then the FDA copied the language from Teva's letter and issued their own warning letter on July 22, supposedly addressing healthcare professionals, and cautioning them that these imported IUDs may or may not have been approved by regulatory agencies in the countries of their origin or may be counterfeit or illegal and potentially unsafe.

These drug safety concerns for these IUDs were Teva's and the FDA's primary concern, or so it seemed. The FDA's and Teva's concern sounded reasonable and legitimate. No one will disagree that any medical product whose safety cannot be verified, one that could be counterfeit, should be a concern to all of us. But what if there was a medical product that could be verified to have been made by a German drug maker, approved by the German regulatory agency for safety and quality? Was it illegal to use it then? There is no mention of any of this in the letter from the FDA. My independent research boosted my confidence that the agents were indeed telling me the truth about the FDA first becoming aware in 2010 of some IUD-related problems, bought by some physicians from web-based pharmacies without verification of the safety of these products. This was almost the exact time they came to interview me on August 17, 2010. The two FDA agents' visit to my office on this date now made sense.

I thoroughly searched my office to see if I ever received either of these letters from Teva or the FDA and I found neither. If I had received them, I would have remembered it. This is not the kind of thing a physician who cares about his medical license forgets. Getting a warning letter from the FDA, a federal agency, is important. I did find in a high stack of papers on my office-desk, a letter sent to me by the Canadian distributor of the generic German copper IUD. In it, the distributor warned all Ob/Gyns in the U.S. that Teva had made false claims to American physicians by alleging that all Cu-380A IUDs from Canada were counterfeit and warning doctors not to buy those brands and to buy only Teva's ParaGard - the only safe IUD. The letter also stated that their European 380A IUD manufacturer was challenging the veracity of Teva's false claims to American doctors, which was meant to eliminate competition for the equivalent generic product Cu-380A copper IUD. This letter from the distributor was apparently sent to all U.S. physicians to counter the FDA and Teva's claims of foreign generics of Teva's copper IUD brands were fake, unsafe, counterfeit, bought from web-based pharmacies and bought on the Internet, etc. Letter from the distributor suggested that Teva was trying to protect its profits and had resorted to a smear campaign to do it.

Apparently, this foreign drug company, the manufacturer of Cu-380A and its Canadian distributors were upset at the FDA — Teva alliance in saying that the U.S. brand, ParaGard, was the only genuine drug and that American women and their physicians must buy that brand or face the consequences for breaking the law.

According to this letter from the Canadian distributor, supported by the maker of the generic copper IUD, Teva was concerned that it was losing market share to the generic IUD as more and more patients and doctors in the U.S. chose not to buy the U.S. brand at quadruple the price of the European brands. The trend of physicians moving from ParaGard to the generic brands did not surprise me. The price of the ParaGard was beyond what most patients could afford, especially if insurance was going to reimburse only a small fraction of the cost, with the patient having to come up with several hundred dollars, provided that insurance covered this benefit at all. Nearly one third of the insurance companies simply did not.

During this two-month period, I made it a point to attend a two-day CME (continued medical education), Conference on Contraception that 400 Ob/Gyns from around the country attended for 16 CME credits. I discovered that one-third of the physicians attending the conference used the T-Safe Cu-380A made in Germany. This was demonstrated by a show of hands in the conference. Others who did not use the generic brand confirmed that they did not offer IUD services because patients could not afford to buy the U.S. brand, ParaGard. These physicians, all Ob/Gyns, did not wish to get involved with the patients' financial problems, so they just gave them a prescription to buy their IUD and return to have it inserted. Patients never came back with the ParaGard IUD because they could not afford it and their insurance would not reimburse them for it. Instead, these patients switched to another birth control method, even if they needed the copper IUD for medical reasons or simply went without it. There are medical conditions in which a copper IUD is the only birth control method that is safe and effective, so this was not a decision they made lightly.

My continued research on this topic further led me to discover much later that a Cu-380A IUD manufacturer had filed an application with the FDA for approval of their brand of the copper IUD. I was not able to verify the date of the maker's application. The name is not clear from reading the FDA's internal documents. Nor was I able to identify the manufacturer applicant's name. My guess is that it was one of the European Cu-380A IUD manufacturers. Considering the striking similarity in the language of both the FDA's and Teva's letters, one did not need to be a rocket scientist to decipher that the FDA letters to all "healthcare professionals and colleagues," sent almost simultaneously with Teva's letters (dated only two weeks apart), were prepared by the FDA in cahoots with Teva. That is why, sometimes I like to address the FDA as the FDC, because I think the FDA is more of a Food and Drug Cartel (FDC) than Food and Drug administration.

I later learned that on February 11, 2013, Teva filed a citizen's petition requesting that the FDA refrain from approving any Cu-380A IUD equivalent to Teva's brand. It is mind-boggling to believe that the female citizens of the United States would petition the U.S. government to not approve a drug that is safely manufactured with proper research presented to the FDA, that is available to them at a fraction of the price, and instead plead with the FDA to force them to buy the U.S brand at four times the price, a price that few American women of reproductive age could afford (Exhibit 9). The 25-page petition filed by Teva to the FDA claims that its brand, ParaGard, is superior to the applicant's Cu-380A and therefore, their IUD brand should not be allowed in the United States.

It is public knowledge that the FDA is funded by pharmaceutical companies. This creates a conflict of interest because, in order to get such funding approved, the FDA must keep Big Pharma happy.

So, it is not a stretch to assume that Teva worked with the FDA to protect its interests and stop the use of other copper IUDs, which are cutting into their profits.

As a seasoned biochemist, and a medicinal and biological chemist with an academic background in these disciplines, I was able to see within minutes of reading this petition that the claims made by Teva based on its research were bogus. Bogus research is considered genuine by the FDA if the research is conducted and submitted by Big Pharma. It reminded me of research papers by Monsanto, a company that makes genetically modified seeds and weed killers, a research conducted by Monsanto's scientists presented to the FDA, which the FDA accepted without criticism, while rejecting or marginalizing research papers submitted by independent researchers on Monsanto's products. That is what our FDA is today. During hearings, John Kerry told the FDA commissioner, Dr. Alderson, that the FDA had 'betrayed the American public' by approving 76,000 carcinogenic chemicals because of the FDA's financial relationship with the food and drug industry. The FDA accepted the fraudulent research data but refused to look at the data by independent researchers that showed that these chemicals were responsible for causing cancer. These chemicals were also responsible for the deaths of hundreds of thousands of people and animals around the globe. It could be millions of dead people, no one has an accurate count, and these were deaths caused directly and indirectly by Monsanto's products.

An example from my own sub-specialty in medicine, urogynecology, is that of vaginal mesh products approved by the FDA without thoroughly considering the safety of these, which has now disabled tens of thousands of women around the country for life. Now there are billions of dollars of lawsuits going on against Big

Pharma, the mesh makers. There are way too many examples of this kind of bogus research accepted by the FDA, too numerous to mention here. Such inner workings of the FDA demonstrate how it is in bed with Big Pharma, how it helps Big Pharma through a wink and a nod in generating false documents and false research to dupe the American public.

Medical Board's Investigation and Decision

I received a query from Donald Krpan, the Executive Director of the Medical Board, on November 12, 2010, exactly 30 days after FDA agent Richard Pueschel's call to my office on October 12, 2010, in which he (Pueschel) confirmed that the German-made copper IUD, Cu-380A, was FDA approved. The Board letter stated that the Medical Board had received a complaint from a patient of mine, Ann Baker (I am changing the patient's name to comply with HIPAA regulations and protect her identity). When I read the complaint, I immediately knew what was going on, because this complaint was also about the copper IUD. This could not have been a mere coincidence. The Medical Board's letter was so close in timing to the FDA's visit that I realized that the most likely reason the FDA agents came to see me was the probability that this patient had filed a similar complaint with the FDA, triggering an inquiry from them, as well. This was mere speculation on my part, however, because the FDA agents said nothing about receiving a complaint from anyone on their visit to my office on August 17. They merely stated that the reason for their visit was to educate themselves about these imported IUDs that they learned doctors were using. It wasn't until three years later when I received Discovery documents from the Medical Board (in

June 2013) that I came to learn that the FDA investigation had been a joint-venture between the FDA and the Medical Board, with the FDA taking the lead role and the Medical Board merely following the FDA's instructions. I also learned for the first time that the Medical Board was just another government law enforcement agency.

This was a rude awakening since I had thought the Medical Board was a uniquely different entity tasked with protecting the health needs of the population and making sure that licensed doctors followed regulations to ensure the safety of patients in a doctor-patient relationship. I never thought that the Medical Board could possibly play any role in serving the financial interests of the pharmaceutical industry. I thought of healthcare as something that society considered sacrosanct, above and beyond private profiteering. Yes, that is how ignorant I was about healthcare in the United States even in my capacity as a physician. I came to realize that the Medical Boards have little to do with patient care or the well-being of healthcare consumers. Board members of the Medical Board are often not even aware of what is going on. Politically appointed representatives and attorneys who have probably elementary knowledge of medicine can accuse physicians, and then determine if a physician should be allowed to retain his/her medical license. The Medical Board is there to rubber stamp their decisions when all the paperwork is done. I sure hope that is not always the case, but it certainly was in my case.

I reviewed the Medical Board complaint filed by Ann Baker attached to the Board's query letter from the Board's Executive Director. Ann Baker's initial contact was with my wife who was covering for my regular employee, a nurse who had called in sick that day. My wife is a licensed nurse in the State of California and the

State of New York and identified herself as "Dr. Singh's nurse." After this initial contact, I saw Ms. Baker and took detailed information about her history and conducted a physical exam.

The patient's initial presentation was for a well-woman exam as well as contraceptive counseling. Ms. Baker specifically requested a copper IUD, a non-hormonal long-term birth control method, because she said she had problems with all hormonal birth control methods in the past including birth control pills. I explained to her everything that an Ob/Gyn would be expected to tell a patient about non-hormonal copper IUDs. I pulled out the actual copper IUD and showed her what it looked like and how it worked, explaining the pros, cons, risks, benefits, and alternatives, and noted such in the chart. (The FDA is still in possession of Ann Baker's original chart, and I only have an electronic copy that I received from the FDA.) I also showed her the hormone-based IUD called Mirena, which she did not want because of her alleged history of health problems with the hormones. I was glad that she rejected it and I would have recommended against it anyway because Mirena, in my opinion, had dangerous side effects. (Mirena is yet another example of FDA approving a fairly dangerous product without proper investigation to please their Big Pharma masters.) After my evaluation based on her history, I requested blood work and performed a gynecological exam to make sure the patient was a suitable candidate for the birth control method she was requesting. My staff made a follow-up appointment for the surgical implant of this IUD, pending results of STD tests and blood work.

The patient returned on April 16, 2010 for the surgical implant of the copper IUD, which I inserted without complications. I scheduled a four-week follow-up appointment with her for an IUD check, which is a standard care protocol. When she returned on May 12, 2010, her IUD seemed to have dislodged a bit from its position as noted from her cervical os (an opening in the cervix that goes into the uterine cavity). I repositioned it back in its intra-uterine position. I scheduled the patient another follow-up appointment to check on this IUD. The patient returned on June 22, 2010, with unrelated complaints of vulvitis, itching, and rash. I wanted to check the IUD to make sure it was still in place even though this was not her appointment for the IUD re-check. On examination, I noted that the IUD had dislodged again. I readjusted the IUD and told her that if it dislodged again, I would have to remove it and replace it with a new one, or she might want to choose an entirely different birth control method. I made a subsequent appointment for her. I gave her a copy of a research paper from an Ob/Gyn medical journal so that she could read the opinions of IUD researcher experts about recommended management for dislodged IUDs. (The term used in medical literature is *malpositioned IUDs.*) My staff made a reminder call to her the day before her next appointment. It was a policy in my medical practice that my receptionist or the medical assistant make a courtesy reminder call the day before each patient's scheduled appointment. Mrs. Baker did not come in for her appointment, despite our reminder call. She did not respond to follow-up phone calls, nor did she ever volunteer to come back after that day.

The patient's complaint was disturbing in many ways, as it contained multiple allegations. The first one was that I violated the patient's Christian faith by not adequately explaining to her that the copper IUD *kills the baby*. She stated she had learned from a friend at her church that the IUD implant *kills the fertilized egg*, not just the sperm. Secondly, the patient claimed that she had done her own investigation, and discovered that my wife, a nurse, was not a real nurse and was practicing illegally – all untrue. She further claimed that she believed that I was not a real doctor. But the most disturbing part of the complaint was that another provider that she sought care from told her (I have changed this provider's name to Dr. Henderson to protect patient-doctor relationship and comply with HIPAA laws) that the brand of IUD she received from me was not what I showed her in the office during her first visit.

The fact that another healthcare provider had told her she did not receive the IUD that I promised her, was especially disturbing to me. Was it a vendetta from Dr. Henderson whose privileges were taken away by the Mercy Hospital Ob/Gyn Department in Bakersfield of which I was an active staff member? Dr. Henderson lost his medical practice due to actions that were taken by the Ob/Gyn medical staff of Mercy Hospital after he was found to have cognitive impairment and dementia. A neuropsychological evaluation had been done, and the findings were that he had become a safety hazard to both his patients and himself, because of impairment of memory resulting in poor Judgment. Against the advice of the Ob/Gyn Medical Staff, Dr. Henderson continued to see patients in a private office at the time Ann Baker saw him in his office to remove the IUD I had implanted. The Ob/Gyn Department complained to the Medical Board that Dr. Henderson was continuing to see patients against their advisement. As a result, Dr. Henderson's medical license was cancelled by the Medical Board of California and the DMV did not renew his driver's license.

The Medical Board's complaint required me to respond to the patient's allegations within thirty days, by December 10, 2010. The Board also asked me to submit a certified copy of the patient's medical records. I could not finish my own investigation of the real cause of the patient's grievance within the deadline. I tried to call the new provider she had seen, Dr. Henderson, but by then his office had already been shut down as he was forced into retirement due to the aforementioned complaints piling up against him. So, I was late in my reply to the Medical Board. I replied to the Board on December 21, instead of December 10.

In my letter to the Board, I gave a chronological account of the care and treatment with dates of service provided to Ann Baker as the Board had requested. I also explained to the Board that the Lot number of the copper IUD noted in the chart was that of a U.S. brand copper IUD, Cu-380A, trade name ParaGard, which to me only meant that if the note said patient received ParaGard brand, then it must mean that the patient received the ParaGard. (As you will learn later in the story, this notation turned out to be a clerical error in the patient's chart.) I also informed the Board about licensing, qualifications, and the credentials of the nurse in question and per their request, attached a copy of my own curriculum vitae to confirm my credentials as an obstetrician and a gynecologist.

About four months later, in or around April 2011, I received a phone call from the Executive Director of the Medical Board, Donald Krpan. Strangely, he started yelling at me on the phone and threatened me with Medical Board sanctions if I did not answer all his questions specified in his letter, including explaining how the Lot number in the medical chart was for the U.S. brand while the patient claimed that she had received a different brand. I informed him that during the three months since my response to him on December 21, 2010, I had investigated what had indeed occurred with this patient. I told him that a clerical error had been made in that I noted the Lot number for the U.S. brand although I inserted the German-made

Cu-375 IUD. It was an IUD I used on a select few patients who had no insurance coverage and badly needed the IUD contraception, with the intention of providing it to them for free. This had been an error on my part, as a result of mistakenly identifying the patient as a research subject at the time of implantation. I informed him that this sort of error of noting the wrong National Drug Code (NDC) number could potentially occur because I often completed all my charts later in the evening or the following morning. The Lot number that should have been noted by the medical assistant was not noted by her, and I added it for her but wrote it incorrectly when I went through the charts at the end of the day. I explained to him how I could have easily made that mistake because writing lot numbers was not my routine job. It was the responsibility of the medical assistant to note Lot numbers in the charts at the time of patient visits before they left the exam room. I provided the Executive Director with an opportunity to inspect all IUD-related charts in my office that would show that Lot numbers were almost always noted in the charts by the medical assistant, and I estimated that at least 95 to 99 percent or more of the files contained correct information, as noted by the medical assistant. I also explained to him that using the word ParaGard in the chart only meant copper IUD. The three words, Cu-380A, the copper IUD, and ParaGard were used interchangeably in all Ob/Gyn medical literature, the actual pharmaceutical name of the drug being Cu-380A. Since Krpan was a physician but not an Ob/Gyn, I provided him with medical journal references so he could verify this information. I provided him with references and page numbers from the yearly Ob/Gyn compendia that all Ob/Gyns in the country read to keep abreast with the continuing education in their field of specialty. I also gave him references and page numbers from

Ob/Gyn textbooks and literature, so he could read and understand how these terms, Cu-380A, Paragard, and Copper IUD etc were used synonymously.

He seemed satisfied with my explanation and curtailed his yelling but brought up several other complaints of his own. He said that I was using the name Dr. Paul Aurora on my website and in many other places and stated I did not identify my degree but just called myself an Ob/Gyn or a doctor. I explained to him that Paul Aurora was a pseudonym, under which I wrote articles and gave public talks and seminars. Aurora is my family's tribal name, and I decided to use it because I did not want to discourage impoverished patients from seeking care from me. Once doctors begin writing and speaking, the perception can be that they're making a lot of money as public figures and may charge more for patient care. That was definitely not the impression I wanted to give, so I opted to keep my practice name separate from everything else I was doing. After a bit of additional upset, he calmed down and told me that he was going to issue me another letter listing further complaints and that he expected a prompt answer from me or I would face sanctions from the Medical Board. I figured that the primary reason he was so upset was that I had sent him a delayed response the first time violating the 30-day response rule. In wrapping up our conversation, he stated he would accept my explanation of it being a clerical error if I submitted a copy of the invoice of the U.S. brand Copper IUD with the same lot number as noted in the chart, to show proof that I had made a purchase but accidentally implanted a different brand. [The Lot number in the chart was not the correct number for the brand that I inserted.]

A week later, I received a letter from him that discussed my failure to address some of the complaints in his original letter of complaints.

One of the complaints was that I failed to accurately identify the brand of IUD inserted (a complaint he called "misrepresentation"), by using one brand but noting another brand in the medical chart.

I responded to the Board within 30 days this time and sent a copy of the invoice of the two U.S brand ParaGard IUDs that I had purchased in September, 2009. In a written response, Krpan accepted my explanation but added that I must fix the problems with my website within thirty days. I had to abandon my website altogether and get a new one designed to satisfy all the medical board's requirements. I hired an attorney, Steve Boreman, to represent me with the Board, and he helped resolve the remaining issues to the Board's satisfaction. Or so I thought. It was all over until the FDA forced the Board to reopen the case in 2013, based on the FDA's alleged Discovery.

March 28, 2012: The FDA Raids My Office

Agent Pueschel, raided my office on March 28, 2012, within weeks of the assumed resolution with the Medical Board. I would like to remind my readers that this is the same person who was accompanied by another senior FDA agent, an Asian American female, when they came to my office on August 17, 2010 — my very first contact with the FDA agency. By 2011, I was under the impression that the case of the FDA complaint filed by Ann Baker had been satisfactorily resolved through the Medical Board, but I was wrong. It would not be until the summer of 2013 when I reviewed the FDA's Discovery documents received from the Medical Board, that the reasons for the FDA raid of my office would be revealed to me. The FDA's new evidentiary documents generated single-handedly by agent Pueschel were now to be made an integral part of the Medical Board's case in its renewed accusation against me — a result of the FDA pushing the Medical Board to do so.

Among other things, the Medical Board's Discovery documents revealed that the FDA had asked the Medical Board to assist it by reopening a Medical Board investigation of me, and also asked the Board if it would assist and cooperate with the FDA during this second investigation, to which the Board agreed. Apparently, the FDA was not happy with the Medical Board's failure to revoke my medical license the first time around.

After reading these Discovery documents, it became clear to me that the FDA and Teva, wanted to have my medical license revoked by any means. This was apparent from the FDA's one-way communications with the Medical Board following the Board's inaction, with FDA prosecutors working behind the scenes in cooperation with Teva. I could not have known any of this on the day of the FDA raid because this was happening in secret behind the scenes.

On the day of the raid, my office was in full bloom. The waiting room was filled with several female patients when about twenty government agents in paramilitary outfits carrying guns barged in yelling, "Dr. Singh, Dr. Singh!!" I heard tremendous noise and my name being called out. Before I knew it, they entered my office and informed me of who they were. Leading the charge was agent Pueschel wearing civilian clothes, accompanied by a man and woman also in civilian clothes. The female FDA agent with him in 2010, was distinctly absent from this army of policemen. Different gunmen had already occupied the examination rooms even before I had a chance to find out what they were doing in my office. According to my staff, FDA agents ordered two undressed female patients who were waiting to be seen, to pull up their pants and leave the premises. The same order was given to those in the waiting room. I was confused because all IUD-related issues were resolved on October 12, 2010, after my staff and I agreed to adhere to all the FDA's instructions regarding the use of copper IUDs. I wondered what was going on as I watched these gunmen ransack every office and exam room in my building.

Agent Pueschel introduced the investigators who were with him as Jesse Townsend, the Medical Board Investigator, and Sonia Rios of the Bureau of Medical Fraud and Elder Abuse (BMFEA). Sonia Rios handed me her business card. I asked for one from Jesse Townsend and he said he did not have one. When asked why they were raiding my office, Pueschel said to me, "Oh, you are not under arrest," and then asked if the other investigators could interview me. "I would be happy to be interviewed, but I have some questions of my own," I replied. He nodded in agreement before telling me that I did not have to agree to be interviewed at all if I did not want to proceed. I said I would prefer to be interviewed. I felt I had to find out what prompted an armed raid in front of my patients and my employees. I was struggling to comprehend it all. So, I set up the conference room for Pueschel, Jesse Townsend, and Sonia Rios to conduct their interviews. The gunmen continued to ransack my office while I waited and watched the FDA gunmen opening and closing doors, running back and forth in the hallways, in and out of exam rooms and offices, and going up and down the stairs searching for — *what,* I did not know — and shouting things that were hard to understand. The only bit I clearly heard was when one agent shouted to another to look for Ann Baker's chart, saying "he [me] altered medical notes." My staff told me later that day that they also heard those comments. Some gunmen took over the offices that had computers in them, including the room with the server that contained all the data, and started downloading everything after obtaining passwords from our IT guy, Fred Miller (Pseudonym used to protect his identity).

Finally, the two investigators entered the conference room that I'd set up for interviews and sat down. Pueschel followed them in and asked me if I minded if he closed the door behind him, which he did as I nodded. I was not, however, going to allow anyone to interview me unless Pueschel first gave me a better understanding as to what this FDA raid was all about.

So, it began with me asking Mr. Pueschel, "What is the reason for raiding my office and this interview? What is new that you've even returned?" He told me it concerned the IUDs. "What IUDs?" I asked. He did not answer me, so I tried again. "Did we not settle the IUD issue in 2010?" There was still no answer.

Because of Pueschel's silence, I had no choice but to ask him questions. I reiterated all the events of 2010 and conveyed the history of the case to the other two investigators. "What is it about the IUD?" I repeated. "What is this all about?" I reminded him of his phone call to me on October 12, 2010, on behalf of the FDA informing me not to use Cu-375 IUD which I never used again. I also reminded him that he informed me during this call in 2010, that Cu-380A, the German-made T- Safe that I bought from a Canadian distributor, was approved by the FDA. I stated it was the only IUD I had been using since the day of his phone call. "So, what is the problem *now* two years later?" I asked.

Pueschel did not make eye contact with me, continuously gazing at the floor. The other two agents looked back and forth at him and me, and seemed bewildered, but did not appear to be concerned, as though it was not their problem or obligation or business to understand it all. It could not have been too hard for the Medical Board investigator and the Bureau of Medical Fraud investigator to understand what I was saying unless they were as dumb as rocks; but they were not dumb as rocks, they were perfectly normal human beings, who simply did not seem to be very concerned. I looked at them from time to time to get some reaction as I interrogated Pueschel, but they showed no sense of surprise. It seemed like they were on a mission before coming to my office. How two government investigators could turn their backs on the most fraudulent of all of the FDA's acts, as they did in my case, is something that I am still struggling to understand.

While reading the Medical Board's Discovery documents provided to me a year after the fact, I learned that these two new agents were there to assist the FDA with its criminal investigation of me, while the Medical Board was independently conducting its own to support the FDA claims against me. The Medical Board was to verify, confirm, and support the FDA's allegations in order to recommend the revocation of my medical license upon the FDA's request. One would think these two new investigators might be interested in learning what I was interrogating the FDA agent about, but it didn't interest them. That didn't stop me; it was my way of making everyone present aware of the events that occurred between August and October 2010.

I continued to ask Pueschel the same question. He did not answer it and continued staring at the floor. To me, this was a tacit admission of guilt. I persisted until he spoke. When I asked once again, "Did we not resolve the IUD issue in 2010?" he broke his silence and said we had resolved it, but that was not the reason they were there raiding my office. He stated my patients were complaining of bleeding, from the IUDs that I had inserted, and the FDA believed I had altered medical records on a patient. He did not name the patient but added that I had refused to remove a dislodged IUD from that patient when she requested removal. He accused me of reinserting a dislodged IUD in her multiple times.

I heaved a sigh of relief upon his acknowledgment that the issues that made him bring the investigators from the Medical Board and BMFEA were not related to the issues discussed in 2010 but involved patient care issues and the side effects of the IUDs. It made sense to bring the Medical Board investigator into it since the Medical Board is an agency that deals with the standard of care and patient safety issues concerning consumers and patients. Since I understood the problem to be an isolated case involving one patient, I was no longer concerned about their presence and was more than willing to answer any questions they had for me. It took years for me to connect all the dots and see what the real deal was.

With no intention of doing so, Pueschel revealed which patient he was referring to by saying that I refused to remove the dislodged IUD upon her repeated requests and that I had altered medical notes. Ann Baker was a rare patient in my practice that I could recall ever having dislodging issues. She was also the one who had complained to the Medical Board and the only one with an erroneous IUD Lot number in the medical chart. I told him that I was not altering medical records of Ms. Baker or anyone else "... if you are referring to Ann Baker." I told him that there was a clerical error in her medical chart because I completed medical charts at the end of the day or the following morning. I informed him that an error in documentation could occur while completing charts later in the day, and not immediately during the patient's visit. I emphasized that finishing up paperwork at the end of the day (or sometimes a day or two later) was not unusual in busy private medical practices. Some doctors did not complete their charts for weeks, which could lead to more serious charting errors. I also informed him that I had discussed this potential error in the medical chart with the Executive Director of the Medical Board in a phone conversation, and that the issue of Ann Baker's complaint with the Medical Board had already been resolved in the prior year. I informed him that Dr. Henderson who removed the IUD from Ms. Baker, might have an agenda in criticizing me because he had a grievance against the entire Ob/Gyn medical staff who revoked his hospital privileges and had his medical and driver's licenses revoked.

To respond to Pueschel's further allegations that my patients were complaining of bleeding and pain from the IUDs, I informed him that heavier periods and intermittent spotting and pain was the most common side effect of copper IUDs and that I always educated my patients about the risks and benefits prior to IUD insertion. "Did I not show you and your partner the IUD package drug insert for copper IUDs side effects in 2010?" I asked. Pueschel didn't respond to me, but the Medical Board investigator, Jesse Townsend, took over and started verbally attacking me with the same accusations as Pueschel's and some new ones of his own.

From this point on, it was all about the Medical Board's investigator, Jesse Townsend, with very few interruptions from Pueschel. Mr. Townsend repeated over and over the accusation that I used IUDs that were not FDA approved, which caused harmful side effects and bleeding complications in my patients. He also accused me of refusing to remove IUDs from patients who requested removal and pushing IUDs on others to line my pockets with profits by defrauding the insurance companies. Townsend alleged that I billed for the U.S.

brand ParaGard, which he said was a fraud. I told him that I had no idea that these IUDs were not FDA approved and that according to the FDA, Cu-380A IUDs *were* FDA approved, as the FDA advised me in October 2010. I looked at Pueschel for confirmation as I stated that, but he kept his head down.

Looking back, it seems to me that this was Pueschel's plan. Jesse Townsend would do the dirty work while Pueschel would maintain his silence and keep his hands clean. As Pueschel sat quietly, I responded to the allegations that the billing codes were for the drug and not for a particular brand. Billing codes were not reserved for a specific brand or trade name but for the drug called Cu-380A, which the FDA told me was an approved drug. Then he accused me of writing "ParaGard" in patients charts when, in fact, I had used IUDs that I bought from Canada. I told him that the words ParaGard, Cu-380A, and copper IUD were synonymous terms in the eyes of all Ob/Gyns and more importantly terms interchangeably used in all Ob/Gyn medical journals. I informed him that I stopped using Cu-375 IUDs in October, 2010 and used only Cu-380A because FDA had told me that it was approved. He asked how many of those did I use. A dozen? Half a dozen? Two dozen? I informed him that I used about 10 — 20 copper 375 IUDs between 2008 and 2009. I only used Cu-380A effective October 2010, per the instructions from the FDA. Nothing I said was going to calm Mr. Townsend down, and he continued to verbally assault me. Then he proceeded to insult me by saying I was not a real doctor and did not know how to insert IUDs, and that I was incompetent, which he alleged was the cause for complications. He asked something to the effect of: *Where the heck did you learn to implant IUDs and just who taught you?* I told him that I was an Ob/Gyn with 26 years of schooling, and 20 years of medical practice and that implanting IUDs was rather a very simple procedure for any Ob/Gyn. My answers only made him angrier, and he became more verbally abusive. The rest of this interview was filled with questions and accusations, starting with why I bought IUDs from Canada. I told him I bought them because they were much cheaper, something that patients could afford, and in my opinion, they were safe products. I informed him that I had never refused to remove an IUD if a patient requested it for any reason, no doctor would deny such a request from a patient, and that I followed the research protocols that existed in medical literature for the management of dislodged IUDs. He continued to badger me verbally.

Townsend's behavior was unbecoming of a government employee, let alone a Medical Board investigator, who interviewed physicians. As this went on, I wondered why my questioning of Pueschel did not simplify everything for the other two investigators and close the case on the spot. But instead, it garnered more hostility from Mr. Townsend. Pueschel remained calm throughout this process. I honestly did not know the best way to proceed in this very hostile environment. Pueschel made it look like there was no dispute between him (the FDA) and me by remaining silent, and I bought into it because I had no idea what had been cooked up by him or his superiors at the FDA behind the scenes. Mr. Townsend was fired up as though he knew something about the IUDs I bought from Canada that I did not understand as an Ob/Gyn. He was accusing me of things he had no knowledge of, let alone expertise in. He repeated the same accusations over and over about harming patients and causing bleeding. He accused me of telling patients that the IUDs that weren't FDA approved were ParaGard brand IUDs. I promptly interjected by saying: "Why don't you ask him [pointing my finger at Pueschel] if they were approved or not?" Again, Pueschel kept his eyes on the floor. Mr. Townsend's questions were rhetorical. He would accuse me of something as though he was asking something and then answer the question himself to justify his accusation without allowing me the opportunity to respond. He was young and rash and so hostile that at times I felt he was about to hit me physically. He did not sit down and conducted the entire interview standing over me very close to my face in an awfully awkward manner making me very uncomfortable. I could not fathom how a so-called FDA interview turned into an accusations spree by a trained investigator from the Medical Board of California. In retrospect, I do not have the slightest doubt in my mind that had I been a six-foot tall, well dressed blue-eyed Anglo-Saxon physician, Townsend would not have had the guts to insult me like this. Instead, here I was a little brown-skinned Indian, with no counselor by my side to intervene, surrounded by gangsters.

As I ruminate over this issue, Pueschel reminds me of early settlers to whom the native Americans offered gifts, love, and friendship, not knowing that these men were planning to slaughter an entire civilization of tens of millions once they had enough guns and a couple of hundred men to overpower an Indian tribe.

How could Mr. Townsend, with little or no knowledge of IUDs or contraception of any sort, relentlessly continue to accuse me, a gynecologist, of causing complications? I thought I was supposed to be the one to educate him about the side effects and complications of IUDs. I was the one with a specialized education in this field of medicine called, Obstetrics and Gynecology, with more than 26 years of formal education. I am still not sure if this Medical Board Investigator was a racist or an uninformed bigot, but I do not wish to dwell on that thought.

It was not until June of 2013 when the Medical Board reopened the case against me upon the FDA's request and provided me with the FDA's Discovery documents, which included 200-page script of Ann Baker's interview by Townsend, that it became clear to me why Townsend believed that I was a not a real doctor. In her testimony, Baker tells Townsend that she believed I was not a real doctor. She had said this in her original complaint to the Board and FDA in 2010. Townsend seemed to have believed Baker, that is why he mistreated me in the FDA interview as though I was someone with fake credentials. Baker's interview script explained why he was accusing me of not being a real doctor in his verbal assaults toward me in asking questions such as, "Where the heck did you learn to implant IUDs in women." The Medical Board is supposed to grant an interview to a physician if the Board suspects misconduct or compromise of patient care. The Medical Board has no legal authority to send an investigator to interview a physician without first verifying his/her credentials. It is unheard of for a representative of the Medical Board to insult a doctor and question his or her credentials. Such tactics are inappropriate and outside the Medical Board's standards and legal duties. In this situation, statutory procedures, policies and legal requirements of the due process were blatantly violated by the Medical Board. It is a serious violation of the law for a Medical Board to secretly dispatch an investigator to go badger, beat up and humiliate a physician by circumventing all the steps of the due process that are well defined in healthcare law that governs a physician's medical license in the State of California. It was like the Gambino mafia sending a hitman to do a job.

I initially believed that these investigators had some misunderstanding about the side effects and complications of IUDs and that

I could easily alleviate their misconceptions by explaining. It became obvious at this point in the interview that these agents had been talking to my patients before coming to my office. I had no knowledge of what they had been talking about, so I did not want to accuse Pueschel or Townsend of things that I did not know with certainty. I could only comment on the one patient Pueschel accidentally identified without mentioning her name, and I did. I informed Townsend that those complications, such as bleeding and pain, were the side effects of the IUD and had nothing to do with what brand of IUD a patient received, whether it was ParaGard or the one I bought from Canada. I also told the agents that the patients were talking about the most common side effects of copper IUDs that I always counseled my patients about in their contraceptive counseling appointments well before the actual implantation. These side effects and complications were also listed in the ParaGard drug insert by Teva (the one he was lobbying for: See Exhibit 15). Townsend then started accusing me of refusing to remove the dislodged IUDs and, in the same breath, of pushing IUDs on patients to profit, lining my pockets with money by billing insurance companies for the Paragard brand. I countered that his accusation made no sense because, first, he accused me of refusing to replace dislodged IUDs and then contradicted himself by accusing me of pushing more IUDs on patients to make money. If it was my intention to make money off patients, I would be removing dislodged IUDs and replacing them with new ones. I informed him that I followed Ob/Gyn protocols to make my clinical decisions as to when to reposition a dislodged IUD, and when to remove it or replace it (Exhibit 17).

But it seemed like I was talking to myself most of this time because he was not interested in what I had to say. I finally told

Townsend that I would not answer any more questions unless he stopped accusing me and changed his demeanor. He asked if I called these patients to come back and have their Canadian IUDs removed. "Why the heck would I do that?" I questioned. "What would be the rationale for removing IUDs from patients? Those who have problems come back and ask for removal, and I have removed many of them. Why would I suggest to patients who aren't having problems that they get their IUDs removed?"

Then I stood up and said the interview was over. Rios, the Investigator from the BMFEA, interrupted and asked me if I would allow her to ask me just a couple of questions. She was very polite and promised that she wouldn't ask too many questions, so, I agreed, but I remained standing.

Rios specifically wanted to know why Medi-Cal did not pay me for some claims that I had submitted. She read patient names from a long print- out in her hand. It looked like a continuous data sheet that had rolled out of an Associated Press teleprinter for the afternoon news. I informed her I had no clue because I was not the biller. I also told her that to my knowledge, a certain percentage of the claims routinely got denied or never got paid unless the biller followed up with denials aggressively, but I would never know because I relied on the biller's ability to collect or follow up on denials. Denial could also be due to lack of insurance coverage for IUD contraception. I had no personal training or knowledge of billing myself, I informed her. She did not seem to have any more questions.

Townsend then went on another bout of verbal assaults, again repeating the same accusations. I said to him, "You are starting to annoy me now." At this point, my Medical Assistant, Sandra Johnson, pushed open the door and told me that my wife had sent for an attorney and that I had been instructed by my attorney to stop talking to these agents. I ended the interview.

Soon after the agents left, Sandra shocked me by stating that she had been trying for about an hour to get into the conference room to tell me to stop talking to these agents per my attorney's instructions, but the hefty gunmen physically blocked her way and prevented her from going into the back room where the interview was being conducted. I had thought what I was doing in that conference room was voluntary. Now I realized that I was being held in that room through deception. I learned from my staff that my wife had contacted a lawyer named Benjamin Gluck with the help of another lawyer named Michael Gonzalez. Gluck instructed my wife to immediately tell me not to talk with the agents until he (Gluck) got there.

I had a meeting with my staff the next morning in which they informed me that the other FDA agents and gunmen conducted employee interviews in the waiting room, asking each of my staff members about my character and my billing practices. Agents told my staff that they knew everything about me, such as where I lived, what kind of clothes I wore, and where and what I ate every day for lunch because I had been under their surveillance. The Discovery documents submitted to me by the Medical Board in the year to follow (2013) suggested that the FDA had already spent millions of dollars on covert operations in their investigation of me, for more than three years without my having a clue about it. This should explain why I frequently make statements such as, "I did not find out until two years later..." The government's cover-up and framing the case required accumulating information and withholding it until such time it would be too late for me (the defendant) to do anything about it. This tactic is consistent with what Sidney Powell and Judge Alex Kozinski explain in the book, *Exposing Corruption in the Department of Justice.* Unethical government agents and prosecutors secretly fabricate evidence behind the scenes because they have access to all the forensics and witnesses without the knowledge of the defendant. By the time the defendant finds out, the real evidence is already destroyed, while the so-called evidence that supports the government's case has already been manufactured.

I also learned from my staff that my wife called the office not once, but several times while I was being held in the interview room, to tell all FDA agents in the waiting and reception area to stop the interview process because my attorney was on his way to represent me. One staff member even had an FDA agent get on the phone, informing him that Dr. Singh's wife wanted to talk with him. My wife told him that she wanted me to immediately discontinue the interview because my attorney was on his way from Los Angeles. The agent challenged her by asking something like, "How do I know that you are Doctor Singh's wife?" "Because the staff gave you the phone and they know I am his wife," she replied. Then the staff in the reception room proceeded to confirm with this FDA agent on the phone that he (agent) was on the phone with Dr. Singh's wife. But the agent hung up on my wife, saying he didn't know who she was. She called back several times, only to be hung up on again and again by the agents.

I had no clue what was going on in any area of my office outside of the interview room with doors shut, where I was being held. After my wife made several calls, the gunmen warned my staff that they were not allowed to open the main door to the office if the doctor's wife showed up. One guard stood at the main entrance blocking it with his gun pointed at the staff. I did not know that my staff was trying to come into the interview room to tell me to stop the interview from the time it began, but they were physically prevented from doing so. Now I understood why Pueschel wanted to close the door behind him as he entered the room to start interviewing me, so that I could not possibly hear any activity outside in the hallway. This was a preconceived scheme that I would not fully understand until years later. Ms. Johnson also informed me that she tried to reach out to me when she realized I had come out of the room during my interview process to use the bathroom with a gunman following me to the bathroom, but she was prevented from coming anywhere near me in the hallway by a large gunman blocking her way. A gunman, twice the size of Johnson, prevented her from crossing the path in the hallway to get to me to deliver me the message from my attorney. I recall the incident as though it happened yesterday. I was coming out of the room during my interview for a bathroom break when a gunman trailed me. When I asked him why he was following me to the bathroom, he replied that he was just following the protocol.

Essentially there would have been no interview that day if my attorney's message reached me the first time my wife delivered it to my staff, without this physical interference from the agents. Two days later, my IT guy, Fred Miller, came in to see me. He was very upset and told me that when he opened the door to my office during the hours of the raid, an agent put a gun to his head asking who he was. Mr. Miller replied that he had come to give them the password for the server because they had requested it by calling him on the phone, and that's when they let him in.

According to my staff, all these hours before my attorney's arrival, the agents continued to ransack the office, taking all the data from computers, and loading up their cars with original medical charts of all patients who had ever received an IUD from my office. They removed about $20,000 worth of merchandise, drugs, Botox, Juvéderm, and every IUD from all the exam rooms including many ParaGard and Mirena IUDs. They also took hundreds of papers and files, including patient appointment books, invoices, electronic billing records – anything and everything that could be helpful to them for their "case" against me. Imagine 20 people working together from 9:00 am to 5:00 pm and all they could accomplish in one day. I confirmed this for myself over several weeks as I started discovering all the files and materials missing from my office.

Finally, the criminal defense attorney, Benjamin Gluck, accompanied by a younger colleague of his, arrived at the end of the day after hours of waiting. It was already 5:00 pm, the interview was over, and the raid was done to the FDA's satisfaction. Interestingly, Gluck happened to be a good friend of Pueschel's. Apparently, he knew Pueschel from other FDA investigations. According to my attorney, Pueschel informed him before the FDA agents' departure that day that he (Pueschel) knew that I was altering medical records and harmed so many patients with complications from these IUDs I bought from Canada, information that he claimed he had gathered based on his interviews of my patients.

Then Gluck and his colleague and I sat in my office to discuss. My wife joined the meeting via phone. Gluck told me that based on his brief conversation with Pueschel before the FDA agents left, it was an FDA case, which he said was good news because it would have been worse if it was a Medical Board case since then my medical license would be at risk. I did not know what that meant, and I still don't know to this day what he was trying to tell me.

Gluck then informed me that the FDA agents had removed all the IUD-related patient charts from my office, but they wanted to know if any patient records were left behind in my office or any other location offsite. I told him that the oldest files from 2006 to 2008 were in storage and a warehouse in the back of my house. He told me that the FDA agent Pueschel wanted all the remaining IUD medical charts from 2008 and 2009 because the FDA case was limited to 2008 and 2009. I took Gluck and his colleague to the warehouse fifteen minutes away from my office and showed him where the charts were. He instructed me not to touch them or open them, and any IUD-related patient charts in those boxes would have to be sent to the FDA agent directly by Mary Young, who was my receptionist, the custodian of the charts with her notarized certification.

Before Gluck left, I informed him of everything I had learned from my staff after leaving the interview room. I informed him that my Medical Assistant was physically prevented from coming into the room to tell me to stop talking, per his instructions. I also told him that agents were hanging up the phone on my wife who was trying to tell them to stop interviewing me per his (Gluck's) instructions. I was stunned to hear Gluck's response. I do not remember the exact wording, but the gist was that it was "business as usual for the government." It was clear that for him it was an acceptable practice by FDA agents and he seemed to be very comfortable with the idea, shrugging his shoulders like it was a normal legal procedure. It was ok with him that he instructed the FDA agents not to interview his client and they ignored him. Then he told me that Richard Pueschel informed him (Gluck) that he (Pueschel) had a search warrant. "Was he not supposed to show it to me if he had one?" I asked. He just shrugged his shoulders again like it was not a big deal; government's *business as usual.* It was a very bizarre experience to see my defense attorney regard all this as normal and acceptable conduct by the government agents.

It was the first time in my life that I discovered that the government of the United States could act like a totalitarian regime, that such illegal conduct was part of the accepted behaviors in the government, behaviors that defense attorneys were also comfortable with. I could not fathom the blasé attitude of my own defense attorney towards the due process of the law.

I had Ms. Young, sort through the boxes in storage to find all IUD-related charts and work directly with my attorney Gluck to send the charts to the FDA through the attorney's office. It took her about three weeks to identify and dig out all IUD-related charts, and she sent them to the FDA with her certification and notarization as the custodian of those records. At this stage, the FDA was in possession of well over 90 percent of the original medical charts of all the patients who ever received a Canadian imported IUD from my office, or any other IUD for that matter, including ParaGard since I first started using them in May of 2008. An estimated 10 percent of the charts were destroyed in vandalism in my old Delano office in the year 2011, so I provided the Medical Board with copies of the police reports, my insurance company's photographic evidence of the vandalized charts and files, and reports relating to it.

My attorney charged me $10,000 for his two-hours visit to my office that day. I emailed Gluck a written detailed summary attachment of all the events that occurred on March 28, 2012, after gathering all the details from my wife and my staff, but again, it meant nothing to him. He did not bother to respond to my email let alone read my detailed summary. I did not understand what was actually happening the day of the raid until I saw the FDA's documents through the Medical Board eighteen months later when the FDA's preconceived scheme started unfolding for the first time. While they were acting as though the interview was voluntary, I was actually being detained and denied communication with others so they could accomplish what they came to accomplish that day.

I made a follow-up appointment with my attorney within weeks of the raid as he had advised me to do. I showed him samples of Cu-380A IUDs in packages including their drug Inserts for both the U.S. ParaGard and the German brand, T-Safe. He read the packages' drug inserts front and back several times. I pointed out to him the specifications of the drug to show that they were the same products. He told me that it was a crime to use the German-made T-Safe. "Why is it a crime when the FDA told me that I was permitted to use the German-made IUD?" I asked. He responded that you couldn't depend on what the FDA or an FDA agent tells you, adding that agents are not necessarily the most honest people.

If you can't trust law enforcement and government agencies in a democracy, then who do you trust? I gave Gluck samples of a whole bunch of other products that FDA agents also took from my office during the raid, which included Botox, Juvéderm, ParaGard and the Mirena IUD, products that were exclusive products of the U. S. manufacturers but purchased from the same Canadian distributor at a fraction of the prices. He looked at me and told me I had committed crimes.

"How is that?" I asked. He replied that it was a crime to buy them cheaper from Canada because their drug inserts had slightly different instructions and in different languages in addition to English, which would show that they were not the same products. "How can you say that they are not the same products with the U.S. manufacturers logos displayed on them by Allergan and Bayer, a subsidiary of Schering Plough?" I asked. He said he agreed with me that it did not make any sense to call them different products, but they were different because the government often made that argument in court cases, because the drug insert was written in German in addition to English.

"Aren't the instructions and the look of the packages expected to be a bit different, when they are from countries such as Canada, France, and Germany?" I asked. "They are products made by the U.S. pharmaceutical companies." My argument meant nothing to Gluck. I finally asked, "It is all about money, isn't it? The drug company is behind all this." He responded emphatically, "of course, it is about money", as though that was the most ethical thing in the world for him to say or believe in. His reply reflected Big Pharma's ethics as well as his own.

It was not until I read the book by the famous American lawyer, Gerry Spence, that I understood for the first time in my life how a typical American lawyer is trained, brainwashed, and thoroughly corrupted by their training in law schools, many of which are now literally bought out and run by corporations. The law schools give rise to new trainees awash in corporate culture ready to commit financial mayhem the day they leave law school and land their first lucrative corporate job. This training starts on day one in almost all law schools, with nearly no exceptions today. It reminds me of my days in medical school where all I heard were students talking about how they were going to make a financial killing as soon as they got out. The students regularly bragged about how successful their families were and how they were making millions in medicine. That was when I knew I was not going to be in a so-called noble profession, but there was no going back because I had already accumulated a quarter million dollars of student loans.

My attorney told me to take the IUD samples back home and not leave them in my car because it was contraband. "How can using the copper IUD be a crime when the FDA told me in 2010 that it was FDA-approved, and then, Pueschel, reconfirmed this during my interview with him a few weeks ago?" Gluck repeated a new version of what he'd already stated by saying I shouldn't necessarily rely on Pueschel admitting to that and that FDA agents can't always be trusted to tell the truth.

"The other two investigators present at the raid heard Pueschel acknowledge this fact," I told him. He suggested I not rely on them either. I asked Gluck what advice he would give me under the circumstances and what I needed to do. He advised me to stop using IUDs imported from Canada regardless of what Pueschel or the FDA told me. He said I should not rely on Pueschel's information and simply stop using all IUDs just to be on the safe side and not talk to anyone about it, nor should my staff discuss this with anyone else.

I called Gluck from time to time during the following few months to find out what was going to happen. He said he knew nothing about what the government was doing and hoped that it would all just go away. He suggested that we keep quiet and that there was no reason to wake up the government. This was followed by a very long silence from the FDA for the next two and a half years – a period that was so long, I almost forgot about it and went on living my life. But having Gluck show up at my office with his colleague at the time of the raid, followed by two short meetings with him, one immediately in my office and another in his office, cost me $18,000 in legal fees, which wiped out both my business and personal accounts.

I want my readers to use this dollar amount as a yardstick to measure the amount of money one may need to defend oneself against the federal government in a case that could last for years. The answer is clear; it could be several million dollars. Such an estimate should help you understand more than ever the truth that we have a two-tier legal system in the U.S: one for those who have tons of money and another for those who have no money or not enough money to fight back.

My face-to-face and one-on-one conversation with Gluck was my first exposure to the relationship of the criminal defense industry with the government agencies and the federal prosecutors. None of this made sense to me at that time due to my ignorance. I later learned that this was an incestuous revolving-door relationship between the government, private criminal defense law firms, and the corporations, which of course depended heavily on who knew who. Gluck was keeping warm and cozy with the government rather than zealously defending me which was his legal duty. There was nothing I could have done at that time.

A former prosecutor who is now an activist and became my friend during these years told me that most criminal defense lawyers think alike because of their similar upbringing in the corporate-driven legal system. Revolving-door corruption in America is such a fascinating subject, and I was under the impression that revolving-door corruption existed between financial institutions, pharmaceutical giants, large corporations, and the government. I discovered that this corruption exists in all areas of the new world order of neoliberalism with no exceptions made, and this includes the legal system, healthcare system, and the mainstream media. You name it; it is part of it and it includes everything.

Facing the Wrath of My Patients

A few weeks after this FDA raid, I received a phone call from one of my patients. The patient had received an IUD from my office, and she told me that she had been interviewed by an FDA agent who had informed her that I was the subject of a criminal investigation by the government for having implanted IUDs that were not approved by the FDA. She was distraught and hysterical and asked how I could do this to her, saying she had always trusted me because her mom, who was a patient, spoke highly of me. She then said that if it were not for her mom, she was not even going to call me because the agent had told her to keep it to herself. Then the patient went right back to crying in the middle of this conversation saying she felt betrayed. She said her mother did not believe that I had done anything wrong and still thought of me as the best doctor she's ever had, adding that she'd been symptom-free for the first time in a long time and had seen many doctors and spent a fortune before coming to me. Her mother encouraged her to give me the benefit of explaining my position which is why she called me. Then she stopped sobbing and gave me a chance to respond.

"Calm down first so I can address your concerns. What else did the FDA agent tell you about the IUD?" I asked. She told me the agent said I had bought the IUD on the Internet, that it was not approved by the FDA, and that it was an unsafe and harmful IUD. She told me she was having side effects such as very heavy periods and cramps and the agent told her that they were complications from the defective unapproved IUD I had implanted in her.

I went numb when I first heard this. I said, "Why don't you come on over to my office for a few minutes. Let me show you something that I would like you to see for yourself with your own eyes. I would also like to answer all your questions and address your concerns." Then I assured her that I was the same doctor that her family had known for years. I told her that the FDA agent had misinformed her and it wouldn't take much clarification for her to change her opinion of me. She said she would be right over. I told my staff in the front desk to let her into my office when she arrived, and within five minutes she was in my office. She sat down, and I pulled out the German-made IUD with its drug package insert and explained to her that this was the IUD she received. I told her that two FDA agents were given a sample of this IUD upon request on August 17, 2010, which the Food and Drug Administration inspected and researched for two months and gave me its permission to use in October of 2010. This was the same drug as the U.S. made Cu-380A that had a trade name ParaGard. I also told her that the German medical devices were known worldwide for being of the highest quality, and superior to any equivalent U.S. brands. This device was used by tens of millions of women in Western Europe. The German-made IUD was a Cu-380A IUD, was CDC approved, and used as the gold standard in England, France, Germany and Canada, countries where healthcare was known to be much better than in the United States.

She asked why she was then having complications. I pulled out the U.S. brand ParaGard's drug insert, and without showing it to her, I asked her to name a complication she was having or ever had had from the IUD that I inserted. As she listed symptoms, I let her read the insert to show her that those were all side effects of the U.S.-made ParaGard. I asked her if there was anything else she could think of that she experienced as a side effect of this IUD. She thought hard and then came up with some more vague symptoms, and I showed her that those were also listed in the ParaGard insert. The takeaway for her was that these side effects had nothing to do with the German brand or the U.S. brand IUD. I also jogged her memory that I counseled her before giving her the IUD that heavy periods and intermittent cramps could occur. I educated her that the actual pharmaceutical name of this device was Cu-380A and that brand names such as the U.S. brand ParaGard or the German-made T-Safe meant nothing; it was like calling Tylenol, acetominophen or paracetamol, they were different names for the same drug. These were trade names for the copper IUD, and both were the same drug and device. I also told her that the IUD could be removed in an instant if side effects bothered her more than she could handle. "It literally takes seconds to remove the IUD if you want me to remove it," I offered. I informed her that she could come back to have it removed any time if she wanted.

She did not want to have it removed after I answered all her questions. I saw her countenance change. She replied that the pain was not so bad and the periods were only just a bit heavier and not bad enough to have her IUD removed. It seemed like her list of complications had diminished dramatically after listening to the facts. This IUD that had ruined her life just a few minutes earlier was now not too bad, and not causing too much bleeding or pain. A thought crossed my mind at this time that the FDA agents could have deceived so many of my patients through this disinformation campaign. I was terrified just thinking about it, and I found myself at a loss as to how I was going to combat this dissemination of disinformation by the FDA.

This was the first time I realized that a nightmarish scenario was lurking because these patients were falsely induced into believing things about the T-Safe IUD and me that were untrue, thus making them exaggerate their symptoms because of this unexpected shock of being alleged victims of a crime. This would be even truer, I thought to myself, because we were dealing with very vulnerable young female hormonal women who were poor and ill-informed and psychologically manipulated in the hands of corrupt trained professionals. She was smart to ask me the question I was waiting for, which was why I would use imported IUDs even if they *are* safe? I responded by asking her if she was willing to come up with at least $600 cash out- of-pocket on top of what her best private medical insurance was willing to pay for all IUD-related services to obtain the U.S. made Cu-380A, the ParaGard? She responded no. "Well, there goes your answer," I said.

"This is the same answer I have gotten from other patients whenever I've informed them the U.S. brand ParaGard was sold at a price no insurance on the planet was willing to pay and almost no one in my patient population can afford it." I informed her that the general formula was that even the best insurances reimbursed one-third to half the total healthcare costs related to the copper IUD at the doctor's office.

She stated I hadn't told her about the price difference during her initial visit. "Perhaps, I did not, but would your decision have been different if I went into all these details then? Would you have chosen to pay a minimum of an extra $600 out of your pocket to get the U.S. brand if you knew the U.S. and the German T-Safes were the same?" She again replied no.

I had her watch the computer screen as I went online to show her scores of patient reviews of ParaGard on Google complaining about their doctors asking for $1,000 upfront cash from them to receive the

U.S. brand ParaGard IUD, and most of those patients chose to go on a different birth control method as a result. Some patients wrote that it cost them $1,200 out of pocket because their insurance paid only a portion of the services or did not cover the benefit. This was the average cost of a Cu-380A ParaGard IUD and related healthcare services when the IUD was purchased from the U.S. manufacturer, Teva. I informed her that the only exception to this would be some government-funded clinic such as Planned Parenthood, and then a woman must prove that she was living way below the poverty line to be qualified for this IUD at a reduced cost. Then I shared with her some patient consumer reviews of ParaGard in which patients complained of bleeding, pain and other horrible side effects from ParaGard, a lot more than she said she had ever experienced herself.

"Do you still believe this device you received is dangerous or unsafe? She came back with another no. I said, "I want you to ask me any other questions you have before you go. I want to be able to answer them all, especially any questions you have related to what the FDA agent told you about this German-made IUD. I also want you to take these package inserts of the ParaGard and that of the German T-Safe with you and share them with other patients you know who received an IUD from my office, and encourage them to come and see me so I can address their concerns as well."

Toward the end of her visit, I asked her to describe the FDA agent. What she described sounded like Pueschel — middle-aged, white male, brownish hair, and tall, but not too tall. I told her that Pueschel and the FDA had been aware since August, 2010 that the Cu-380A IUD that I implanted in patients was manufactured in Germany by a German Pharmaceutical company EurimPharm, although I purchased it from a Canadian distributor. I explained that this German generic IUD was used and approved in Canada, Europe, and every first world nation around the globe. I assured her that the IUD was not bought on the Internet and that the agent knew this and the FDA had all records of when and how I purchased IUDs. I informed her that the FDA agent was guilty of perjury because he had known for two years that the IUD was made by a German Pharmaceutical Company and a safe product bought by me from a physical distributor in Canada and was not a dangerous or harmful product purchased from the Internet. I also told her that this German Cu-380A IUD was examined and inspected by the FDA in August, September, and October of 2010 and I was given permission by the FDA to use it as an FDA- approved device. I showed her a copy of the original prescription with my signature faxed to the Canadian distributor, which was a standard regulation for physicians in both Canada and the U.S. I could not order something like it from a website and the Canadian distributor did not sell it online. It was strictly by a prescription signed by an MD like it was done in the United States. That was the law. I informed her that the agent had lied to her. The same would apply if a patient wanted to obtain an IUD from this Canadian distributor. She would have to get a prescription from her physician in the United States and have it faxed directly by her physician to the Canadian distributor for an IUD to be dispensed directly to the patient.

After she left, I called her mother and told her what had transpired. She apologized for the doubts of her daughter, and the mother, like her daughter, promised to help me by testifying on my behalf if that became necessary. I told them I did not care about anyone testifying for me; what I cared about was that my patients were being deceptively misinformed. I asked them if they would tell any other patients they knew who received German brand IUDs to come forward and visit me in my office to help me diffuse the situation as much as possible and lift the fog of disinformation that might have been spread by this FDA agent.

At that juncture, I had no idea how many such patient interviews had been conducted by the FDA and by whom. All I could decipher at this stage was that these agents were masterful in conducting their business. I wanted to start calling all my patients who had obtained IUDs from my office, but my attorney soon put a gag order on employees and me. We were not supposed to talk to anyone. My receptionist delivered a phone message she received from Gluck that the physician or the staff were not to speak about the case to anyone. I wanted to adhere to my attorney's advice because I might later regret it if I didn't. After all, I was not a lawyer nor did I know at the time how things would unfold. I thought my defense attorney was trying to make the FDA go away by clarifying the FDA's misunderstandings.

I wish I knew then what I know today, which is that when it comes to government accusations, an opportunity to discuss anything at all with the government can exist only if the prosecutors are willing to allow the defense to debate or argue a point. If the government does not wish to allow that, then your criminal defense attorney is not allowed to do his or her job. The defense attorney can say nothing; he must shut up and listen. The government does what it does without consulting anyone else. A defense attorney has no legal powers of any sort. I could not have possibly known that one needed the U.S. government's permission to speak the truth or to speak at all. I don't think any American citizen not involved in a criminal accusation by our government knows that. From that perspective, there is no difference, as I learned, between a defendant and his defense attorney. You might as well not have a defense attorney if his/her role is to wait and watch and hope for the best. You might as well save your money.

In retrospect, I can tell you that what the so-called defense attorney provided was no better than what my wife, who has no legal experience, could have done, simply because the knowledge of the law or court procedures did not matter. In addition, Gluck did not have the best social skills and wasn't equipped to effectively take on an egotistical prosecutor. He had a big ego of his own, which made him clash with a narcissistic prosecutor who was endowed with the power of gods by the U.S. government. I was at the mercy of the government. In fact, he did not call himself the prosecutor, he addressed himself as "the government." I was told I must say yes to every one of the prosecutorial demands unconditionally if I wished to save my family and myself by avoiding prison. I was told repeatedly that I must take responsibility for everything, and I mean *everything* they were accusing me of, and to do so without putting up resistance or else the consequence would be catastrophic.

Sounds strange, does it not? Taking responsibility for the government's wrongdoing becomes a prerequisite for a defendant at some point during the government's Discovery leading to the government's accusations. It is not uncommon for any criminal case to be suicidal for the defendant if he has no money and yet chooses to resist the prosecutor's demands. And these demands have nothing to do with law, order, justice, truth or untruth. It is just what the government wants. Imagine the pressure you would feel two miles under the ocean per square inch column of water; it will squish you to death in a nanosecond. Try to resist that pressure, and you will die before you have a chance to take one breath.

My prosecutor, Delahunty, reminds me of a high school bully in the 70's when I was in high school. The bully was beating a little guy to a pulp after school hours, with blood all over the place. Every time the little guy tried to raise his head above the ground, the bully pounded on him again, throwing him right back on the floor, and the little guy was not even putting up any resistance. He beat him until he could not get up and laid there in a pool of blood. If a teacher, who was still there after office hours, did not happen to pass by the bicycle parking lot and stop the beating, the bully would have killed the little guy. That is our government to those who are defenseless without financial resources.

In the months and years to follow, many patients who had received IUDs from my office stopped being my patients. Some called for the transfer of care and asked for their IUD-related medical records. I was forbidden to contact patients, but whenever a patient called, I took the opportunity to have her come in so I could remove the misunderstanding that patients had, but to my surprise many of these patients had been brainwashed, or perhaps instructed by the FDA to abstain from talking with me, let alone call me to discuss their complaint. I am sure that if I were a patient, I would not want to see my doctor either if the government informed me that the physician was under criminal investigation for implanting unsafe and counterfeit devices in patients' bodies.

We trust our government, don't we? There is no doubt in my mind that my patients had been instructed by the FDA not to speak with the doctor regarding the FDA's investigation. How else could the FDA continue its uninterrupted criminal investigation in secret for years behind my back without my knowledge? That would have been impossible. I learned later in this case that this was a widespread technique that government agents and prosecutors use to isolate potential witnesses by inducing fear and bias in them and keeping the lid on the facts of the case. There was no doubt in my mind that my patients who loved me at one time now could not wait to see me destroyed.

Only a handful of my former IUD patients knocked at my door, perhaps encouraged by these mother and daughter patients of mine. Those who came wasted no time in changing their opinion of me when I revealed the whole truth to them. Some even got very angry with the FDA and offered to testify on my behalf against the FDA if I was ever sued. The patients who dared to come forward to see me and give me the benefit of the doubt, walked away knowing that nothing in life was more important to me than to do right by my patients, which was consistent with what they had already believed about me. The result of this criminal accusation was less critical to me than restoring their good faith in me.

I had devoted my entire life helping patients in unusual and unconventional ways. For example, my wife and I decided to take care of the poor and the disadvantaged since we both came from needy families and had suffered healthcare issues due to a lack of money in our days of poverty. I rejected high-paying jobs in favor of working in disadvantaged areas to work with the poor where there was no Ob/Gyn available within 50 square miles. There had been only one rule in my practice, which had been that no one would die on my watch. If I saw a patient being unfairly treated because she had no money or insurance, I would always help. I have a history of driving many patients to emergency rooms and pregnant patients to labor and delivery sites. My wife always reminded me that every time I drove a laboring female to the hospital in my car, I lost $500 of revenue for my own family. Also, being away from the office for

2 or 3 hours as I drove back and forth resulted in unbillable hours, and added enormous liability in the event I had an accident with a pregnant patient in my car. But what can a doctor do in a small town where many pregnant patients do not have insurance coverage for an ambulance? This explains why it is not a coincidence that our family's net worth was just over $1 million after 26 years of education and 20 years of medical practice. That figure is one-fourth the average net worth of another average Ob/Gyn physician of my age not far from retirement. And this net worth of mine was primarily the result of a dramatic appreciation in the value of our primary home, luckily bought during a real estate depression. Otherwise, my family would not have a pot to piss in, pardon my language. My wife, a nurse, and I, a physician, a specialist, and a sub-specialist, never turned a poor patient away from my office door. The only exception was when we discovered that the patient had the financial means to pay but lied about her monthly income to get free care. My patients always knew my reputation, and some took advantage of that. Sadly, there are some people who are dishonest when it comes to their financial situation. That is why they call money the great evil.

I told the patients who had returned that I would go to the end of the earth to prove to them that the Cu-380A IUDs I inserted were safe and a well-tested product. I gave some of these patients a 145-page long World Health Organization Report on the safety and procurement procedures of generic Cu-380A IUD, supported by research that was spearheaded by the U.S. Center for Disease Control and multiple healthcare organizations in Germany, France and the United Kingdom (Exhibit 2: WHO Research under CDC.) The United States has been dependent on Germany's medical technologies and devices throughout the century, especially after World War II because of the unparalleled superiority of its healthcare products and devices. They are recognized all around the world as number one in healthcare technologies, second to none.

A clear majority never came to talk with me. I was told they were so worked up against me by the FDA that they were going around spouting venom and spreading rumors, adding fuel to the fire. A few patients who informed me privately what was going on in the small town of Tehachapi also informed me the FDA had promised patients restitution and/or money for their cooperation. The FDA had scared the living Jesus out of them in terms of what they were made to believe I had done to them in wrecking their lives with this FDA-unapproved IUD. In retrospect, I regret the day I followed my counsel's advice not to talk to my patients regarding IUDs. I wish I had taken the risk, and gone door-to-door to tell them all the truth. It was a small town and I could have easily accomplished that by driving around for two hours every evening for a couple of months. I had their addresses from their medical charts. There is no doubt in my mind that I could have restored their faith in me, and I could have deprived the FDA of the luxury of scores of falsely induced witnesses.

FDA Urges Medical Board to Reopen Case

Medical Board Files Charges

I received a call from the Medical Board Investigator, Jesse Townsend, several months after the raid. He informed me that he and Richard Pueschel had decided that an administrative action by the Medical Board against me to revoke my medical license would be an appropriate action, and that he had already made his recommendations to the Medical Board.

At that point, the only memory I had of Townsend was that he was an obnoxious guy who was supposedly sent to interview me by the Medical Board. It seemed odd that he was not coming across as offensive during this phone call. He was talking politely like a rational human being would. He gave me his phone number and asked me to have my attorney call him if he had any questions regarding the action he had recommended to the Medical Board.

I immediately contacted my attorney, Gluck, via email. He promised me that he would call Townsend to find out what was going on. In a follow-up email, Gluck informed me that he had called Townsend and left messages, but there was no response. Knowing what I know now about Gluck, I am not even sure if he bothered to call Townsend at all. I sent him many email messages urging him to find out the details from Townsend, but he stopped answering my emails. I was left in the dark and did not know what to do. Two years later in 2015, during the FDA's criminal charges against me, I found out that it was Gluck's usual style of conducting business with his clients in only selectively responding to emails or responding only when some money was to be made. It was way too late for me to change lawyers, although I am not suggesting that changing attorneys would have made any difference at all, considering that they play little or no role in changing the government's resolve in criminalizing its targets.

It was very quiet for many months after Townsend's phone call. I was simply bewildered as to why I had not yet received any formal accusation for an administrative action from the Board. As I was just about to forget the whole thing, the Medical Board filed the promised accusation against me on April 10, 2013, with allegations of altering the medical records of Ann Baker, being dishonest, grossly negligent, and causing serious complications to patients with the non-FDA approved IUDs. It included other accusations like billing fraud and robbing IUD patients of their money and property. They also stated the IUDs were dangerous devices that were bought on the Internet. The Board filed the accusation but did not submit any Discovery documents with the complaint. When the Discovery documents finally arrived months later, it became clear why the Board took so long to file: FDA Pueschel took a long time to provide the FDA documentation that the Board was meant to use in its own Discovery. The whole Board investigation was initiated at the FDA agent's request. The Discovery primarily contained documentation generated by the FDA agent Pueschel and some of his FDA colleagues.

In describing one of the Board's allegations against me, the Medical Board's attorney, John E. DeCure, working on behalf of his superior, Steve Diehl, quoted all the laws that apply to podiatry (foot doctors who are not physicians) and then asked the judge to revoke my license as a gynecological surgeon, based on these laws. How much education does a man needs to know the difference between a foot doctor and a gynecologist?

Review of FDA's "Discovery Documents"

After a court battle to obtain the Medical Board's discovery documents to prove its allegations, and the judge giving a final warning and a deadline to the Board, I received them on June 20, 2013, about three months after the filing of the case. When I read the 250 pages of discovery provided to me, I found some things that traumatized me so much that it has become a source of post-traumatic syndrome ever since and something that won't go away for as long as I live. Time has not alleviated my symptoms so far, and it's now 2016. This trauma has been the equivalent of what my brother-in-law's therapists described when he came back from the Iraq war and went into treatment. Now he is permanently emotionally disabled. He saw at arm's length Iraqi soldiers' brains blown up and literally scattered in pieces in front of him. This traumatized him so much that he is now on veteran's mental disability for the rest of his life because of post-traumatic stress disorder.

My trauma from reading the Medical Board's Discovery, has had a similar effect in the sense that whenever I remember reading those pages, I feel helpless, defenseless, and completely violated and abused. It has been extremely difficult for me to write this section of the book because it triggers the trauma, my heart starts racing, I sweat, and I panic when someone comes around to say hi to me as I am writing about this in my prison cell. What I found in these 250 pages were *two things* that unbeknown to me were going to change my life forever. First was that the FDA investigator Pueschel had completely omitted any script or memorandum of my meeting with him and the female Asian American agent conducted on August 17, 2010 in my first encounter with the FDA. I wish I had saved the business card of that female FDA agent who interviewed me so that I could at least tell you her name. I read the entire thing over and over to see if I missed it, but never found a reference to her anywhere. I also did not find any mention of the two months of interactions with the FDA that occurred between August 17 and October 12, 2010.

I did find a couple of vague and false references to August 17, as though what was being mentioned was so trivial, insignificant and irrelevant that it deserved allusion of a sentence or two in what would later morph into thousands of pages of the FDA's Discovery of the government criminal investigation case in 2015. What should have amounted to hundreds of pages of transcript of recorded interview by two FDA agents had simply been omitted by reducing it to two sentences. Then I carefully pored over the documents again and again to try to find any mention of the female Asian American FDA agent but saw no mention of her existence. She, along with her interview, had vanished from the government's Discovery.

Second, I discovered that the first 10-15 minutes of the FDA agent's interview on March 28, 2012 (the date of the raid), was omitted from FDA agent Pueschel's official memorandum of March 28, 2012 FDA interview. The first 15 minutes of the interview would have contained my interrogation of Pueschel, (essentially my interview of Pueschel), before I allowed the investigators to proceed with their interview of me (exhibit 3). I further noted that this memorandum was carefully crafted and framed with an objective in mind. It was a mixture of bits and pieces of skillfully designed fabrications that were out of context, replete with lies, edited, and crafted with omissions, false additions, and misleading statements throughout the three-page-long narration. To spice up his report to make me look like a bad guy, Pueschel also had rumor and hearsay incorporated into his report as his evidence against me. The sources of this hearsay were many shady characters among whom were some physicians, insurance companies (such as unnamed employees of Kern Family Healthcare) and some hospitals (such as unnamed employees of San Joaquin Community Hospital) who had bad things to say about me. He stated that he had heard that I lost privileges at hospitals which was false. Such parts of his report sounded like a woman who is bad-mouthing a neighbor whom she does not like very much for unspecified reasons without providing evidence how her claims about the neighbor being a bad neighbor were true. Even if this gossip, rumor and hearsay were to be true, it had no relevance to his allegations, the report was crafted to psychologically influence anyone who would ever become a reader of this report. Ironically, this was a report written by a Federal agent who is supposed to write a legal document with evidence provided to back up his claims. Instead, he made a clear attempt at digging up the dirt by talking with people who had a history of a conflict of interest with me in the past, those who were willing to impart to him erroneous information, gossip or rumor, which Pueschel used as his evidence.

After reading the discovery, I felt betrayed by the legal system, which I always believed was a reasonable one. We all know that evidence has to be grounded in facts, not hearsay from people who do not like you for one reason or another. I knew that some level of corruption existed everywhere, but I never thought that corruption in the legal system could go that far. I had agreed to be interviewed by the FDA agent without a lawyer present because I believed in at least an elementary integrity of the legal system and in the agents representing an agency as important as the FDA. Despite this atrocity of falsification of Discovery, I still had some faith in the system, and planned to bring this up in front of the Medical Board when I went to the Medical Board Hearing. Little did I know that once the government decides to target an individual and starts destroying evidence, a defendant must be willing to relent in trying to save his life, or be prepared to go to jail for a very long time. The government has the sovereign right to withhold evidence from the courts, and the fact that judges gladly participate in these unforgivable crimes makes it impossible for an ordinary citizen to fight back or seek justice.

The very foundation of this Discovery was based on the documentation created by Pueschel, and it was evident that Pueschel had been asking the Board to delay taking action against me because he was working on more documents that the FDA wanted the Board to incorporate in its accusations. I know this because when my attorney demanded that the Board provide us the Discovery right away as it was violating rules of Discovery by not providing it within a reasonable period after filing the accusation, and he finally threatened the government attorney to file a Motion to Compel Discovery (Gov. Code Section 11507.7, California Administrative Procedure Act.) that the Discovery was finally provided. The Medical Board's attorney kept saying that they were working on generating more documentation and intended to file Amended Accusations as more evidence came in. It was all about Pueschel trying to get as many patients to testify against me as he possibly could to incorporate additional information into the Board's Discovery before the Medical Board case went forward to make the FDA's claims (now the Board's claims) against me as damning as possible. Here are some excerpts from the medical board investigator's reports, where FDA agent Pueschel is clearly identified as the sole person behind these investigations even though the accusations are filed as accusations of the Medical Board:

1. "According to information, the BMFEA (Bureau of Medical Fraud and Elder Abuse) was asked to assist the FDA with their investigation" (Page 3).
2. "The BMFEA's investigator, Sonia Rios turned to Medical Board for help; Sonia Rios of BMFEA requested assistance from the Medical Board of California" (Page 3).
3. "Sonia Rios of BMFEA also provided me (the Board Investigator, Townsend) the name of the FDA special agent, Pueschel who she said was head of conducting the investigation."(pg 3).

The Board broke every law and regulation stated in the California Administrative Procedure Act that governs the administration of doctors' medical licenses in the State of California. These gross violations included the fact that the Board, by law, was required to afford me a recorded Medical Board Interview with an investigator, with a medical consultant assigned by the Board present at such an interview, an expert who, unlike the investigator, understands medical issues, prior to filing any accusations against me. The reason for such violations was clear; that is because it really was not a Medical Board accusation, but the Board had agreed to illegally engage in doing the dirty work for the FDA under the garb of the Medical Board's accusation. Because of this, none of the statements in the Accusation were attributable to me. I only needed to see the dates of the patient interviews conducted by FDA agent Pueschel presented as part of the Medical Board's Discovery to connect the dots.

A small part of the overall Discovery was an Investigation Report by the Board's medical investigator, Jesse Townsend. More than two-thirds of Townsend's independent investigation report was cut-and-pasted, a reiteration of all the FDA allegations prepared by Pueschel and presented in direct sentences by the Board investigator as though they were the Board's independent findings. It was written as though Townsend was present in the 2010 FDA interview at a time he did not even know that I existed. Townsend framed his report cleverly to try to fool even a careful reader unless someone studied it carefully, read between the lines, and cross-referenced every statement during the reading process. Jesse Townsend had become the FDA's (Pueschel's) mouthpiece.

Townsend's investigation report also made me aware that the FDA had suspended its own case against me on June 1, 2012, after the Medical Board had agreed to honor the FDA's request to officially take over the case to discipline my medical license. (Discovery Document Page 14: "Jesse Townsend, the Medical Investigator, discovered on 6/1/12 that the FDA had suspended its own case"). Elsewhere in the Discovery, the Medical Board's investigation states multiple times that the FDA agent called the Medical Board and requested to reinvestigate me, and Donald Krpan, Executive Director of the Medical Board, agreed to oblige. Townsend and the Board attorney handpicked specific documents from the first Board investigation of me in 2010 and 2011 — records that did not tell the complete story of the resolution reached with the Medical Board — and made these select documents part of this new Discovery. He also withheld all documentation of Donald Krpan's phone conversations with me.

I will never know for sure, but it would be fascinating to find out if the documents incorporated into the discovery from the previous Board inquiry and resolution were selected by Townsend with Pueschel in the driver's seat. My two extensive phone conversations with Krpan, and the final letter of resolution that Krpan sent me, was carefully withheld by Townsend — apparently in consultation with Pueschel. The documents submitted by the Board gave the reader the impression that the case with them was still hanging in the balance from the previous Board inquiry, which was not true. The alleged evidence against me included approximately fifty patient interviews primarily conducted by Pueschel and a few by his FDA colleagues. It also had fifteen patient interviews conducted by Sonia Rios, of Medical Fraud Bureau, which was meant to support Pueschel's allegations against me, but actually contradicted the patients' responses in interviews conducted by Pueschel. All patients interviewed by the FDA said they had complications, whereas Sonia Rios specifically asked them if they had any complications, nearly all patients said they had no complications beyond what was described to them as the common side effects of the IUD. Again, every single patient in Sonia Rios' interviews also said that they did not stop seeing me for their care because of the IUD, but because I had stopped accepting their Medi-Cal insurance. The FDA agent repeated the same patient statements in all of the FDA's patient interviews. It was as though the agent had given a fill-in-the-blank form to all patients to complete and it was filled with questions that would purposely mislead patients to elicit the same answers, for example, what complications have you experienced since having the unapproved IUD implanted? versus have you experienced any side-effects beyond those you were told were normal side-effects of the copper IUD? The Discovery documents also informed me that the FDA had been asking various other state agencies in California to help investigate me for using what they called FDA's non-approved IUDs that they claimed caused complications in patients.

It's understandable why the Medical Board was withholding and delaying the Discovery; the FDA wanted to go after me with as much manufactured evidence as possible to take away my medical license and put me out of business for good.

I called Steve Boreman, the same attorney who had helped me resolve some of the Medical Board's complaints in its first investigation of me in 2010-2011. He was a former government prosecutor who held a political position as Deputy Attorney General for the Medical Board in the past and had gone into private practice to defend doctors against Board actions. He said he knew Donald Krpan. He was enticing me to engage his legal services, which cost $400 an hour. Boreman already had some familiarity with the background of my case, so, it made sense to hire him again for this second investigation, a situation that appeared to be a lot more serious.

He turned out to be an incompetent attorney for this much larger Medical Board case compared to the first one, which he had handled well. After he read through documents and spoke with the Government's Board's attorney, Steve Diehl, he phoned me and immediately started accusing me of the Board's accusations without ever asking for my side of the story. What defense attorney is trained to believe that his client is guilty before his client shares his experience? I began to wonder what kind of a human being I was dealing with. He said that according to his conversation with the Medical Board's attorney, I would be facing the revocation of my license. He said he could try to get me seven years of probation instead, adding that he was friends with Donald Krpan, the Executive Director of the Medical Board, because of his former employment as the government's Deputy Attorney General for the Medical Board.

I did not know what he meant by this, but I later discovered he was one of those revolving-door attorneys who had been a political appointee as the Medical Board's attorney before going into private practice. His political appointment had been replaced with the current political appointee, now my prosecutor, Mr. Steve Diehl. This was my first introduction to the revolving-door phenomenon, which I became more familiar with during my years of trials and tribulations with the FDA.

As I came to learn, Boreman was as incompetent as he was corrupt. In my phone conversations with him, I tried to interrupt him many times to tell him that my review of the Discovery documents revealed to me that the Board's accusations were fabricated and masterminded single-handedly by one FDA agent, Pueschel. I attempted to point out specific sentences and paragraphs that made the integrity of the Discovery highly questionable. I tried to show him the inconsistent statements that raised questions about whether the FDA agent might have lied to the Medical Board. I insisted that he demand that the Medical Board provide a recording of the FDA agent's interview of me on August 17, 2010, which was being used by the Medical Board as the basis to prosecute me. He agreed to do so and also assured me that it was Medical Board's burden to provide us the tape of the recording if it was going to accuse me of anything. In an email that he sent me on May 20, 2013 (see Exhibit 24) he agreed with me and stated, "I understand Paul. The investigators are not always above board. We need to review the interview tape and see what evidence is that they have. Their accusation refers to admission you may have made. I will check the tape thoroughly." He then requested that the Medical Board provide us the tape and the Medical Board refused. I insisted that he demand to be given that tape or any handwritten notes or memo of that interview by two FDA agents - information the Medical Board seemed to be hiding. I also informed him that the FDA agent fraudulently induced my patients into making false statements, and given a chance I could easily demonstrate Pueschel's claims to be untrue by providing supporting documentary evidence that contradicted his claims. As I tried to tell him this on the phone, Boreman would not shut up. He disregarded what I had to say and talked over me each time I attempted to discuss it. I wondered how an attorney could lack any interest in checking the authenticity of what his client was being charged with. At this time, I had thoughts of firing him, but wanted to wait until the Board filed their Amended Accusation, which was to include more evidence from the FDA. To bolster his case with additional evidence, the FDA agent Pueschel was still continuing to interview more patients who had received IUDs from my office.

I waited for that Amended Accusation from the Board, and it did not come through, so I decided to stop waiting and went ahead and fired Boreman. Steve Boreman charged me several thousand dollars for having a couple of phone calls with the attorney for the Medical Board and reading 250 pages of its Discovery. I asked for a detailed invoice, a request he first resisted, and then eventually sent me an inflated bill, which I paid. The last thing I wanted was to get into a battle with a crook in the middle of this important challenge of trying to save my medical license, which was already on the line. I had to pick my battles.

To replace Boreman, I did some research and got a recommendation from a local attorney of someone he described as the "best of the best" in the business for Medical Board defense. This was a celebrated attorney, Russell Iungerich from Los Angeles, one who had made his name by being one of the main trial attorneys in the assassination case of John F. Kennedy when it was reopened. Ironically, when I called Boreman to tell him that I no longer needed his services and requested a transfer, he told me the same thing, that Russell Iungerich was the best in the business. Surprisingly he had good things to say about his rival.

As it turned out, Iungerich was old and sick. His partner, Paul Spackman, did most of the work for him. Iungerich showed up to the office only for an hour or two a day as I discovered later during my initial contacts with his law firm. Iungerich agreed to meet with me to discuss the case. Before meeting with him, I had a phone conversation with Paul Spackman to see if his law firm would be a good match for me. I briefly described my story to him, and as I was talking about the *omissions* from the Discovery documents, he asked me if I knew whether the FDA agent had a recording of the FDA interviews. "I don't know, all I can tell you is what happened. I am not sure if the FDA agent had a recorder on him," I replied. Then he proceeded to tell me that my testimony would be crucial if the FDA could not produce a recording to prove that Pueschel's memorandum accounts were accurate. Spackman said that it was a requirement that the Medical Board records its interviews with any physician that it accuses of misconduct or wrongdoing. It made sense to me. I saw a stark difference between his approach and that of Boreman and knew right away that Iungerich and Spackman were likely a good choice.

My wife and I met with Iungerich and his partner Spackman for three hours in their office in Rolling Hills, Los Angeles, California, one late afternoon. I gave them my analysis of the Discovery documents to show them how the entire foundation of the case was based on lies that were manufactured by Pueschel. Based on their own reading of the Discovery and additional information that I provided them, the two lawyers were able to clearly see exactly what Pueschel and Townsend had done to craft a case against me based on lies and deception.

In addition to the previously discussed tampering and falsification found within these Discovery documents, and refusal to provide the recording of the FDA agents' 2010 interviews, the Board's attorney, Steve Diehl (possibly in concert with Townsend), withheld some of the Board's documentation from the 2010-2011 Board inquiry that stated the IUD issue with regard to patient Ann Baker had been resolved between the Board's Executive Director, Donald Krpan, and myself. They did include communication letters between the

Medical Board Investigator, Townsend, and the Medical Board's expert witness, Ob/Gyn physician, Shirley Wong, supposedly "an IUD Expert." It had certification from the Board's Expert that she had read and reviewed the entire Discovery, including all reports, Townsend's investigation report, memos and patient interviews of FDA agent, Department of Justice reports, and patient interview reports conducted by the Bureau of Medical Fraud Investigator, Sonia Rios. It had the expert's final opinion and conclusions based on her review of the FDA's evidence (presented as the Board's evidence). The only statement she made that was not in support of me was about using FDA-unapproved IUDs, which she said was a violation of the standard of care, and she agreed with the FDA on this. That one point was the only thing she supported the Medical Board on in reiterating the FDA agent's accusation. The expert did not make any distinction between the side effects of the German IUD, T-Safe, and the U.S. drug maker's IUD, ParaGard.

The Board did not disclose how much they paid this expert for her review, but I was told she was paid well for her effort. She did not question the safety of the T-Safe brand. She stated that I had provided Ms. Baker appropriate care just as the patient had requested when she came to my office. Apparently being a paid consultant for these government agencies, she was aware that she was expected to agree, and perhaps rightfully so, that doctors were not supposed to use FDA-unapproved IUDs. But I cannot complain about her findings since she did not make any statement uniquely harmful to me in her conclusions. In fact, her testimony was more supportive than harmful to my case, despite all the perjuries committed by the FDA agent and submitted as government evidence for the Medical Board's pre-hearing.

I showed my attorneys the proof that Wong was an Obstetrician and Gynecologist with qualifications that were not credentialed and recognized by the ACGME (Accreditation Council for Graduate Medical Education), although her conclusions were correct for the most part, and mostly all in my favor. The one minor exception was when she stated that the adjustment of a dislodged IUD, rather than replacement of it, was a minor deviation from the standard of care. She was incorrect on that point, and I showed my attorneys papers by experts engaged in IUD research from Harvard, USC, NYU, John A. Burns School of Medicine, Hawaii, and Florida State to prove that the way I handled dislodged IUDs was in accordance with their recommendations, and inconsistent with the opinion of the Board's expert (Exhibit 17).

I provided my new attorneys with all the information I had and was fortunate that Iungerich, who had not read the Discovery, seemed to believe everything I told him. I knew he understood it all when he commented that it made sense to him. Spackman, who had read the Discovery ahead of our meeting, agreed that there were many contradictory and questionable statements to be found throughout.

To my dismay, there was a catch. Spackman stated that regardless of all the damning evidence we might gather to show that the FDA had falsified its case against me, I would not be able to accuse the FDA agent of perjury before the Judge because if I did, the judge would revoke my license immediately. One of them said you cannot seek justice from the government by calling the government a criminal.

"What about the fact that the FDA did not provide a recording of the interviews?" I asked the question with confidence, as this was the critical point Spackman made during our initial phone conversation that helped me decide that they were the right set of attorneys to represent me. Suddenly, this lack of a recording did not seem to matter to either one of them. Their response was like the one I got from my previous attorney, Gluck, which implied that anything illegal the government does was okay, as though the law does not apply to them, it only applies to accused defendants.

I was disappointed that Spackman had used this argument to lure me as a client, but it was not a good enough reason to go and look for other lawyers, especially after my traumatic experience with Boreman. Overall, they both looked competent and seemed to be evaluating my case fairly and logically. They informed me that the most powerful defense I would have was that the Cu-380A that I used was manufactured in Germany and was approved, researched and recommended by the U.S. Centers for Disease Control and we had written evidence of that. This evidence could not fail despite the FDA's claims. As far as the Cu-375 IUD was concerned, that was no longer an issue because I worked out that misunderstanding with the Board's Executive Director in my first Medical Board case two years prior, and I had stopped using that IUD more than three years prior, upon the FDA's advice. The case boiled down to whether or not the Cu-380A made by a German Pharma company was U.S. FDA approved. And if it was not, then why did the FDA tell me in 2010 that it was? There was also the ethical question of why American women should have to pay four times the price for a U.S. brand when the same high-quality drug made in Germany was available at a fraction of the U.S. price.

I did not expect a good outcome before meeting with Spackman and Iungerich because I was still jolted by Boreman's mistreatment of me, but I went home that night with some optimism and hope.

But, as they say, there is no such thing as a free lunch. Iungerich wanted to get started with a $30,000 upfront non-refundable fee and a rate of $500 an hour for every billable hour each of them was going to put in after the initial $30,000 were used up. That was a lot of money for me to dish out! I had no choice because I needed to save my medical license to continue to make a living for my young family and my business, which had suffered when FDA agents went around town speaking with my former and current patients telling them I was under criminal investigation. There was no other option than to try to save my medical license and work toward regaining the trust of my patients.

After several months, on September 13, 2013, the Board filed an Amended Accusation. It did not have any new information as the Board had claimed but more of the same thing: additional patient interviews conducted by Pueschel, leading to the same guided conclusions. The date of the pre-hearing was set in February, 2014. It was postponed for several more months and finally rescheduled in August, 2014. Among the reasons for the delays was that the Medical Board was waiting for the FDA agent to spice up the case a bit more, in an attempt to seal my fate.

August, 2014: Medical Board Hearing

A week before the Board hearing, I learned that Iungerich, the attorney I specifically hired was not well enough to attend and his partner Spackman would be attending instead. I was disappointed but had no control over the matter. I met with Spackman in a restaurant midway between his office in Los Angeles and my office in Tehachapi to discuss what to expect at the hearing so I would be prepared for it. We spent two hours talking. I brought with me tons of literature from the medical journals in the United States as well as Europe about German T-Safe and U.S. equivalent, ParaGard as well as Cu-375 (three-year copper IUD used only in Europe), and the safety studies and approval status of these IUDs in Europe. I also showed him research papers from Harvard University and the University of Southern California on comparative studies of the effectiveness of Cu-380A and Cu-375. I informed Spackman that I intended to tell the judge everything that I knew about the fabricated documents concocted by FDA agent Pueschel and the suppression of actual evidence. Spackman reacted dramatically to what I said. He warned me that the judge would revoke my license in a heartbeat if I accused the federal government of wrongdoing, repeating the warning both attorneys had already given me once before in their office. "I just want to tell the judge the truth," I said. "Isn't court supposed to be a place where the truth comes out and people testify to reveal what they know?" He warned me about accusing the FDA agent and politely threatened that he would not represent me if I were planning to make any statements of the sort in front of the judge. He also informed me that the Board Attorney, John E. DeCure working on behalf of Steve Diehl, had called to tell him the Board would not settle this case for any less than a revocation of my license, but DeCure promised he would try to get it settled for 7 years of probation on my license by talking with the Board.

The enthusiasm of my stellar attorneys about the nature of my claims seemed to have already petered out. I wondered why all those great defense arguments of theirs had disappeared. It was time for a reality check about how the system worked and the fact that truth would not be allowed to prevail when it comes to our government. I told him I would fight for my medical license, and if he allowed me to speak in front of the judge, I promised not to directly accuse the FDA of any wrongdoing. I assured him I would be very judicious in conveying my concerns and making my statements.

During the week before the hearing, I thought hard about how I could tell the judge what I knew without offending him since the fate of my medical license was in his hands. I was not sure what else Spackman might forbid me from talking about in court, so I did not discuss it with him any further. I brewed thoughts in my own mind as to how I was going to try to indirectly expose the FDA agent's suppression of evidence to the judge.

In early August, 2014, I appeared in court for my hearing. Also present were John E. DeCure, representing the Medical Board, and Paul Spackman who was representing me. The Administrative Law Judge's name does not appear on the final decision document, I was told that she was substituting for the judge who was meant to originally hear the case that morning — a change that was unexpected and without prior notice to anyone. Before we entered the courtroom, John E. DeCure reminded my attorney that the Board would not settle for anything less than revocation of my license, but added that he was trying to convince the Medical Board to give me seven years of probation on my license instead. I did not say a word when Spackman informed me of this. I knew I could not leave matters solely in the hands of Spackman if I wanted any truth to come out that day. I also knew that he would forbid me from saying certain things if I gave him any indication of what my statements would be. I kept quiet and was prepared to take my chances. I knew it was going to be a long day for me, and it was I who was going to be doing the talking. I was also very aware that if I prevented my attorney from presenting the case by simply taking over, it would be an unusual situation and he wouldn't be happy about it. But If I did not take charge, my attorney would beat around the bush in order to be respectful to the court, avoiding the truth because of his concern about offending the judge leading to a potential negative outcome for my medical license.

As soon as we sat down, the Board attorney read the Board's recommendation to revoke my license or put me on seven-year probation. In response to this opening remark by the Board's attorney, I took over the floor instead of waiting for my attorney to respond. I wanted my presentation before the Administrative Law Judge to be a mirror image of the presentation I made before the two FDA agents on August 17, 2010 with the only exception being that I would remain respectful this time because this was the courtroom. I chose my words carefully and refrained from accusing the FDA agent of forging evidence, withholding information, and omitting things – all points I wanted so badly to tell the judge.

I gave the same persuasive talk to the judge that I had given to the two FDA agents in 2010 with a slightly different twist to help her understand the underlying issues at some length. I opened two packages of copper IUDs, the U.S. manufactured, ParaGard and the German brand, T-safe and spread their drug inserts on the table. Then I politely challenged the judge to look at them and tell me that they were not the same drug by two different pharmas, one U.S. and the other German. They were the same. My exact words were, "God could not tell that these are not the same drugs, because they are." Then I went on to read the list of side effects from the package inserts of both devices to demonstrate that the side effects were from the device and had nothing to do with what the brand was. I specifically focused on pointing out the side effects from the ParaGard insert so that the judge would be able to immediately decipher that the questions asked during patient interviews conducted by the FDA agent, and presented in the Discovery, must have been worded in a way to get damning responses. I also emphasized to the judge that the Board's hired expert, Shirley Wong, had testified in a letter that she reviewed the entire investigation report by the Medical Board investigator as well as reports of the Department of Justice, the FDA agent and those of the BMFEA, and did not independently report any difference between the side effects of the T-Safe and the ParaGard, except paraphrasing the FDA words against me in her report before stating her own findings. Spackman intervened and backed me up on my statements. I offered to show the judge scores of Ob/Gyn research papers from medical journals demonstrating the safety and quality of the German-made T-Safe and the Cu-375. I had brought with me a duffle bag that weighed 50 pounds full of these research papers. I also offered to show the judge the medical literature on Cu-375 by the U.S. researchers demonstrating that it was safe to use as well. This was the IUD that, although not approved, I used for research studies and provided for free and then immediately stopped using it effective August 17, 2010, upon receiving instructions from the FDA.

Surprisingly, both the judge and the Board attorney seemed to be receptive to all my statements and showed no hostility or opposition. As I attempted to open my bag, the judge did not seem to be interested in looking at research papers but asked my attorney to bring over the IUDs and their drug inserts for her inspection. She examined the packages back and front, and looked at both brands of IUDs, the ParaGard and T-Safe, a few times. She casually looked at the drug inserts of both. My impression was that she heard the sincerity in my voice and measured the confidence with which I spoke. The package inserts were there only to confirm what I was claiming to be true.

Then I switched over to discussing the predatory pricing of the copper IUD by Teva. I offered to show the judge my billing records to demonstrate financial need and the price differences between the products. I was prepared to show the judge that I did not charge patients who could not afford the IUD but needed it for medical reasons, or if their insurance plan did not adequately cover the benefit. I offered to show her the billing records I brought with me to demonstrate that those who had the T-Safe from my office were given it at the bare minimum cost of the IUD device and the necessary services such as ultrasound and surgical supplies, which were not paid separately due to bundled billing code for Cu-380A, and that I did not seek salary or emoluments for the related healthcare services that I rendered for free, including multiple doctor's office visits. I informed the judge that the accusation of altering medical records of my patient, Ann Baker, was a clerical error and that no other mistake had been found in any IUD patients' charts who received IUDs from my office since 2008. Occasionally, my attorney jumped into the conversation to support me, especially about the predatory prices of the U.S. brand IUD ParaGard, but otherwise stayed silent for the most part. He explained to the judge how Teva was raising prices of the ParaGard copper IUD each year to make it out of the reach of most patients. He also informed the judge and DeCure that according to a recent ob/gyns CME Conference on Contraceptives, one third of the gynecologists in the country were using imported Cu-380A IUDs, while others did not offer the IUD services at all because patients could not afford to buy the Paragard.

Spackman also interrupted my speech to say that one of the Board's witnesses, a physician named Dr. Coelho, wrote medical notes that the Board provided to Spackman to support its claim against me — notes that failed to support the Medical Board's allegations against me. Days before the hearing, Spackman had asked the government's attorney if Dr. Coelho would be available for questioning or deposition and was informed that he would not be available, as he had moved to Guam. I wonder why he skipped town or could not travel from Guam for a deposition.

I was surprised that Spackman let me speak so much and so forcefully, even while making statements he had forbidden, perhaps because he noted things were going well. I was able to make all the necessary and relevant points about my case, without explicitly bringing up my accusations against the FDA's suppression of evidence. Of course, in my view, destruction of evidence by the FDA should have been the first thing brought up before anything else in this court of law, but I had been warned against doing so.

I waited for the Board's attorney and the Judge to give me one counter-argument, but they had none. I wondered how the Board could level such serious allegations against a physician and then dial it back so quickly when the federal government (the FDA) had invested so much into this investigation. It was possible that millions of dollars of taxpayers' money had been wasted over the years trying to fabricate this case against me, so I found it unlikely that anyone would say, "Sorry, we made a mistake, let's go home."

I told DeCure that I would rather go to a full trial than accept any probation on my medical license. He stepped out of the courtroom and supposedly called Donald Krpan (the same guy who yelled at me on the phone in the Board's first inquiry), came back and made the "Board's new offer" to me to accept "a letter of reprimand" as a settlement to avoid unnecessary legal expense for both sides. He said that the Medical Board would leave my medical license intact if I agreed to bear half the cost of the Board's investigation. Fortunately, he did not ask me to pay for half the cost of the FDA investigation, which could have been millions. He also said that I should attend a course on medical ethics and a course on medical record keeping. I refused to settle for a letter of reprimand. The Board attorney and my defense attorney both informed me that the letter did not have any effect on my career nor restrict my medical license in any way so it would be wise to sign it to prevent the heavy cost of litigation for both parties. The Board's attorney kept explaining to me that it was a prima facie case, which he said meant that I was not admitting to any of the accusations leveled against me in the Discovery. He said, "Prima facie means that the Board's claims could be proven to be true from the viewpoint of the Board if I decided to go to trial." My attorney took me out of the room with the judge's permission and advised me to accept it, explaining that a letter of reprimand meant nothing — it was just a slap on the wrist. He said it would save me tons of money instead of going to trial only for a moral victory, which could be very costly.

"Have I not provided the evidence against all accusations made, why should I accept a letter of reprimand?" I asked. The FDA had drained me financially for five years, not to mention the emotional impact on me and my family, and the loss of business and revenue. Considering the economic consequences of going to trial, I took my attorney's advice and agreed to accept the letter. I just wanted to restore peace in my life by avoiding any further cost and financial burden on my family. I had been through a lot already and was emotionally drained. I questioned my attorney as to what it meant to attend a course in medical ethics. Did it mean that it was unethical for a physician to provide affordable healthcare? On the other hand, did it mean that it was ethical for Teva to sell IUDs to American women at predatory prices? What ethics were being discussed? Who needed the ethics? What was the definition of *ethics* according to our government? Going to a medical record-keeping course, on the other hand, I believed would be a good idea, because I needed a reprimand for not keeping proper medical records due to the error I had made in noting the wrong Lot number in Ann Baker's chart. Besides I would get Continued Medical Education (CME) credits, which I had to get 150 of them as a requirement for the renewal of my medical license every two years anyway. I had made an unfortunate record-keeping mistake, although I knew for a fact such errors were within the standard curve that one would find in any busy medical office. In the end, it was an economic decision to accept a letter of reprimand from the Medical Board. It left a sour taste in my mouth though, since the Medical Board was supposed to look after the needs of consumers, and not the profits of Big Pharma.

September 5, 2014: Accepting Medical Board Decision

I told Spackman that before I agree to sign any Settlement Agreement with the Board, the Board must agree to insert language in the written agreement that said that I provided not just affordable care to my patients but contributed money from my pocket for them to be able to get medically necessary IUDs from my office. He discussed with Mr. DeCure about it who inserted the following language in the final draft stating: "IUDs were not FDA approved. In mitigation, the Respondent did so without a motive of pecuniary gain but in an attempt to work within the limits of the patients' allowable insurance benefits" (Exhibit 19). I did not like the fact that the Agreement drafted by DeCure did not say that I contributed money from my pocket to help my patients obtain IUD services. I also did not like the fact that DeCure, the Medical Board attorney, cut and pasted Pueschel' s false statements from the Discovery, such as IUDs I used to be not FDA approved. Regardless of whether the IUDs were FDA approved or not, the fact remained that the FDA informed me in October 2010 that the T-Safe was FDA approved. The Board's language in the Agreement also had no details of the fact that I provided patients IUDs at my bare minimum cost of the device and related bundled services and did not take any salary or profit for myself. No such details were incorporated. Spackman did not want me to make fuss about the omitted details and advised me to put this behind me by signing the agreement and moving on with my life since my medical license was untouched and unrestricted. He made a good point. I wanted this nightmare to end, and I decided to go on with my life.

Two months later, on October 31, the settlement order was filed in the court on October 31, and became effective in November, 2014. In the Stipulated statement the government attorney stated: "For purposes of resolving the First Amended Accusation without the expense and uncertainty of further proceedings, Respondent does not contest, that at the administrative hearing, complainant could establish a *prima facie* case with respect to the charges in the First Amended Accusation, and Respondent hereby gives up his right to contest those charges" (Stipulated Settlement, p.3).

A week after signing this settlement agreement, I announced on my website the launch date of my next book, which I thought would be titled, *FDA's Betrayal of the American Public*, words that I took from John Kerry's hearing of the FDA's Assistant Commissioner, Mr. Alderson, aired on C-SPAN TV in 2011. During the hearing, Senator Kerry told the FDA commissioner, "You have betrayed the American Public" for being in the pocket of the food and drug industry. Indeed, it is a breath of fresh air when a politician speaks the truth, even when it's only to win the hearts of the public or for the sake of votes for an upcoming election.

Shortly after the settlement with the Medical Board, a local newspaper, *Tehachapi News*, approached me for my version of what happened before covering the story. I took advantage of this and gave a full account of the abuse of Big Pharma and the corruption in the FDA. The newspaper published at least half of what I told the reporter as my side of the story. I had also encouraged the reporter to go to YouTube and listen to my public seminars criticizing the FDA for being in cahoots with Big Pharma so that he could gain some understanding as a journalist about the corruption in the Food and Drug Administration.

Perhaps it was a rash decision on my part to start advertising a book about the FDA almost immediately after the conclusion of the Board case. My wife advised me not to speak with the press or announce the release of my book on the website, but being the stubborn person that I am, I never listen to my wife and dismissed her concerns. (Note to all male readers: *Do not* dismiss what your wife is telling you. As I have learned, ignoring one's wife may result in nothing, or it may result in years of pain. Women have some insights that we men don't.) I felt somewhat vindicated, given the fact that the FDA and Teva's scheme to have my medical license revoked did not work. I naively did not realize that it might not yet be over. I should have reflected a bit more on what my staff had told me following the FDA raid when they said the FDA agents who had interviewed them boasted that I had been under massive surveillance during the previous two years, they knew what I wore, where I had lunched each day, and that I wore the same clothes every day, etc. I should have known that any federal agency that would spend years spying on me, building a case, and falsifying records to ruin me, would not be stopped by a State Medical Board decision.

Within a month of the local newspapers reporting my settlement with the Medical Board, I once again began to hear rumblings about the FDA hitting the Tehachapi streets in pursuit of damning information about me. Since the Medical Board refused to do the bidding for the FDA, Pueschel now ramped up his efforts to ruin me. This is obvious by looking at the dates of Pueschel's interviews with my patients, as found in the documents generated by the FDA. Occasionally a patient would call to ask questions about an IUD that she received or ask for a copy of her IUD-related medical records, the kinds of inquiries that had gone away for a while but had sprung up once more within a month of the Medical Board's soft decision. That could not have been a coincidence. I could tell something was not right, and figured the FDA was planning a renewed assault. I immediately went to my website and deleted the announcement about the launch date of my book, and temporarily canceled the plans to release it. But as you know, once something is posted on the internet it gets picked up by search engines and never goes away. I realized how bad things were when a patient who had received an IUD from me came to my office and complained that FDA agents were knocking on her door every month and asking her if she would cooperate with them by testifying against me. The patient informed me that she had told the two men to stop harassing her, but they kept coming back to her house even though she told them many times that she would not help them because "I trust and believe in my doctor and have had no problem or complications from this IUD. I can't help you."

I was dealing with the fallout from the Medical Board's decision and a new wave of the FDA's propaganda on behalf of the drug giant, Teva. I could not have measured how unhappy the FDA and Teva were with the Medical Board's final decision, given how much time and money the FDA had put into crafting a carefully thought-out case, and covertly recruiting the Medical Board to act as its executioner. Now the FDA had to take matters into its own hands. Allowing a gynecologist (with YouTube videos and speaking engagements) to continue advocating for copper IUDs from Germany, posed a threat to the financial monopoly Teva so enjoyed.

Now that it is all over, I can only draw the logical conclusion that the FDA had targeted me to make an example of, perhaps even before the agents first arrived in my office in 2010. They never did state why I was the one they decided to visit to ask fundamental questions about IUDs, and at the time, I didn't think to ask. I will never know the truth unless someone in the government reveals everything that has been concealed, which is highly unlikely. But who better than someone born in another country, idealistic about this one, and unsavvy about the ins and outs of the legal system? I will go to my grave feeling I was targeted as someone to be framed so they could use me as an example to threaten other doctors.

In the months that followed, I paid my half portion of the Medical Board's investigation cost and attended a course in medical record keeping and ethics at the University of Southern California.

The class was called Professional Boundaries, a government-run program given by a psychiatrist who was an advocate for government regulations. That completed, all of my obligations as outlined in my agreement with the Medical Board had been satisfied, and I was more than ready to move on from this nightmare. I have learned since then that there had been some other IUD cases during the same time period I was being prosecuted by the federal government but none where the prosecutors and the FDA engaged in unlawfully criminal behavior in pursuing their set goals.

CHAPTER 3

GUILTY AT GUNPOINT

Mounting Threats of Arrest and Indictment

SIX MONTHS AFTER THE BOARD'S DECISION, IN MAY, 2015, I received a phone call from Gluck, my attorney on record with the federal government. Gluck informed me that he received a phone call from an FDA prosecutor telling him that the government was going to indict me for purchasing and using the IUDs that I bought from Canada. The prosecutor, Patrick Delahunty, also said that "the defendant" (me) did not have much time left. I asked Gluck what was meant by 'not much time left' and what charges I was facing. He informed me that Delahunty did not tell him what the charges were, but that the prosecutor said I didn't have much time before they came to arrest me, and that I would be indicted. "Why don't you find out what the charges are?" I suggested. Gluck replied that my account with his law firm was closed in 2014, two years after the raid and that this one would be regarded as a new case. Therefore they would first need a $50,000 retainer before he agreed to call the prosecutor back to find out the details. I informed Gluck that I did not have that kind of money and that there were no grounds for a federal case anyway because all issues related to the FDA's allegations and accusations, had been investigated and resolved through two investigations by the Medical Board, between 2010 and 2014. I apprised him of all that had been happening for three years, since he had not been in the loop.

Gluck was not interested in a word I said. He would not call Delahunty, the prosecutor until I agreed to pay him $50,000 upfront and reiterated that his fee was $700 an hour. I told him that I had already lost a lot of my business due to FDA agent Pueschel maligning my good name and ruining my reputation and that I did not have any money left, and would have to start tapping into my retirement account. "What are your worries and your concerns that you would require such a large deposit?" I asked. I questioned whether it was essential since there was no case. All IUD-related issues had been amicably resolved through the Medical Board. But Gluck said he would not take the case without $50,000 upfront, and that it was the policy of his law firm. Feeling my hands were tied, I offered to pay him $30,000 from my retirement account, but he said he would have to consult with his partners to see if they would allow him to accept $30,000, and he would get back to me with their decision.

Days passed, and he did not call me back. I became worried that they would come and arrest me in the middle of the day while I was seeing patients. I still suffered trauma from the FDA raid in 2012, mainly when I thought about how frightened my patients and employees must have been. I didn't want any of us to have to endure another incident like that. After leaving Gluck several voicemail messages, he responded and said that he had not yet had a chance to speak with his partners at the law firm and that he would get back to me soon.

I knew he was playing games, after already scaring the hell out of me by conveying the message from the prosecutor about "not much time left." I sensed his answer to $30,000 was going to be 'no' so I called him and suggested taking on the case for $40,000, even though it would take a couple of weeks to get the money out because of tax liability and regulations surrounding early withdrawal from a retirement fund. He said he would ask his partners if they would accept $40,000 and call me back. Two days later I was still waiting to hear from him, so I called him, ready to buckle to his demand for $50,000. When I finally reached him, he told me he had not yet spoken with his partners but decided he would accept $40,000. It appeared the decision was his to make all along – so he was playing psychology.

Perhaps I should not have told him about my poor financial condition. I am not sure how it affected his long-term commitment to represent me. I assured him the money was on its way, adding that he needed to call Delahunty immediately. After speaking with Delahunty the next morning, Gluck informed me that the prosecutor did not want to tell him what the charges were, but stated he was sure that I only had little time left before an arrest and indictment. It was this vague message that forced me to relent to Gluck's demands for money sooner rather than later, even before it was clear what the crime was.

In other words, the prosecutor was already threatening me with consequences as though saying, "I assure you that I will charge you with a crime, even though I don't know what it is yet. Don't even think about pleading not guilty." That was Delahunty's technique to manipulate me to plead guilty regardless of the merit of his case, and irrespective of its legal basis.

Gluck informed me that he had another phone call set up with the prosecutor the following day and would let me know what he found out. He called me back after speaking with Delahunty the second time and told me that he informed him (Delahunty) that all the FDA's issues had been determined by the Medical Board, and we would like to know what the FDA charges were that had not already been addressed. Delahunty responded that the Medical Board did not know what he knew. The prosecutor then proceeded to claim that I had been using Cu-375 copper IUDs after being told by Pueschel in 2010 to stop using them. Gluck asked me if that was true, and I informed him it was not true. I also informed him that I did not implant any IUDs in the two-month period between August 17 and October 12, 2010, while awaiting Pueschel to inform me of the FDA's verdict about the approval status of these IUDs. Gluck called Delahunty back to tell him that his accusation that I used Cu-375s after October 12, 2010, was untrue. Gluck informed the prosecutor that I had stopped using Cu-375s after August 17, 2010, and that he (Gluck) believed I was telling the truth.

I sincerely hoped this exchange would clear up any misunderstanding on the part of the FDA and Delahunty, but soon it became clear they were not going to be deterred by the facts. Delahunty called Gluck with a new allegation. Now he accused me of continuing to use the CU-380A I bought from Canada after the FDA raid on March 28, 2012. When Gluck conveyed this to me, I told him that this new claim was not true either. I jogged Gluck's memory to help him recall his conversation with me in his office in Los Angeles in April of 2012, weeks after the FDA raid, in which he had advised me not to use any IUDs bought from Canada, even though the FDA had been telling me for two years that T-Safe was an FDA-approved IUD. I had decided to follow Gluck's advice at that time, even though I disagreed with him in principle. Gluck remembered that conversation and called the prosecutor back to tell him that the new allegation was not true either, to which Delahunty replied with something to the effect (and this is not the exact wording), 'Now you are going to tell me that your client is perfect, aren't you?' Gluck replied, and again, I'm paraphrasing, 'I am not saying that he is perfect, all I am saying is that this accusation of yours is not true either. My client did not use any IUDs at all after the date of the raid because I had told him not to, and he says he complied and I believe him.' Delahunty seemed to accept that answer, so I was optimistic and hoped this would now lead to a quick resolution of all remaining misunderstandings.

Two days later, when Gluck called the prosecutor back to see if everything was now straightened out and the matter closed, the prosecutor reiterated to Gluck that I needed to plead guilty sooner rather than later and that I was running out of time, and would soon be indicted and arrested. I was completely distressed and bewildered that the prosecutor wanted to publicly arrest and humiliate me, continuing with his threat to indict me, despite accepting my responses to his charges as truthful. At least that is the clear impression Gluck gave me based on his conversations with Delahunty. The accusations Delahunty had leveled against me thus far, he now seemed to accept as being untrue. I felt like I was already guilty in the eyes of the prosecutor even though he had no idea as to what his charges against me were.

After this conversation, Delahunty sent FDA agents to my ex-employee and former Medical Assistant, Sandra Johnson's current workplace, which was another doctor's office in Bakersfield. Ms. Johnson was my employee till 2014 when she took a local job in Bakersfield because she could no longer commute 80 miles a day, a two-way trip to Tehachapi. Ms. Johnson had handled copper IUDs in my office as was apparent from her handwriting in the medical charts confiscated by the government. The FDA agents informed her that the FDA prosecutors would depose her. I spoke to Gluck and insisted that if such a deposition were to occur, I wanted Spackman, the attorney who represented me with the Medical Board, to be part of that deposition/interview of Johnson. I wanted Spackman to witness the story that was unfolding since he was directly aware of the facts of the FDA case as presented through the agency of the Medical Board in the years 2013 and 2014. Getting Spackman on board was financially burdensome for me because I would primarily be paying him just to be a witness. Spackman had told me that he would be happy to be a witness to the events that were unfolding because he knew my Medical Board case well, but could not directly defend me, because criminal defense was not an area of his expertise. It meant I would be spending more money I did not have. They say a penny is too much if you don't have it, but it was going to cost thousands of dollars for Spackman to travel and be present during the deposition, at a fee of $500 an hour.

Gluck immediately suggested hiring a former prosecutor and a friend of his, Stephen Jones of Holmes, Taylor & Jones LLP, to represent Ms. Johnson in her deposition, and asked me to pay for it since Ms. Johnson did not have the money. She was making $12 an hour with three children to support. Gluck told me that this attorney was a former government prosecutor and could be, in his words, "helpful to my case." I accepted Gluck's recommendation thinking that Ms.

Johnson would be able to unmask Agent Pueschel's cover-ups since she was familiar with all the events that took place between the FDA and me between August 17,2010 and October 12,2010. There was no way Johnson could have been able to afford an attorney, and who knew what these guys were up to. Perhaps she could further clear up Delahunty's misunderstandings at her deposition and put an end to this case for good. I was quite puzzled at this point because I did not understand why it was necessary to depose Johnson or anyone because the answer to every possible question Delahunty could ever want to know was in the medical charts and billing electronic records in his possession, why not look up the charts and billing records.

Ms. Johnson called me in a panic over agents showing up at her house and her workplace "every day." I called Gluck and told him that Johnson called me and was very upset, wanting to know what was going on. Gluck told me that I was not to speak to her at all through this process because I was the defendant and that was the law. I stopped talking with her from that point on. She called me again, and I advised her not to call me because I had been warned not to speak to her about the case due to concerns that I could influence her.

After receiving a proffer agreement and a written immunity from the prosecutor, Ms. Johnson was interviewed and recorded for eight hours on May 29, 2015, in Bakersfield, California. At the deposition were prosecutors Delahunty and his supervisor Kirk Sheriff; FDA agent Pueschel; Johnson's defense attorney, Stephen Jones; my defense attorney, Gluck; and my former Medical Board defense attorney, Spackman. Spackman later reported to me that he had never *seen such a vicious* human being like the younger one, referring to the government attorney taking the lead in the interview. Spackman did not know who this man was, but he was referring to Delahunty, the younger of the two federal prosecutors. Spackman's observation was very similar to Gluck's, as he also described Delahunty as being young, obnoxious, immature, inexperienced, and nasty. In his dealings with Delahunty, Gluck noted that he seemed to be a zealous prosecutor, who seemed to want to score convictions, perhaps to advance his career and that his behavior was grossly unprofessional.

The morning after the deposition, Gluck called me and said that he needed my permission to speak with Stephen Jones, Ms. Johnson's attorney to ask him to disclose his conversation with the government prosecutors about how the deposition went in the eyes of the government. Since Johnson's attorney was a former prosecutor and a former colleague of government prosecutors, he could obtain the status of the case from the government and give us a heads up about the results of the deposition. I gave my permission to Gluck, of course. Gluck then immediately revealed to me that Ms. Johnson's testimony corroborated my claims and assertions to be true. He did not give me any details but did note that her testimony 'could not have been any better.' It would not be until much later after my conviction that I would learn the details of what happened before and during the eight-hour interrogation. It is quite revealing about the way our government, and law and order, work in this country. After hearing what had occurred in Johnson's deposition, there was no doubt in my mind that I was dealing with a criminal who happened to be a prosecutor working for our federal government. More on this later.

Days after Ms. Johnson's deposition, my medical biller at the time, Amy Jones, who was my biiller up until the day of my conviction (her name has been changed to protect her identity), informed me that FDA agents knocked at her door, and intimidated her by saying something to the effect of, "We wanted to let you know it's not over yet." That was a threat. And seeing how this knock on Amy's door took place days after the prosecutor's spent eight hours badgering Ms. Johnson, they decided to give the warning that Amy would be their next target.

Amy Jones had been my medical biller for years and her interview during the FDA raid was one of the many documents that had been altered, edited, falsified, and narrated out of context by Pueschel, and submitted to the Medical Board during the Board's second investigation that concluded on October 31, 2014.

There was silence from the prosecutor for several days following Johnson's deposition. The question remained what could Delahunty be up to now that Ms. Johnson had also cleared up any misunderstandings Delahunty might still have. Frankly, I was very hopeful at this point that my integrity had shined so many times from so many angles that Delahunty had now nothing else that he could make up against me even if he intended to. In my opinion, all issues had been resolved to everyone's satisfaction including Delahunty's at this juncture. But within days, Gluck once again, started delivering me messages from Delahunty that I would be indicted very shortly, within a week or days, even though he couldn't tell me what the charges could be or would be. Only Delahunty or his God knew what Delahunty was planning.

I felt like an army had surrounded my house, closing in from all directions to break down the doors and shoot me, although they couldn't tell me what I had done wrong. I was now an enemy combatant with no human or legal rights. It was clear that Delahunty had made up his mind that there would be an indictment, no matter what. Now all he had to do was get me to buckle and tell him I would agree to a plea deal with the hope of somehow saving myself. If I didn't, he would continue digging until he could manufacture something new.

In a follow-up conversation between my attorney and Delahunty, the prosecutor came up with yet another new theory. This theory was his surefire rationale for indictment, and it was that my patients had given very emotional testimonies to the FDA agent about the complications they experienced from the IUDs that I implanted in them. It was indeed more of a threat than it was a justification for indictment, with the prosecutor insinuating to my defense attorney that he had this weapon of mass destruction to use against me. Strangely, my defense attorney seemed to be very comfortable with the idea of this novel offense that might stick. He told me there was no way I could escape the influence on the case from those moving, heart-wrenching, emotional, testimonies to be given by crying patients in front of the jury if I chose not to plead guilty. Gluck said that the patients' emotional testimonies would reduce our chances of success at trial. It gave me a pause when he also informed me that the defense did not have the right to tell the grand jury what was true and wasn't true about the testimonies. We could not dispute the credibility of any of the prosecutor's claims. Delahunty could say anything to the Grand jury and we would not be able to counter it with the truth, because we were not allowed to present our case at this point.

I clearly recall a phone call from Gluck in which he told me that it would be outside his capability to successfully defend me against those heart-wrenching testimonies. That was bad news for me, he said. Gluck did not have the time or the patience to listen to what I had to tell him about these patient reports and how they were masterfully elicited and falsely induced by the FDA agent, Pueschel.

He was mainly repeating to me what the prosecutor had told him. That was an existential threat, to witness false testimonies by patients against me who would cry in front of the judge at trial, who had been psychologically convinced by Pueschel that their bodies were subject to great harm. And then Gluck made it clear to me that defense was not allowed to give their side of the story to the grand jury at the time of indictment if Delahunty chose to present his case to the grand jury painting me as a vicious human being who endangered the lives of vulnerable patients and caused them serious bodily harm. That would surely seal my indictment rubber-stamped by a duped grand jury.

As I have stated earlier in this book, I spent a lot of time trying to explain to Gluck that the side effects described by patients in interviews conducted by FDA agent Pueschel were thoroughly reviewed by the Medical Board's hired Ob/Gyn IUD expert physician, and she did not make any distinction between the side effects of the two IUDs, the German brand that I used and the U.S. brand. I also informed him that the patients' complaints in their testimonies were fraudulently induced by FDA agents deliberately spreading disinformation that the IUDs patients received from my office were dangerous, counterfeit, and defective, and bought on the Internet. Testimonial complaints (interviews by the FDA agent Pueschel) were fill-in-the-blank formats, asking leading questions, after spreading disinformation about the German T-Safes. I requested that Gluck go over the Discovery documents carefully to read sections that showed that FDA scientists inspected all the Cu-380A IUDs removed from patients and found them to be "T-Safe", the German-made Cu-380A manufactured by EurimPharma, and not something "dangerous" bought from the "Internet" as the FDA agents had described to all my patients over and over. Gluck did not read this Discovery despite my repeated email requests. He often ignored my emails. I then made it as easy as possible for him by providing him with page and line numbers that he should read, to minimize his reading responsibility. Instead of doing his due diligence to look at the evidence, he came up with a theory as to how he would impeach FDA agent Pueschel, only if he could establish that Pueschel's notes of the 2010 interview were not signed off by his supervisor at the FDA. The question, however, remained that we have to first get those notes from the government.

He laid out three arguments in his email to me as to how he would approach this to prove that the FDA agent was concealing information (Exhibit 22 and Exhibit 24 of *Companion Book: The Death of the Rule of Law*). Gluck was starting to lose interest in my objections. I believe that Gluck tried to convey my concerns to the prosecutor, or so he claimed, (I have no way of knowing), but he met with another threat. The prosecutor told him the Statute of Limitations was running out, and that I now had only days before I must plead guilty or face the consequences of public arrest and indictment. This is the strangest of all things, how does one plead guilty to a crime if one is not officially charged with anything? The pressure was on, building up and starting to become immeasurable. And still, no charge had been made.

It was at this time that the prosecutor also alleged that I fraudulently billed patients for U.S. brand ParaGard IUD, when in fact I used the generic Cu-380A. I explained to Gluck that the billing code was not reserved for a specific brand but for the actual pharmaceutical drug and device called Cu-380 A and that it was not fraudulent billing. The prosecutor alleged that I enriched myself by pushing those IUDs on patients and profited greatly in buying cheaper IUDs, and billed for insurance reimbursement that was reserved for the U.S brand, ParaGard. I insisted that the opposite was true in that I helped indigent patients obtain an essential healthcare service they so desperately needed but had no access to because of the exorbitant price of the U.S brand IUD. And I made no profits but took a financial loss in the process. But again, my attorney ignored my objections. I was not allowed to explain - my opinion did not matter, and any evidence I had to prove my point, was not relevant.

I asked Gluck if I could have the opportunity to present my evidence to the judge face-to-face for just five minutes. I felt confident if I could get in front of the judge and show him all the evidence that this would be cleared up once and for all. Before I even finished completing my sentence, Gluck told me I would "never be allowed" to speak directly to the judge. I informed him that I spoke directly to the judge in Los Angeles, and it cleared all doubts in the judge's mind within minutes, which made the judge reverse the entire Medical Board case. He responded that this was different as it was a criminal case where different rules applied. I knew I was in big trouble in the hands of the FDA prosecutor, Delahunty, who was not willing to listen to the facts, regardless of who presented them. Gluck told me that like most young prosecutors, Delahunty was young, ambitious, and overzealous, and lacked experience. The prosecutor wanted convictions. He was a tyrant, no doubt, but Gluck also had a big ego which stood in the way of his minimal social skills.

Gluck and Delahunty argued with each other at one point, and Gluck quickly backed off as he realized he was making it much worse for me. According to what he told me on the phone, he was also being rough and told the young prosecutor that he did not know what the hell he was doing wasting his time making a federal case out of a few thousand dollars of billing. That did not make things better for me.

Gluck wounded this madman's ego. Now Delahunty was pissed. He wanted me at all cost after that. He would make this conviction stick no matter what he had to do.

In reading between the lines of everything Delahunty was doing and saying, and not doing and not saying, I was certain that he was fully aware of the fact that the IUDs I used were safe. He had to have known this since he would have read the decision of the Medical Board based on the Board's Expert witness, and the fact that he had physical possession of a T-Safe IUD which he could have easily verified from the German Pharmaceutical company to make sure it was their genuine product. But I was naïve and did not know how the system worked with the Department of Justice. The due process of law does not apply to defendants. That is just a clause that sits in the Fifth Amendment and looks pretty never to be employed by the government. The laws do not matter, the only thing that counts is what the prosecutor wants. The question now was, what were the charges going to be since Delahunty was days away from fulfilling his promise of arresting me publicly?

This entire drama was played out within a few weeks from the day my defense attorney received that first ominous call from Delahunty. It happened so fast. The prosecutor said he had to rush it before his Statute of Limitations ran out. Gluck objected that Delahunty had five years to investigate and now that he had a week left before his time was up, he was pressuring me to plead guilty without discussing the merit of his case. It did not matter what Gluck had to say. Now it boiled down to the idea that I must first plead guilty and then the two opposing attorneys would figure out the details as to how they would frame the charges. How do you plead guilty without knowing the allegations? 'What are you going to charge my client with?' my attorney asked the prosecutor one more time. Delahunty informed him that the government had decided to charge me with a single count of Mail Fraud and that the decision was made with the approval of Delahunty's supervisor, Kirk Sherriff.

Gluck informed me that there was no way around this because the Anti-Drug importation law made it illegal to import any drug, brand or generic, from Europe or Canada. I asked him why then would the FDA told me for two years that the brand of Cu-380A I bought from Canada was FDA approved. I asked why the FDA did not charge me with mail fraud five years earlier when I point blank told the FDA agents on August 17, 2010, that I bought these German T-Safes from a Canadian distributor? Gluck chose not to answer my questions or address my objections.

I wondered if there was something else behind all this - five years after the fact and a week before the Statute of Limitations? It did not make any sense. Did that also mean that the FDA was guilty of a criminal act by informing me that the generic Cu-380A was FDA approved? Perhaps, the FDA as a government agency was at greater fault and should be held to higher standards than I, since all I did was obey the government's instructions in 2010. Did that mean people in the FDA - Pueschel, his supervisors, and FDA scientists should all go to jail for committing a crime if following their instructions was a crime? Imagine a scenario where federal agents show up at your door one morning, (referring to 8/17/10) and you tell them that you had been engaged in committing mail fraud crime for three years, (in using these mail fraud IUDs since 2008), provide a physical proof of that crime to the agents, and they respond, 'Well that's all right. We agree that you have committed a crime but take it easy for now because we're very busy doing some other important stuff. We'll be back in five or six years when we get a free moment, and we'll charge you with mail fraud a week before our statute of limitations is about to run out, right now we have more important things to deal with. See you then, good bye!' Of course, they didn't say this, but if I'd been committing a crime and told them that I had been, why not arrest me then? I wanted someone to answer that question if the charges were going to be mail fraud.

I was becoming so bogged down under this ever-increasing agonizing pressure from Delahunty's threats that I did not have the strength to carry on this argument any further, mainly because my attorney did not give a fig about what I had to say. I was expected to shut up and listen to what the government (i.e., the prosecutor) was accusing me of, and that would be that. I did not know what to do. I did not know how to save myself from this impending doom. All I could think about was how to protect my family financially, how we would be able to keep our heads above water, how we would keep breathing and what could happen to my kids and wife.

Gluck's legal theories of impeaching Pueschel were rapidly disappearing. I emphasized to him that he did not have to have arguments, there was enough in the Discovery documents that showed that the FDA agent covered up the exculpatory evidence. In his emails and phone calls to me (Exhibit 3, 22, and 24), Gluck informed me that he called Delahunty and asked him to produce documentation of the 2010 interviews of Dr. Singh by two FDA agents, which formulated the prosecutor's basis for accusations. The prosecutor, Delahunty, according to Gluck, replied that he didn't have it (Exhibit 3, 22, and 24). Gluck asked prosecutor Delahunty if he would give him the handwritten notes instead since he didn't have the recording or the written documentation, and got nowhere (Exhibits: 3, 22, and 24).

That was when Gluck started spitting out his theories as to how he could impeach the FDA agent for lying. Seeing what the two FDA Agents had written up during their 2010 interviews was vital to me because I felt it would be critical to my defense. Being repeatedly dismissed as though I was asking for something unnecessary, significantly added to my stress. When I insisted that Gluck question the prosecutor about having concealing information about the 2010 FDA interviews, they dropped the ultimate bomb to shut me up for good. Gluck called to deliver a chilling message from Delahunty stating that if I did not plead guilty, the prosecutor was now ready to indict my wife and put her in prison, as well. It was both incredibly frustrating and disturbing to know that I was not entitled to due process and justice did not exist. I asked Gluck if he would ask the prosecutor what happened to the female agent who interviewed me in August 2010 and inquire about why her name vanished from the discovery, but Gluck continued to tune me out and was annoyed that I insisted on asking questions. The government had already made their decision, and there was nothing he or I could do about it.

I've come to doubt that Gluck ever communicated my questions to the prosecutor. No competent attorney dedicated to defending his client would so quickly and consistently ignore the facts. Nor would he disregard the need to gain access to documents. In fact, I now know a good criminal attorney would use the fact that the prosecutor admitted that he didn't even have them as evidence to dismantle the charges. But as I came to realize, I didn't have a competent attorney.

Fortunately, I have a lot of Gluck's exchanges in the many emails he sent to me, although he was smart enough to say some things only by phone to minimize his liability. I will never learn the truth about what Gluck was up to, whether he was cooking a deal with

Delahunty or was just in it for the money without having to put a lot of effort into the case. He only selectively answered my emails and avoided answering hard questions. It was clear that Gluck regarded the behavior on the part of the prosecutor as business as usual, as though the government not providing evidence to the defendant was an acceptable legal practice, and dismissing the client paying you or treating him with animus, was to be expected. For him it was normal; for me it was shocking and disconcerting.

Gluck started to feel me out to see if I still wanted to plead not guilty. He again theorized that he would be able to prove that Pueschel's handwritten notes of the 2010 interview were a forgery if they weren't signed by his supervisor, but this was a pipedream since we couldn't get our hands on those notes. It was just like Spackman's somewhat exaggerated claim that if the government did not provide the interview recorded statements, we could somehow hold the government agent responsible for unproven accusations. These are the kind of comments attorneys often make to their clients to solicit business by giving false hope without revealing the whole truth to the client that the government does not necessarily follow the rule of law and that some prosecutors have unlimited and unilateral tyrannical powers. Frankly many prosecutors could not care less about the law or the due process of law and they piss on the Constitution of the United States, the supreme law of the land, every morning they wake up.

Gluck informed me that he would file for the Impeachment of FDA agent Pueschel, but he did not tell me what the catch was. I did not understand until later that I would have to plead not guilty and then come up with $750,000 for the first year of litigation before any possibility of such impeachment could remotely become a reality. And it would be an impossibility if the government continued to deny the existence of any notes on the August 17,2010 interview; no amount of money then spent by the defense could or would lead to Pueschel's impeachment. Was I supposed to know that a citizen cannot hold the government accountable unless one first pleads not guilty and hands over a million dollars for legal defense? Isn't this putting the cart before the horse? I had already spent $250,000 to deal with lawsuits and legal hassles with the Medical Board initiated by the same FDA agent, Pueschel, during which time he ruined my business with his false allegations, causing irreparable financial loss. Had my primary home and my rental property not appreciated dramatically in value, instead of having gone reverse like those of many other unfortunate homeowners, my net worth would have been zero.

I knew that Gluck had not read the Discovery documents despite my requests. And if he did, he did not go through everything thoroughly, because there are so many contradictions, despite the FDA agent's masterful crafting of those documents, that Gluck could have constructed a solid case in my favor despite the carefully fabricated documents. In at least two of his emails that I have in my possession, Gluck admitted to not paying close attention to my complaints and made a renewed promise that he would start paying closer attention and answer my emails, but that didn't happen. Even though he knew I was broke, Gluck upped the ante without ever increasing the effort he put into my defense.

Out of desperation, I requested that Gluck approach the other side with a deal. I would surrender my medical license if they dropped the case. I knew that my medical license is what the FDA and Teva wanted. The prosecutor immediately accepted the offer with one exception. He said I would have to plead guilty to a felony charge for a single count of mail fraud, and as a tradeoff of surrendering my license, there would be no jail time for me. Gluck asked the prosecutor if he would trade a felony charge for a misdemeanor. The prosecutor did not go for it for reasons that I did not understand at the time, but became very clear to me much later. The only way to ensure the revocation of a physician's license is to charge him with a felony crime. Felony charges would make revocation a certainty, an automatic spill-over from having committed a felonious crime.

In a three-way phone call that Gluck set up with my wife and me, and my Medical Board defense attorney, Paul Spackman, Gluck confirmed that he made the offer to Delahunty who readily agreed that if I surrendered my medical license, there would be no jail time. I would have to accept a felony on my record for a single count of mail fraud, but that would be it. Gluck informed us that he tried to persuade the prosecutor to reduce the felony to a misdemeanor, but Delahunty said that wasn't an option. Gluck then tried to convince me not to waste any time and to surrender my license to the Medical Board the very next morning. My understanding is that Gluck wanted to show the prosecutor that I had already surrendered my license as per my promise. My wife Gina interrupted and asked Gluck if he had ever seen a case like this in his experience as a criminal defense attorney, and he replied that they see it all the time and have seen guys coming out of jail after seventeen years who never committed any crime. Gina asked Gluck what my chances of winning were if I were to not plead guilty to a felony. Forty percent was his response, adding that Delahunty was planning to send her to jail, too, if I didn't plead guilty. "Why forty percent, why not a hundred percent?" she asked him. Gluck said that the prosecutors would bring in patient witnesses to testify against me, with emotionally charged tales of how the "dangerous" IUD I implanted wrecked their lives. Then he rationalized in saying that the jury already thinks that you are guilty of *something* the moment you are brought into the court as a criminal, all of that would lower our chances of success.

My wife and I shared a look that I knew meant I would have to plead guilty. We would accept one count of mail fraud and be grateful for no jail time, I'd have a felony on my record, and surrender my medical license to close this deal, which would allow me to stay home to take care of my disabled son. My wife told me later that day that she had never seen me so hysterical. I repeatedly told Gluck on the phone about the cover-ups and lies that FDA prosecutors were engaged in, proclaiming that I was innocent while the real criminals, the FDA agent and the prosecutors, were getting off scot-free. I was hysterical, and I was crying. I vaguely remember that, but since I was under tremendous pressure, my mind must have suppressed some of these memories deep in my subconscious, perhaps for the preservation of my sanity. All I remember is that I was hysterical. I also remember my world was turned upside down. And I knew that my life was about to change forever, and in a direction that may not ever be reversible. I was worried about my kids and my wife more than anything else, concerned that we would not financially survive with my medical career over. My wife would have to find a job that paid enough to support three kids. She had not worked full-time for twenty years and would not make a large enough salary to support the family. Perhaps she would have to go back to school to get an advanced degree, allowing her to find a higher paying job. Needless to say, her life was going to become very difficult.

My motivations for giving in to the prosecutor's demands were to avoid imminent arrest and public humiliation but more importantly, to avoid having my wife thrown in jail. She had nothing to do with my choice of IUDs. She came to the office only once in a while to fill in when the medical assistant was sick or we had shortage of staff. But seeing how this prosecutor was capable of forging documents to indict me, he could quickly falsify some more to put my wife in jail, as well. And the indictment, in my opinion, was a sure thing. There was no way a grand jury would not indict me when a prosecutor told the jurors how a greedy physician bought cheap, counterfeit, unsafe IUDs on the Internet to line his pockets with profits, thereby ruining the health of many patients. I could imagine these former patients of mine who once told me that they loved me, now crying in front of the judge to support the prosecutor's claim because they'd been told I had committed a crime. But my most significant motivation in pleading guilty in all this was that Delahunty's consistent behavior thus far had made it abundantly clear to me and my attorney that it did not matter what I had to say, or what the laws were, he was determined to get his conviction by hook or by crook by using the unlimited abusive power that the government of the United States had endowed upon him. It was clear to me that if I continued to object to the wrongdoing by the government and asking for Brady materials, (which are supposed to be given to the defense upon request by law), the prosecutor would show my attorney and me his middle finger, because he already had, no matter how many times we asked. The only thing that mattered, in this case, was what "the government", a synonym for Delahunty, wanted. I was told I must plead guilty by Friday that week or face public arrest. I was given a deadline, an ultimatum. That was my last chance to avoid public humiliation, and it was only hours away.

Spackman informed Gluck that he was going to research the process on how to surrender my medical license. He was at a loss as to what reasons for surrender should be given to the medical board. Spackman never had a situation like this before in his decades of medical board defense experience. He was at a loss. Gluck and Spackman communicated directly with each other to follow up on the process of surrendering my medical license. I am in possession of many emails exchanged between the two to figure out this dilemma. I was starting to have second thoughts about surrendering my medical license, but the fear of my wife being sent to jail if I refused to surrender paralyzed my limbs.

My Conference Call with a Former Prosecutor

The same night as the three-way phone conversation with Gluck, Spackman, my wife, and me, I had a two-hour phone conversation with a former government prosecutor, someone who had become a dear friend through my tribulations during my Board case. I will not get into how and where I met this person nor will I reveal his/her name or gender. I will call him Raul from this point on to simplify my writing. Raul does not necessarily imply male gender. I am keeping my promise not to reveal any information that would help identify this person who had warned me that *the lives of too many former employees had been ruined for speaking up.* He had seen it all and was quite disillusioned with the system and tired of it all, as he put it. I wanted to seek a second opinion from him to see if I had made the right decision to relent to the prosecutor's demands. He knew the details of my case as I had extensive discussions with him throughout the medical board case in 2013 and 2014 and he had reviewed the Discovery papers for me. Raul had a change of heart when one of his close relatives went to prison after being charged with a crime he never committed. He admitted to me at one point that he had engaged in some unsavory acts of the government's unlimited power in his early career for which he was not very proud. He no longer worked for the government, had been an activist for a while now (perhaps to redeem himself?). When I told him about the decision I had made, he asked me why I would surrender my medical license since none of this is the FDA's business in that it falls under the jurisdiction of the Medical Board. I informed him that it was part of the agreement made between my attorney and the prosecutor to avoid jail time, or else the prosecutor was threatening me with a long sentence and to imprisoning my wife.

I asked him, who had decades of experience as a prosecutor, a series of questions. Following are the quotes from the question/answer session I had with him.

Q: I have decided to surrender my medical license and accept a felony on my record, but I am still considering pleading not guilty. I need your opinion. The prosecutor has promised not to send me to jail if I surrender my medical license to him and plead guilty to a single count of mail fraud. The prosecutor has now added a new threat: to jail my wife, as well, if I continue to resist his demand to plead guilty. You know my story, what are the chances of my success if I plead not guilty?

A: Zero percent.

Q: Why do you say that? You know that the prosecutors and FDA agent Pueschel falsified documents. Why shouldn't my chances of winning be 100 percent? My attorney told me in a conference call today that I only have a 40 percent chance of winning because the prosecutor was planning to use my patients as witnesses who he claims would give very emotional testimonies against me.

A: You have answered your own question. More importantly, remember, once prosecutors destroy evidence and start lying, you have no way out. They are committed to keeping the evidence concealed. And there is no way they would ever allow exculpatory evidence to surface. They would use every device to keep it hidden from the court. If you continue to bring it up, they will retaliate by asking for a maximum prison sentence, and the judge will accept whatever manufactured evidence the prosecutor chooses to present.

Q: Why can't I expose the FDA and the prosecutors in my testimony?

A: (He laughed at my question.) There is one planet I know of where defendants can expose prosecutors, that planet is Mars, and you don't live on Mars. You know what I am trying to tell you. First, who do you think they are going to believe, you or the prosecutor? Besides, the more you insist on trying to expose him, the harsher the punishment he'll insist on, so it's a certainty that you'll end up with 20 years in prison. And the guy is right; he will find a way to put your wife in jail if you challenge him. Do you really want that? The threshold for the credibility of evidence before the court is ten on a scale of ten for the defendants, while the threshold of evidence furnished by the prosecutors can be as little as the prosecutor's word, which means no evidence at all, just his word. His word is the law.

Q: Is there any way I could speak with the judge privately in his chambers? I did that with the Judge in the Medical Board case, which turned my case around 180 degrees.

A: Any such request you make needs permission and cooperation from the prosecutors and the judge in a criminal case. Do you think the prosecutor is going to let you speak with the judge privately, so you could try to destroy the basis of prosecutorial arguments against you?

Q: My attorney says it will cost me $750,000 for trial. I have already spent well over $200,000 in legal expenses over the last five years; add $750,000 and it is my entire networth. But several of my patients who believe in me have decided to start a website, and a drive for donations through social media, in an appeal for donations for my case.

A: Your patients will not be able to raise enough money, or they might not know what it will take. You can't count on donations entirely. In the end, this responsibility will fall on you. Besides the cost may be $7 million, not $700,000; $750,000 is not the real cost if you want to go all the way to an extended trial to expose the lies you have been wanting to expose. It could take years and millions of dollars, $750,000 is just a bait from your defense attorney to get you to go to the so-called trial.

Q: But Gluck told me $750,000 would be the total cost.

A: (He laughed.) That is to lure you in. Didn't you tell me your attorney's fee is $700 an hour? With at least two attorneys working on the case at that rate, what makes you think $750,000 will be the total cost? They will be billing you $50,000 a month; $750,000 could be the total cost of everything leading up to the trial, not the trial itself, not the kind of trial you want. This could be the total cost if your attorney were planning to negotiate towards the end and had no real intentions of doing the hard work it will take to bring up issues of fabrications, omissions, and forgeries by going to an extensive trial and simultaneously trying to find forensic evidence of the many things you are concerned about in order to be able to file for impeachment of the FDA — agent. Asking for exculpatory documents from the government is a whole new challenge for any defense attorney. I bet your attorney has no intention of doing any of that. Also, your attorney with this 40 percent chance thing already knows the outcome. He is not telling you everything he has up his sleeve. You'll be surprised to see how the claim of his 40 percent success rate magically starts to dwindle the moment he realizes you don't have much money left and are on the brink of losing everything. His true colors will start to shine like a rainbow at that time. Rest assured, he wants your money more than he is interested in justice. He'll reveal what his real motives are when you have no money left, you've sold everything, and your kids are homeless. It's hideous business, my friend. Even the days of IBM are history now. IBM could bring the government down to its knees by spending $50 million on defense and that $50 million those days is the equivalent of a billion dollars today, and you are no IBM. The Obama Administration is taking down companies with assets worth hundreds of billions of dollars, often putting many lower-level innocent employees in jail, while making deals with the real criminals on the top and letting them off the hook. The system is corrupt - don't even try to challenge it. Ninety-five percent of the cases end up settling in the government's favor before the trial, defendants always ending up relenting to government pressure after spending all their hard-earned money. The government has a 99 percent conviction rate on the remaining 5 percent cases that do go to trial. So, what are the odds? If your prosecutor were an honest person, you would have a chance, in fact, you would not be facing these problems in the first place, but any prosecutor who destroys evidence is very dangerous to the defendant and the system of justice. Once we prosecutors decide to suppress evidence, there is no going back - we must win.

Q: Who are the one percent who fight and win?

A: I didn't say, one percent wins. What I am saying is that one percent of the defendants of the five percent that go to trial will be vindicated, which means we are talking about not even one-tenth of one percent success rate for those defendants who do not have financial resources. Vindicated defendants are often not just innocent but also have a lot of money for defense. The general rule for most prosecutors is that if they accuse you of something, they must win, and they always do. And if you don't have the money, then it doesn't even matter if you're innocent or guilty, you will be found guilty regardless. It is extremely rare, in fact, unheard of, for a prosecutor to admit a mistake and say, sorry I made an error and I take it back. Once the government falsifies a document, then there is no going back unless someone is going to blow the whistle, and whistleblowers simply do not exist.

Q: Is there any way I could subpoena FDA records that the government is hiding, and how about FOIA?

A: Yes, you'll be able to do whatever you wish. What makes you think they will give it to you? Remember, you're not Senator

Stevens. That was a very unusual situation where an FBI agent broke ranks with the FBI and exposed the liars in the DOJ. That is incredibly rare. Judges don't even order exculpatory evidence from the government if your defense attorney were to request it. If your attorney managed to convince the judge to order the government to divulge information, the prosecutors often ignore judge's orders and give some excuse, and there's no consequence for them. There's not a thing a judge can do or will do. In theory, he can, but he won't. He works for the government, not for you. On the other hand, if you, the defendant, defied a judge's order to divulge information that you possess, you'd get a longer prison sentence for obstruction of justice, for perjury and so on and so forth. [The earth slipped from underneath me when Raul revealed all this to me.]

Q: Is there any way you could take over my case?

A: I'm a government target and have already paid a hefty price for exposing people.

Q: Is there any way I could ask the judge to allow me five minutes of his time to speak privately and directly with him in his chambers? Or is there a way I could talk directly to the grand jury if it appears that the grand jury might indict me after the prosecutor presented his case?

A: You have already asked me this question multiple times. No, that's not going to happen. You will need to get the prosecutor or the judge's permission to do anything like that, and they will never grant you that permission. Do you think a prosecutor who is going to present his side of the case to the Grand Jury is going to let you go before the Grand Jury and give your side?

Grand Juries are just rubber stamps for the prosecutors. Grand juries and the juries at trials often do not know the whole story. Prosecutors always manage to hide information from them, or just won't allow the facts to surface. They have many devices and techniques they use and extraordinary powers to suppress relevant evidence or to prevent the defendants from bringing it up to the attention of the judge or the jury. Judges and prosecutors often talk behind the scenes in solidarity without the defense attorney's knowledge. The defense often does not know what transpires between the judge and the prosecutor. The rule of law and procedures to be followed are found in the books, reality is different.

Q: What do you think I should do, or can do?

A: I can't tell you what can do or should do, but keep in mind that whatever you choose to do, be cautious. You can certainly choose the option of the public defender but don't expect a different outcome. It will save you money, but the outcome may be much worse. Public defenders are overworked, overwhelmed, and underpaid, and they work for the government. Public defenders may be overwhelmed with as many as 200 cases put on their plate at a given time. They're not interested in going to trial for you. They'll be intermediary brokers like your current lawyer, only ten times worse because they don't have any time for you. They are there to intercede between you and the government to try to get you a better deal. That is the most you can expect. The public defender may listen to you for five minutes, but he is not particularly interested in your innocence or the facts of the case. He is there to make a deal and get it over with and move on to his next case. The public defender could buy some justice for you only if your case were the only case he was dealing with throughout the year and his other 200 cases could be put on hold just for the sake of your case. It's not impossible to have a positive outcome by engaging the services of a public defender, but it's extremely rare. And the public defender would be assigned to you; you don't get to interview and choose the one you like. I'm sorry to sound so cynical, but I don't want to mislead you in any way.

Q: Well, you said my chances of winning against the government is zero percent? Did I hear you correctly? So, what is the point?

A: Yes, that is what I said, and I meant it. I don't mean to discourage you, but you have an extremely low probability of winning even if you had millions of dollars to fight against the government's unlimited financial resources, but for what, for a moral victory? The reason for lower chances of vindication in your case is that the prosecutors have already fabricated a story and there is nothing you can do about it. Allegations are more difficult to fight when the evidence is suppressed by those who are expected to uphold the law. You don't know what you don't know. Once the government has chosen you as a target, they are determined to win. And you have been saying that you don't have the money. I am sure you know what is best for you. I wish I could help you decide as to how to proceed, but perhaps I already have.

Q: Is this the norm in the Department of Justice?

A: No, I believe many prosecutors and government agents are just trying to do their job responsibly. They're a bit aggressive sometimes and overcharge people. But it is not uncommon for prosecutors to hide information, obstruct justice and break the rules to win convictions because that's how they get promoted inside the Department. The more convictions they have under their belt, the more they're rewarded. This kills those who try to do an honest job, like myself, and want to do the right thing. The honest prosecutors are left behind and never rise through the ranks. They often end up quitting in the end if they continue to refuse to be team players with others in the department.

Q. Team players?

A: Once a government agent or prosecutor lies, they're in it together. No one is going to break ranks with the government unless you were a celebrity and some insider desired to make a name for himself by blowing the whistle, which is extremely rare.

Q: Shouldn't it be the easiest thing to prove that FDA agent Pueschel concealed the name of the female FDA agent who interviewed me on 8/17/10 and deleted it from all FDA reports written single-handedly by him, which are major forgeries for the most part?

A: Yes, easy maybe, but if you try to force the government to admit that fact, the government will make some excuse for this omission, and the judge will accept any explanation from the prosecutor. Like I told you, the judges accept any explanation prosecutors present, even if the government's violation is of the most egregious kind. The standards of law that are applied to the prosecutors and the defendants are very different. The prosecutor will reveal the name of this female agent if you force him to do so, and the FDA will give some excuse why her name and interview records are missing. Then they'll bring her forward and make her say anything they want her to say. She will testify that she doesn't remember because it's been a long time. Or they might even privately coach her to tell a bunch of lies to support the story of Pueschel. She's probably a junior agent; she better say what they want her to if she cares about her job and her future.

Q: What happened to equality before the law?

A: Tell me about it.

Q: Well, the female Asian American FDA agent who interviewed me with Pueschel in 2010 knows all the details of the one-hour interview, which the prosecutors are now saying does not exist. No recording, no transcript, no memo, no handwritten notes. How can all that disappear just like that? How are they going to justify all that? How could she get away with saying, "Well, I don't remember, it's been so long?"

A: Make no mistake, if you continue to insist that the government reveal her name and bring her forward for testimony, which you can through the trial, and they will have to oblige for a legitimate demand, but they will make sure that she does not destroy the government's narrative. She will be instructed to lie. As I said, the best you can hope for from her is, 'Well, yes, I was there and interviewed the doctor, but I don't remember much of anything, it has been a long time.' They can make her say anything. There is no way she is going to blow the whistle on the FDA or the Department of Justice if she cares about preserving her job. She knows if she cares about her future and the future of her family, she can't mess with the government. She knows it is going to be not just her job, but her life will be over if she did anything that might ruin the reputation of the Department of Justice. Even when honest people work for the government, they feel trapped in this institutional imperative that they must protect government secrecy in working together as a team player even if what the government did was criminal.

I informed this former prosecutor that I had again started working on my book, *FDA's Betrayal of the American Public,* in light of the new knowledge I had acquired about the legal system. It was the book I'd put a launch date for on my website which might have triggered these problems in the first place or so I thought. And I told him I decided to name the public officials who committed perjury and concealed evidence in this book.

His response was, and I paraphrase: Good luck and brace yourself because you will be their target for the rest of your life if you publish their names. Just don't mention my name *anywhere*. You are welcome to call me anytime though if you have questions. I'd like to help you as much as I can because I truly feel sorry for what's happening to you and your wife and kids.

A: Things will be stacked up against you at trial. You face the real possibility that the government witnesses are going to perjure themselves. Patients know they must deliver the goods if the prosecutor has promised them restitution or money. The prosecutor will coach them ahead of their testimonies, teach them what they have to say and how they have to say it in front of the jury. The prosecutor will shape their testimonies and chisel them in critical details to make sure that the jury finds you guilty. It's the part of our justice system that isn't just. If you bring in medical experts to prove to the jury that the patients' testimonies make no sense, or are fraudulently induced by the FDA agent and the prosecutor, then your cost for the trial will skyrocket with no upper limits in sight. It's a disgrace, but also the reality.

Q: Will the judge know that these things are happening, such as patients making things up?

A: It depends, but the judges don't care. You must understand that odds are against you if you choose to go to trial. And if you go to trial and you lose, this character [meaning, the prosecutor] will ask for upward departures to your sentence. That is a price you pay for making these prosecutors work harder to establish their claims and accusations, a job which is their legal responsibility anyway. The prosecutor will get what he wants. And rest assured that your sentence will also change from no jail time to plenty of jail time.

Q: So the public defender is also out of the question, right?

A: If your own lawyer who charges you $700 an hour does not bother to read the Discovery, and he does not answer most of your emails, what are the chances that a public defender or a private attorney appointed by the government who is making $125 an hour is going to be so diligent to study and understand your case thoroughly? And I'm not suggesting that there is necessarily a correlation between hourly rate and getting better representation. The issue is that if the government's case is built on concealments, collusion, conspiracy and perjury, and I believe it is, based on what I have read and what you have been telling me, an unethical prosecutor like this will fight tooth and nail to continue to tell more lies and do anything he needs to do to continue to cover up the facts of the case to preserve the credibility of his own story. Whether you have a public defender or private attorney appointed by the court, you must realize that it is often in their best interest to convince you to plead guilty as quickly as you can when the situation is ripe for them. The only exception is when an attorney knows for sure that he could win the case at trial, and an attorney can never be sure of that. A rare public defender may want to go to trial to make a name for himself if he's dealing with some celebrity, and you're no celebrity. Besides, your case has already been made so much more complicated with these phony Discovery documents. The fact that the prosecutor has fabricated this case is precisely the reason I say the odds of your success are zero. Are you trying to expose the government of the United States? It won't work. No amount of money or fundraising will help you in this endless uphill battle. You may win small battles here and there, but you'll lose the war, and they'll retaliate by locking you up for a very long time. They always do my friend, I have yet to see an exception.

Realize that the appointed attorneys for those who are poor often become sly and deceitful when they see they can scare you. It's a shame because it's the poor, or those without enough money such as yourself, that they should be helping more. Regardless of who is the public defender, they'll proceed to handle your case as one that is destined to end up in pleading guilty, even though they will give you the impression that they are preparing to go to trial for you. They just won't tell you what their real plan is for you when you're hopeful of finding some justice at trial. Believe it or not, the same is true for your private attorney who is charging you $700 an hour. He'll lead you on as long as he knows you can continue to write him a hefty monthly check. The truth will come out the moment he figures you have nothing left in your bank account to give to him. All these attorneys, whether they are private, or government appointed, are like the dump trucks that are ready to deliver you to the prosecutor's garbage heap at the end of the day. There are very few out there who are interested in public service. Most think it is not their problem that the government wants to target you. A typical corporate lawyer has the same logic when he engages in corrupt practices. He justifies his behavior by telling himself that it's not his fault that the system is unfair. He's just trying to make a living because he has $200, 000 in student loans to pay back.

Let us say that you are that rare lucky person who got a heroic public defender who takes your case to trial, the probability of which is abysmally low, the government agents, ready with their false testimonies and a cabal of false witnesses, already know that they are up against an appointed attorney who could not afford to do the investigation and preparation necessary to defeat their argument, let alone impeach these crooks for their criminal activities. Your defense attorney will not be able to conduct essential investigation and use forensic tools that he is going to need. He won't be able to mount an expensive defense that comes anywhere close to what the government can do, given their resources. That's why so many people plead guilty even when they are innocent.

So, when your lawyer tells you that he'll file for impeachment of the FDA agent, do not buy that. The judge has to be able to order the government to reveal all sorts of exculpatory evidence that you believe the government has. The judge will not order the government to produce Brady materials upon the defender's request, and if he did, the government would not provide it, and there is nothing your private lawyer or the public defender can do, and they know it. Know that in this type of circumstance, your attorney wants your money, not that he does not want to help you, but he knows he can't. He won't break this news to you until he's taken all your money and caused you to go bankrupt. On the other hand, many public defenders and attorneys who depend on court appointments, are frequently lazy, incompetent, and unmotivated. Those with the best intentions burn out in no time because they're so overworked. You told me that your lawyer doesn't answer three out of four emails. What makes you think a public defender is going to be on top of everything? What's going to motivate him? They're all busy making deals with the prosecutors behind the scenes.

You can undoubtedly fire this attorney if you want me to find another one for you. It might save you some money, but I doubt it would make a difference in the outcome of the case. If you find someone else, I strongly recommend, do not hire someone who worked for the government before. That's a trap. They tell you that they know your prosecutor and will get you favorable results. Most of these people were co-opted by the system while they were working for the government, so much so that they do not know how to begin to fight a

> case honestly. They take your money and then smother you with their bullshit. Don't believe a word they tell you. Worse yet, many of them will try to impress upon you the value of their prior work with the government, to get a higher fee from you.
>
> Perhaps ten percent of criminal defense lawyers, in my opinion, are decent, honest, and conscientious lawyers, and they are helpless before the government like everybody else in many circumstances. Lawyers who charge you more based on their previous employment history, achievements, and credentials says nothing about their honesty or integrity.

Raul's comments jogged my memory of the two attorneys that worked for the defense in my case history. Boreman, who represented me, and Stephen Jones of LA, who represented Sandra Johnson, sold themselves as superior because of their ties with the government due to being ex-government prosecutors. They both turned out to be collaborators for the government.

He went on to tell me that the most significant thing working against me were the patients who were fired up by the FDA. He agreed with Gluck's assessment.

> The testimonies of these cooperating witnesses could have the most devastating effect on your trial. If your lawyer tells you that he'll cross-examine these government witnesses, how is he going to prove that they're lying to the court? How does he even know which of these witnesses will be present at the trial? The government can use hearsay statements against you, which the judge accepts as evidence. To the judge any nonsense, hearsay or rumor brought up by the prosecutor as evidence, is evidence. The government doesn't even have to

> tell the court the sources of their witnesses. The rules for the government and the defendant are very different. There is no equality before the law for resourceless defendants in the U.S. criminal justice system. Judges, for example, encourage such false witnesses and in fact reward them in many ways and they call them "witnesses cooperating for justice" when they know that, they're cooperating with the prosecutors.

I said to Raul that he was essentially telling me that my decision to plead guilty is the best decision that I could have made. He responded, "I am not telling you anything. I just want you to understand how the system works so you can make better choices and do what is best for your family.

Raul gave me a lot of information to digest, and I decided it would be best to sleep on it. The next morning, I awoke with even greater determination that I would stick with my decision to surrender my medical license and perhaps start a new life in a different profession or make a living from my part-time career in journalism and writing. I processed my conversation with the prosecutor all night in my dreams. I thought to myself that at least I would be home with my kids and not have to sit in prison for 20 years, if I took the deal. As angry as I was and as stressed out as I had become, I couldn't help but ride one wave of optimism and hope after the next. But as the saying goes, we make plans, and God laughs.

Federal Government– A Story of Sodom and Gomorrah

The morning after the conference call between my wife and me, Spackman, and Gluck, where I agreed to give in to the prosecutor's demands, Gluck called Delahunty to give him the good news that I would take his offer and plead guilty to one count of mail fraud in exchange for no jail time but a felony on my name. Delahunty got his wishes before his Statute of Limitations deadline, saving him the trouble of a formal indictment. In response to this good news, the prosecutor sent me a message through my attorney, who called my wife to ask her if I knew anyone who robbed a bank, was dealing drugs, or committed a crime. Gluck selectively started talking with my wife from this point on because he knew I was disgusted with him and did not want to speak to him unless I had to. When my wife conveyed this to me, it caught me by surprise. What did he mean by asking such a rude question? I informed him (through my wife) that I did not know any such people. He hinted that offering up such information to the prosecutor might further mitigate my case. This is called "cooperation with the government."

The following day, my wife called Gluck and told him that a world-renowned researcher, Dr. Minot of the Sleep Medicine Department of Stanford University, had treated our nine-year old son and caused permanent injury to his brain by using an FDA-restricted drug with a black box warning (called Xyrem). She informed him that Dr. Minot had deep financial ties with Jazz Pharmaceuticals that sold the drug and that the doctor had put everyone on this drug indiscriminately, nearly 100 percent of his patients were on this drug. It had been dispensed in very high doses to my son by the doctor's personal secretary, Ms. Mali, who was not a healthcare professional, who also worked for Jazz Pharmaceuticals. It turns out that even an average physician was not permitted to prescribe or manage this drug unless the physician or a sleep medicne specialist had signed a special safety protocol agreement with the FDA. The net result was that such criminal behavior by a secretary working under the direct supervision of Minot disabled our son for life, and we had irrefutable evidence of everything that we claimed about this doctor. My wife told Gluck I wanted to give the FDA prosecutor the name of this doctor, since I had been asked if I knew any criminals. Experimenting by using a rare, restricted drug on children, a drug approved only for adults under very special circumstances, put him in the criminal category. What made it worse was when we filed a complaint with the Health Department, and they requested medical records from Dr. Minot, Stanford University said they had lost those records. Dr. Minot's research Lab was also funded by Jazz Pharma and he was on the Big Pharma's payroll in many ways. Jazz sold the drug at $60,000 a year per patient. This was the most heinous crime a physician could commit to profit from his economic relationship with a drug company. I won't go into the details of my son's case but will tell you the response from Gluck was something like, 'The government does not mess with a big entity like Stanford. Tell us about some regular person who committed a crime.' My interpretation of what Gluck said is that the system is designed to jail the poor, those who are without sufficient funds to withstand years in a courtroom and spend millions in attorney fees, not the wealthy and the powerful who are part of the establishment and thus immune to prosecution.

Gluck assured Delahunty that he would personally guarantee him that I would keep my verbal commitment of pleading guilty and that he would get his desired conviction even if the prosecutor missed his Statute of Limitations while waiting for the paperwork. In return, he asked Delahunty for some additional time so I could plead guilty after a psychological evaluation that Gluck now wanted me to get, thinking that it would help mitigate the severity of my case. In exchange for his personal guarantee to Delahunty for a conviction,

Gluck asked the prosecutor to give him a couple of weeks of extra time to have me evaluated, whatever that meant. At this time, Gluck was communicating with me through my wife for the most part, for obvious reasons. She asked Gluck what all of this meant, and he told her that he was going to have a forensic psychologist, a friend of his, evaluate me and write a report for the judge that would show mitigating circumstances.

What I am about to describe in the following paragraphs may not be the most interesting reading for my readers but it is very important in the sense that this shows how criminal our criminal justice system is. Gluck immediately started coming up with creative ideas of all kinds of mitigating factors that he could bring to the judge to help reduce my punishment. First, he took seven years of my tax filings to try to prove that I was under financial stress that led me to make poor decisions – such as buying IUDs from Canada. I never once told him that I made poor choices, nor did anyone else. Instead, I had always maintained that I thought that I made the right decision in helping patients who were poor by providing an affordable option for birth control. My judgment was unclouded on this matter and my mind was clear. Gluck made me work very hard to pull out all those old tax filings, but the prosecutor quickly trashed his argument of financial stress as a mitigating factor. In fact, he didn't even look at it, or so it seemed, because it was something we never discussed any further. Then Gluck suggested to my wife that we could use my son's medical records as a mitigating circumstance the moment he found out from her that our son was disabled. I found this ridiculous since my son's disability had nothing to do with my case. Gluck informed my wife that this was my only hope for getting a favorable opinion from the judge and assured her that he was trying to help me. I relented, and when he got the medical records from my wife and presented his argument to Delahunty, he (Delahunty) showed no sympathy and was not at all moved by the fact that I had a disabled child who I was financially responsible for and taking care of. My wife, terrified for my safety and that of the family and our children, would give my attorney anything and everything that might help my case, mostly behind my back.

The whole angle bothered me. Yes, my son had this terrible disability, but it had nothing to do with the case. Still, I understood why my wife was persuaded to provide such documents and reports to help my case. How would she be able to work a full-time job and pay for all living expenses and the care needed for our children? I did not want to get involved with any of this and was still in shock that Gluck wanted me evaluated. I was also uncertain of the credentials of this forensic psychologist, a friend of Gluck's who worked to assist the government with criminal cases by often manufacturing phony reports to help mitigate the crimes of white-collar criminals, a fact I discovered when I went to see him. So, the whole scheme involved finding something they could use as a contributing factor to my alleged impaired judgment and blame that for my actions. I felt like I was losing my mind. How is it that the truth would not suffice, but some fanciful fairytale might aid my cause? I let my spouse deal with this, however, because I couldn't be upset at a time I needed to try and figure out how my family would survive without my income and very limited occupational prospects as a felon.

The psychologist charged a minimum of $8,000, a non-refundable upfront fee from white-collar criminals, assuming that white-collar criminals had lots of money, and most of them probably do. All I know is that I was not one of them. His name was Richard

Romanoff, and he told me that he charged $400 an hour, but his actual average hourly rate turned out to be $800 an hour, and his quoted total of $8,000 soon turned into $10,000.

When I saw Romanoff, I noted that his office in Los Angeles was enclosed and secured like a bank vault. As distasteful as it was to me, I agreed to meet with Romanoff hoping it would help the outcome of my case. I realized how ironic it was to be sitting in front of this man as a criminal, a physician whose income had been reduced to zero because I had provided IUDs to indigent folks at no personal gain, while this man contracted with the criminal justice system was allowed to legally gouge me at $800 an hour, just like Teva, for personal gain, with nobody calling either one of them criminals.

As soon as Romanoff promised me that he would not share anything with anyone until his report was complete, that I was free to tell him my story confidentially, I laid out the facts of my case. He didn't seem to be surprised or outraged by what I had to tell him, nor did he appear to have any doubt that I was telling him the truth. It was as though this was the usual business practice for him and the government. Did he believe me because he wanted my business? Or did he believe me because he knew how the system worked and had knowledge of the deep-rooted corruption among government agents and prosecutors? He was very comfortable with the system just like his friend Gluck who referred me to him. It was as though these people had no moral compass or a conscience leading them to think anything was wrong with what had happened. I have to wonder – How many people would learn to become comfortable with a corrupt system that brought you an income of $700 an hour like my criminal defense attorney made, or net average of $800 an hour like this forensic psychologist made? My guess is that most people would find their personal bar for what is ethical could be moved to accommodate this moral dilemma. It may well be part of human nature, to some extent. In one sense, I was very grateful that no one who I had to speak with about my case ever doubted me. On the other hand, I had to question these people who seemed immune to how egregious it was to be in a position of power and to abuse that power.

This epiphany about our criminal justice system has bothered me enough that I will be talking about the U.S. government's corruption for the rest of my life and I know that I will become known for that years down the line. This is just the beginning. It makes no sense that an accused person is not allowed to say a word about his case before the judge or the grand jury. The only option made available to the accused is to come up with millions of dollars in defense funds before he can hope to get anywhere near a point where he will be allowed to open his mouth in front of what is going to end up being a misinformed, and thus biased, judge and jury.

I proceeded to tell Romanoff that an FDA agent named Pueschel had fabricated a case against me by first telling me that the T-Safe IUD was FDA approved, then completely change the story two years later that it was not, and refusing to produce documents of the 2010 FDA interview of me that the FDA was now withholding. Psychologist, Romanoff replied that he believed my version of the story, and then he proceeded to tell me that he believed in the system and that it's a legal system that is the best in the world. I felt sickened when I heard that. He went on to suggest that I go to the media with my story if I wanted justice. It was at this point that I realized I was speaking with someone so ignorant that it was frightening. Part of what I had told him was that one of my biggest mistakes was talking to the press, as it resulted in the same result one would get in poking a hornet's nest. I did not respond to his suggestion and informed him that his friend Gluck wanted me to come up with $750,000 if I chose not to plead guilty. He laughed at $750,000 and said that it would cost me millions. Once again, he uttered these words with confidence, arrogance, and shamelessness, as though he was very proud of the fact that he had imparted some great wisdom to me, an esoteric knowledge that only he had. I thought to myself, 'Of course, you believe in the system because you have found your niche in it and it is working well for you.'

After my two-hour conversation with Romanoff during which time he took my mental history, he gave me what he called a controlled document - a government's questionnaire to be completed by criminals over a period of four hours. As I began reading through the questions, I quickly realized that it was drawn from the late nineteenth - and early twentieth-century deviance models no longer considered scientifically valid by any academic standards, anywhere in the world and it was a test being given to me by a psychologist who charged $8,000 for a single evaluation. It included questions about religious guilt, redemption, sinfulness and repentance, and several questions about hearing voices and mental illness. The questionnaire was based on an outdated social deviance model and what were considered to be perverted behaviors once upon a time, also thought a form of mental illness. It confirmed to me that in the American justice system, mental illness was a crime for which people needed to be incarcerated. This type of questioning demonstrated the kind of misunderstanding for which the British government killed one of the greatest scientists of the twentieth century, Alan Turing, by giving him harmful drugs to cure his homosexuality. It was a deviance model in which everyone who was different or did not conform to the beliefs of the religious culture of the early twentieth-century, or the government's religious laws, was considered mentally ill. I told Romanoff that this was old science and that I had written a book on it, to which he responded that he was aware of the weaknesses in the questionnaire, and always adjusted for it when he scored the results. Then he told me that he was a forensic psychologist, thus inquisitive by nature, a creature of habit, and that he would look me up for my research on this subject matter. I asked him if he could make me a photocopy of this questionnaire for my records, but he said it was "a government's-controlled document" and therefore he could not provide me with a copy.

I thought it would be easy for me to obtain a copy since I was a licensed physician, but I was not successful. I would love to share this "controlled document" with social scientists in our universities, who would be shocked to discover that our government is using this kind of nonsense to determine the mindset of people to decide who has criminal intentions — criteria that would determine who deserves to be incarcerated and for how long. The kind of questions found in this questionnaire would give even those with no formal education a good laugh.

Our government keeps these documents secret, documents that are exclusively used by psychologists and psychiatrists who work for the Bureau of Prisons or are affiliated industry contractors, who have exclusive access to the inside world of our government. The visit to this psychologist's office was the beginning of a never-ending cycle for me because from that point on I have repeatedly been asked to sign document after document requiring me to state again and again that I am regretful, sorry, and remorseful for what I did. Every step I've faced in this ordeal has been reminiscent of the stories we read of political dissidents in the former Soviet Union. It was a high crime in the Soviet Union to disagree with anything the government said. By definition, you had a mental illness if you disagreed with the Soviet government. The psychological breakdown of my body, mind, and spirit had just begun, and it reminded me of Solzhenitsyn's (a famous Soviet dissident and Nobel prize winning author) description of breaking down dissidents in body, mind, and spirit in the former Soviet Gulag. Frankly, despite my own knowledge about the corruption in our government, I was surprised that our system worked the same way as it did in the military, feudal, or totalitarian regimes such as the former Soviet Union. There is no difference. I never thought there would come a day when I would arrive at the sad realization that our U.S. government operated under the same suppression of opposition found in fascist regimes, and it did it in the name of justice.

Romanoff completed his report, 17 pages of which can be easily regarded as total bullshit. I think I am justified in calling it total bullshit for one and one reason alone. I believe that Romanoff's first obligation was to write in the report that he believed that injustice had been done based on the fact that he told me he believed my version of the story. That one truthful statement alone should have weighed against the rest of his entire report. I only had to skim over it to see what it was, just as his friend Gluck had said it would be, making attempts at mitigating my case by telling my life story and mental health evaluation. I could not understand why anything said in his report should have any relevance, direct or indirect to the truth about my case. Defense attorneys use these kinds of psychological reports in an attempt to cover-up the crimes of white-collar criminals who truly belong in jail. They engage the services of these self-proclaimed forensic psychologists working for the criminal justice system who can make a fortune out of it. This is a money game; a psychologist will write a favorable report for anyone in exchange for $10,000. His report, of course, made no difference in the outcome of my case, and the judge probably tossed it in the garbage bin next to him. The report contained many accurate descriptions of my life, but it had nothing to do with the case.

A few days after my psychological evaluation, Gluck emailed me a guilty plea document two hours before Delahunty's deadline. I printed and reviewed the guilty plea agreement unilaterally drafted by Delahunty. I noted that the terms were nothing like the terms that he had conveyed to Gluck and that I had agreed to, which was a single count of mail fraud felony with no jail time in exchange for surrendering my medical license. There was no mention of surrendering my medical license, and he asked the judge for a maximum of a 20-year imprisonment, but recommended 22 to 41 months based on what he called his "offense calculations according to the sentencing guidelines." Later I learned that these calculations are done based on the amount of financial fraud involved in a criminal offense. This agreement included every accusation that had been resolved over the years through two Medical Board cases, including multiple allegations that Delahunty had tacitly acknowledged being false during his conversation with my attorney between Delahunty's first phone call to Gluck in May, 2015 and July 28, 2015, the date I signed the plea agreement drafted by Delahunty. It reiterated accusations of causing complications to patients, risking death or bodily injury to female patients by using an IUD that was not approved by the FDA, using unsafe IUDs bought on the Internet, partaking in insurance fraud, lining my pockets with money to enrich myself, and so on. There was no mention of the history of the FDA's interactions with me in 2010, which he tacitly acknowledged to Gluck in their phone conversations. All exculpatory materials and references had vanished as though they never existed. There was no mention of my interview with the two agents in August 2010 and the discussions with the FDA that took place as a follow-up. There was no explanation as to why the government could not produce the 2010 FDA interview memo or notes when requested by Gluck. There was no mention of FDA Agent Pueschel calling me with the FDA's position about the approval status of the T-Safe IUD on October 12, 2010. Instead, Delahunty magically buried the entire history of the FDA and DOJ's deception and collusion by writing one single sentence: "Sometime between 2008 and 2012, Dr. Singh found out that the T-Safe CU-380A IUDs were not FDA approved." Then the prosecutor repeatedly quoted Teva, as though it was the source of his knowledge about laws that mandated buying CU-380A IUDs only from Teva's direct distributors, ParaGard Direct, which is located in the United States.

An hour after emailing me the guilty plea document and about an hour before Delahunty's deadline, Gluck called me to perform the ritual of reading the guilty plea terms out loud to me. He started his phone call with a dire warning about Delahunty's ultimatum regarding his deadline that day. He stated I must sign and return the document that day, by 5:00 pm, and if I failed to do so, I would be indicted the following Monday. Delahunty made sure Gluck conveyed this message to me. Gluck also pointed out to me a clause in Delahunty's agreement to show me that Delahunty had also sealed my fate by stating that I would not be given any rights to appeal my case once I plead guilty through this agreement.

"What happened to the agreement that if I surrendered my medical license, there would be no jail time?" I asked. He said the prosecutor must have realized that he was stepping on the toes of the Medical Board, so he eliminated the medical license part. Prior to Delahunty drafting this agreement, I had sent an email to Gluck saying that I would like to surrender my license a bit gradually because suddenly abandoning pregnant patients in the middle of late gestation would be risky for them because OB/Gyns often do not accept new pregnant patients in their late pregnancy due to liability. I did not want to be responsible for patient abandonment, which was a malpractice liability for me. I can only speculate if resistance to the surrendering of my medical license played any role in Delahunty coming back with a vengeance. (Please refer to published emails in this regard in Exhibit 24).

I asked Gluck why the details of the FDA's interview and decision in 2010 and the history of communications between the FDA and me were omitted from the agreement drafted by Delahunty, and the whole story buried under one vague statement? The document used one vague sentence covering up the whole story that spanned over five years. Omitting all specifics illustrated this was another attempt to cover up all the previous cover ups in a never-ending effort to continue to cover up as necessary. Gluck's response was that he had already questioned the prosecutor about it and the prosecutor had told him that he was not going to change the wording in his statement. Essentially, we were being told to take it or leave it. It was Delahunty's way or the highway.

As Gluck continued reading through the guilty plea, I started interrupting him with objections, because every sentence was a lie, except for statements that referred to logistics inconsequential to the case. After a few of these interruptions, Gluck suddenly metamorphosed into Gregor Samsa from Franz Kafka's, *Metamorphosis*. This was a side of Gluck I had not seen before. I knew he cared about money as the decisive criteria for representation, but I assumed he would be a professional in his demeanor. I did not expect to see him react this way to my questioning him about the integrity of the prosecutor. He raised his voice and started shouting at me repeatedly asking over and over if I understood what he was reading to me. This was his way of telling me to sign the damn agreement — what the prosecutor did was not his problem, and I was not paying him enough to worry about my crap! Yes, I am reading Gluck's mind, but this is how it felt. I will explain later about the corporate training of these lawyers to show you that they could not care less about the due process of law or justice. They will work hard on technicalities to defend someone they know has committed a crime if there is enough money to be made. But they will let an innocent be found guilty in a heartbeat if there is no money in sight.

Gluck was two-thirds of the way through the document when I interrupted him and said, "Read no more, I know what you want me to do, and I will sign it." That suddenly calmed him down and he told me he wanted it signed and returned to him before 5:00 pm, or I was going to be indicted the following Monday. "Understood," I said. I signed it and scanned it back to him at once, as the deadline was only minutes away. I asked him to send me confirmation of receipt of my signature by email, which he did.

The following day, I asked Gluck in a phone call, "If I were to invite you on a C-SPAN Book TV show, what would you say about my case?" He replied that he would find me not guilty if he were on the jury. "That doesn't answer my question," I said. "I want to know what you would say, based on what you know about my case." He dodged the question. I asked a second time, and he avoided it again.

The following day, he called and asked me to give him my billing records for IUD services because he wanted to do his calculations. I had no idea what he meant by calculations. I told him the prosecutors were already in possession of my electronic billing records because FDA agents had downloaded all the billing data from the server in my office during the raid in 2012, but Gluck wanted me to give him the data I had in our computer. He asked for specific records for specific dates and wanted them presented to him in a certain manner such as alphabetical names of patients, and for years 2008 — 2009 and for years 2010 — 2012, and then for all the years on one excel sheet, etc. Gluck made many such requests in a rapid succession over the course of the next few days. My biller Amy Jones, an accountant and one of the best in the field because she was a perfectionist, very quickly retrieved the data for IUDs billed from my office between 2008 and 2012 within a day or sometimes within hours when requested, and gave it to me so I could forward it to Gluck. She used her handwritten notes on the billing print-out itself to explain what might not be clear to a non-professional from just looking at the electronic data. She gave specific information in her handwriting which disproved Delahunty's allegations against me (Exhibit 18.)

I like to say a word about Amy, my medical biller, simply because I cannot resist it. My staff described Amy as a person who was "sickeningly honest". For example, when an insurance accidentally overpaid me 49 cents, she would not rest till I wrote her a check for 49 cents in the name of the insurance company so she could mail it to them the same day before she went home for the day. She would not make a personal local call from my office without asking my permission and in fact always offered me to charge her for the phone call. She would not use a postal stamp from our office supplies until she first offered to pay me 45 cents for it, because she said she was going to use it on a personal letter to a relative. I guess such behavior qualified her for such epithets as "sickeningly honest" but it spoke volumes about her integrity and character as my biller and as a person. I scanned everything she gave me to Gluck immediately as and when I received it from her. Gluck asked me if the data was correct. I told him that errors in billing data were possible because I had a previous biller whose work I was less familiar with. I also informed Gluck that my biller and I could get on the phone with the insurance companies and ask for any missing billing or reimbursement information but cautioned that it might take several days to verify the accuracy of every single reimbursement received over those five years.

Meanwhile, I learned that the prosecutor took it upon himself (and understandably so) to investigate each IUD patient billing record directly from the insurance companies using the medical charts and the billing data that was in his possession. The government had the resources and the workforce that my staff and I did not have. I cannot imagine how many people the prosecutor assigned to the job to gather information that spanned a five-year period. It was apparent by looking at the prosecutor's Excel Spreadsheet, that the government had contacted each insurance provider for every single patient that had received an IUD and got the billing reimbursement information.

I began working on filling in the blanks on my records by calling insurance companies and getting the missing information. It took my wife and me, between taking care of our kids and running the business, several weeks to verify the billing reimbursement data for all patients (which turned out to be a total of 149 IUD recipients over a period of five years, spanning from May of 2008 to March of 2012.) In the end, there were about only four patients that we could not trace because we did not have enough information about these patients to provide the insurance companies with. For example, there might be a missing date of IUD insertion, or a lost medical chart, or missing date of birth and so forth. the sort of minimal data an insurance company would ask for to search for billing and reimbursement records of a given patient. Just the first and last name of a patient is not always adequate information. With the assistance of our biller, my wife and I managed to investigate 99 percent of the billing data when all was said and done.

Delahunty gave Gluck his final version of billing reimbursement data on a spreadsheet based on the government's research, which showed that I received a total of $47,452 from all insurance companies for all IUD-related services during the five-year period. The spreadsheet totals looked credible, and I accepted that as an accurate amount of total reimbursement dollars in good faith. I had no reason to suspect that the prosecutor would have tampered with the data in any way. Even if I had considered the possibility, I could not have gone through his numbers in the very brief time available to me. To even notice anything wrong would have taken time and a genius to see there was a problem with the data they were coming up with, especially considering the agonizingly painful stress I was under, which had thrown me completely off balance. To this day, I still cannot fathom how I survived that month with tons of calculations and sheets being thrown at me by the prosecutor in a rapid succession.

I was busy spending countless hours sifting through hundreds of pages of documents that contained a web of lies while preparing to pack up to go to jail and trying to prepare my family as best as I could for my absence. It was impossible for me to precisely figure out how the prosecutor had arrived at different sets of calculations on his billing spreadsheets, with revised versions continually being churned out by an entire team of people, at the prosecutor's beck and call. I was a team of one person dealing with this agency that had vast resources and numerous people working on the case Delahunty had constructed. My lawyer was no match for this, even if he had been motivated in getting to the truth, which he wasn't. Of course, I could have had a trial in the end if I wanted to prove my innocence, but it would have been like climbing Mount Everest with both legs cut — off, precisely the reason I decided not to go down that path.

I was trying my hardest to update Gluck with the total dollar amounts billed to and received in insurance reimbursements, as I filled in the gaps of missing billing information by contacting the insurance companies, but I did not have the resources and staff to thoroughly analyze the prosecutor's data spreadsheets against my numbers. As I discovered numbers in the prosecutor's spreadsheets that were inconsistent with mine, I updated Gluck, but it fell on deaf ears. I told him on a regular basis that the prosecutor's data was not correct. But to Gluck, it was immaterial. Gluck was now coming across as though he was the prosecutor. He remained busy working out details with the other side about what length of imprisonment would be commensurate with billing fraud per the sentencing guidelines - billing fraud that hadn't been proven and had been unilaterally determined by the prosecutor. It was crystal clear to me from observing Gluck's behavior that the data I was providing him to counteract Delahunty's was probably not being looked at or understood and was perhaps going straight to the trash bin. Gluck's entire focus was on what the prosecutor was claiming about billing. Telling Gluck that I thought the prosecutor's numbers were off was like talking to myself. It wasn't until much later when I had the time to analyze the data presented by Delahunty that I found it to be deceptively fraudulent, the equivalent of falsifying accounting. I doubt it would have mattered even if I had gathered enough evidence on time to prove Delahunty's fraudulent accounting method, however, because only one thing seemed to matter to the prosecutor: I must be found guilty.

Gluck ignored my warnings about the government's spreadsheets and when his colleague, Ashley Bowman, took over the case she did the same. I continued raising my concerns and informing her the data was incorrect, up to the day before my sentencing. But when the government targets someone, puts a lot of time and money into gathering information on that target, and falsifies records to support their lies, they're not going to let the truth or anything else get in the way of finishing their job. I had been rushed to sign an agreement to plead guilty, and they later changed the deal, something I could do nothing about. I was guilty at gunpoint, a third-world justice in what I once considered the greatest, most just country in the world.

My Inner Turmoil Leading up to the Court Date

A court date was set for August 24, 2015. The most ironic thing about going before the federal judge to plead guilty was that a book I had recently finished writing was about the biological basis of human nature in terms of free will, consciousness, and the self in which I also discussed the criminal justice system. Little did I know that I would personally get a glimpse of what the system was indeed about, based on performing what I believed was a public service and not criminal activity.

The case was now in the hands of a younger defense lawyer, Ashley Bowman, who had taken over the logistics of the case the moment I signed Delahunty's guilty plea agreement on July 28, 2015. The law firm of Bird and Mirella, for whom Gluck and Bowman worked, took the case from Gluck and gave it to the law firm's youngest lawyer, one who had only been out of Stanford Law School a few years prior. It made financial sense to assign it to someone with less experience because the law firm did not see any funds coming its way from this case. I understand businesses do what they must, to make things as cost-effective as possible. They knew I had no cash left. My first thought was that it was going to be a disaster having a young attorney, without much prior experience, representing me. But overall, Bowman turned out to be significantly diligent compared with Gluck. Unlike Gluck, she responded to her emails, most of the time, though not always. The only time she did not respond to my emails is when I pointed out an illegal activity of the prosecutor or of my own defense attorneys, which included herself. Bowman reminded me of my young third-year medical students who did a clerkship under me for Obstetrics and Gynecology. They did a better job at taking patient history and doing physical exams than the senior and chief residents, and even some of the attending physicians. Students and those who are new to a profession, are often enthusiastic and eager to prove themselves. But it wasn't long before Bowman proved she was a team player caught in the wheels of a profit-driven machine.

Bowman called to prepare me for the court date. She wanted to inform me as to what I could expect moving forward from that point on. Being my new attorney, I wanted to review the case with her all over again to make sure we were both on the same page. She did not want to discuss it, however, saying she knew everything about it and assured me that Gluck had seen to that. I tried to address the FDA agent's fraudulent inducement of patients, subornation of perjury, prosecutorial concealment of evidence, obstruction of justice, and tampering with evidence, but she politely told me that her role was not to address any of that. She acknowledged that by pleading guilty, I did what was best for my family, but that what I was telling her was not relevant and was outside the scope of what we would be doing next. She told me her concern was in seeking mitigating factors and writing a good sentencing memo to convince the judge to let me stay at home with my kids instead of sending me to prison. She started talking about my son's disability, and the fact that I was my son's only caretaker now that my wife had to get a job outside the home because I had lost everything including my career. I was also taking care of my own disability from a spinal injury I had incurred in 2013, with a recurrent injury in 2015, which Bowman said would be a mitigating factor, as well. She quickly sensed that I was not going to provide her with information about my children, so she started obtaining information about my son's medical condition directly from my wife. My wife was ready to give these people anything they wanted because they were supposedly trying to help me minimize my sentencing, and I guess they were. All the mitigating circumstances in the world had nothing to do with the truth, however.

During this time, I started receiving phone calls from the psychologist, Dr. Romanoff, who had prepared his report for the judge. Romanoff tried to convince me that I should go into therapy sessions, which could be used as a mitigating factor. He went on and on about why it was a good idea for me to have these sessions, but I declined. He then resorted to calling my wife and asking her to talk some sense into me. He said I was inflexible and stubborn, implying that I'm not too bright, without coming out and using the word stupid. I suppose when you work with the attorneys he was working with, doing the kind of work he was doing, you figure that anyone with principles must be short on brain cells. My wife later told me that he mocked me several times in his appeals to her, implying that I was someone who was too dense to have a basic understanding of how the game is played. He went so far as to feign surprise over the fact that someone like my wife would be married to someone as obstinate as me.

Naturally, my wife did not ask me to go along with the recommended psychotherapy sessions. She knew me well enough to know that I would not add to their charade, and she had already heard enough about Dr. Romanoff to understand that this was coming from someone who magically created a report for the court constructed around a narrative of poor judgment on my part, which was a lie. The suggestion to go to therapy to show the judge I was willing to be rehabilitated for my alleged crime was even more offensive than being mocked. My wife knew the only crime that had taken place was *against* me, not *by* me.

An essential element in all of this is that the government expects defense attorneys to play along and not oppose the government, or they are perceived as not helping enforce law and order. It's also career suicide for those who hope to eventually work for the government. Even criminal defense attorneys who are competent and ethical must obey the government by accepting the prosecutor's interpretation of the law, so I believe they have to compartmentalize and convince themselves that what they're doing is for the greater good, or that they have no choice. A rationale you'll hear from them is that it's a problem with the system and they are just doing their job, and it's not their fault that their client doesn't have the money to defend himself, or they're just trying to make a living like everyone else. The more one is surrounded by corruption, the easier corruption is to accept. It's like living with a crack in the wall that you cannot fix. After a while, you stop seeing it.

August 24, 2015 – Pleading Guilty Under the Gun

On August 23, 2015, the day before my court date, I called Gluck and requested that he be present at my hearing even though he was no longer officially on the case. On the day of the hearing, he showed up with Bowman, meeting me outside the courtroom on the 14th floor in Fresno, California. I had a large duffel bag with tons of research papers on European brands and generics of Cu-380A from several medical journals to show Gluck in person, information that I had tried telling him previously through emails, which he had ignored. This was the same duffel bag I brought to my Medical Board hearing in Los Angeles in 2014 when I was exonerated from all FDA allegations. I informed Gluck that I had numerous research papers on the IUD I used that supported my claim that the IUD was approved and recommended by the CDC and the NIH. Nowhere in the 145-page 2010 WHO report did I see a comment by the CDC against using European-made copper IUDs in the United States; the CDC considered these IUDs safe and effective and highly recommended to the entire world (Exhibits 1 and 2).

Gluck refused to look at what I had to show him. He quickly dismissed me with a wave of his hand and started walking away from me. I did not expect him to read it since he had not even read the government's Discovery documents, but I was hoping that he could easily use this information as a genuine argument before the judge. But none of this mattered to Gluck. As he began walking away from me, he whispered something to Bowman about the government still being able to argue that the IUD was counterfeit. He said it as a loud aside, so I believe he wanted me to hear it.

It was a bit early to go in, so Gluck suggested that we go to a lawyer's lounge in the courthouse. The entire time we were there, Gluck sat looking down at his cell phone, not saying a word to me. He knew I was mad as hell at him. I'm not a violent man, but if I could have, I would have beaten the shit out of him at that moment. He did not make any eye contact with me during the fifteen-minute period we were there. To be honest, I did not want to talk to him either. I had lost all respect for him, and I think he knew that, as well.

When I appeared before the judge, Gluck stood next to me. The judge read the government's fiction-based guilty plea, which had my signature on it. Every so often, the judge asked, "Do you understand that?" It was as though he was reading my rights and giving me an opportunity to change my mind. I answered that I understood each time the judge paused to ask. Then he told me to surrender my passport and informed me that the date for sentencing would be on November 7, 2015. From there, Gluck took me to the Probation Department so I could be processed. I did not know what being processed meant and he didn't bother to explain. We sat outside the Probation department, awaiting our turn, in complete silence.

I finally broke the silence and said, "I hope that you fully understand that this entire case was orchestrated by FDA agent Pueschel with Teva probably working behind the scenes." He said, 'I know the feeling." "Know the feeling? I am not talking about feelings - I am talking about facts!" I yelled at him as loud as I could. He did not respond to my outburst, and refused to look me in the eye. He sat quietly until they called me in.

Gluck handed my passport to the clerk at the window, shook my hand and left, and I went inside. It was a large, dark room with no windows and one door. Two 300-pound-plus muscular guys patted and frisked me as I stood with my hands against the wall. Then they took my fingerprints, mug shots, a DNA swab from my mouth, and then released me half an hour later.

I had driven thirty minutes from the courthouse on my way back home to northern California when my cell phone rang. It was my wife. She told me that the news about me was running on both television and radio. She said that TV reports portrayed me as an example of American greed. She went on describing what was being said, but I could hardly process the words. I was numb, but for her sake, I pretended to be calm and attentive. I would not discover until later that there was a press release, (Exhibit 21 of *Companion Book: The Death of the Rule of Law)* prepared ahead of time by Delahunty to be submitted to the media, as soon as I pled guilty. It was the prosecutor's moment of fame by getting his name on television.

Once I pled guilty I was once again free to speak with Sandra Johnson. I contacted her to find out if she would be willing to share the details of her deposition, which was conducted by FDA agent Pueschel and the two prosecutors, Mr. Delahunty and Mr. Sheriff, with my attorneys, Gluck and Spackman present three months prior.

Ms. Johnson informed me that before her testimony began, she was taken for a car ride by a former prosecutor, Stephen Jones (Exhibits 6 and 12), who was hired by Gluck to represent her. Jones intimidated her and threatened her with being dragged into court if she tried to help me in any way. She told me he was insinuating that she must follow the prosecutor's lead as to what the prosecutor wanted her to say or else she might face prosecution. He was threatening her with this despite the fact that she was given immunity prior to this anticipated testimony.

Ms. Johnson said that Stephen Jones began the conversation by making some inappropriate comments, such as, and I paraphrase: We know that you have had an affair with Dr. Singh. You better not try to help him with your testimony. Then he told her that he was aware that my wife was jealous of her, which was, of course, a lie, just as the accusation of an affair was a lie. She said she was terrified to hear him make such outlandish statements and she told him that her relationship with me had been strictly professional and never anything other than an employee — employer relationship. She said that she had never been so afraid in her life. She was shocked by these threats and allegations. I was not at all surprised when she told me the younger prosecutor who interviewed her "wanted me on the chopping block" (her words). She was referring to Delahunty.

Despite the needs of my family, I was not about to completely give up. It had been a week after my plea hearing, I continued to ask Bowman to dig up any exculpatory documents from the government records if there were any to be found. I also requested that she obtain a complete transcript of the press release that the prosecutor released to the media. From Bowman's viewpoint, it was all irrelevant because I had already pled guilty and was now waiting to be sentenced. It bothered her that I still had questions, the game was over as far as she was concerned. She felt uncomfortable when I continued to make demands. I informed Bowman in one of my emails (Exhibit 24: email # 5) that it was not over yet, and that I would expose

Pueschel's crimes; my exact words in this email are, "I promise you that this will all come back to haunt this FDA agent one day for what he has done to me and my family". She did not respond. In the week that followed, I sent Bowman another email (Exhibit 24), in which I informed her that I would one day hold everyone responsible for their crimes against me.

I am in possession of the print-outs of all the emails that I exchanged with Bowman in the last week of August, 2015, the week following my conviction, and scores of additional emails between my conviction and going to the prison nine months later. I can publicly make these email exchanges available to any American citizen who asks for it. There are hundreds of emails exchanged, but I have only published some in Exhibit 24 and other exhibits, for the sake of keeping in check the length of this book. I firmly believe that this atty-client product is under exceptions to the rule of atty-client privilege or product. We all know that when an atty helps hide a crime committed by his client, the atty-client privilege no longer exists, I believe that by the same token, an atty-client privilege or an atty-client product does not and cannot exist if the defense attorneys are engaged in participating in unlawful actions that violated my civil and constitutional rights. It is my job to show you how my attorneys actively participated with the prosecutor in many unlawful behaviors during the course of my ordeal. I make the offer of making all these emails public to prove to law students and citizens how corrupt our legal system can be, behind the scenes, and that the criminal defense industry is very much a part and parcel of this unjust and corrupt system.

In doing additional research, I had found many convictions reversed with the help of the Innocence Project and other activist organizations, when it was discovered that prosecutors lied to the court, forged documents, or concealed evidence. But there have been no consequences for the corrupt prosecutors who ruined the lives of innocent people.

When you read Bowman's emails to me in Exhibit 24, you should be able to see that she was getting tired of me badgering her and accusing the FDA agent and prosecutors of obstruction of justice and falsifying information. My emails to her show that I provided her vast amounts of evidence of the government's wrongdoing, which she conveniently dismissed by saying, such evidence was no longer useful, it was too late, it was outside the scope of her legal arguments, it did not fit her "new framework", that Benjamin and she had devised based on the fact that I had already pled guilty.

Bowman agreed to contact Delahunty who promised he would give her digital records of everything he had. This was great news to me until she told me the disc she had received from Delahunty was "tens of thousands of pages long" and that there was no way she was going to look at it. I asked her repeatedly to please go through it because I knew the FDA had manufactured documents but she insisted she did not have the luxury of time to go through it all. She became increasingly annoyed with me when I was desperately trying to find something from this disc that could prove that I was right in my assertions. She had the same response when I asked her to review the so-called Anti-Drug Importation law and regulations drafted by Big Pharma and rubber stamped by the FDA. I wanted to know where in the law it states that a physician cannot import a safe, well-regulated and approved drug from a German pharmaceutical company that was of equal quality and safety to the U.S. drug equivalent. She said the law was thousands and thousands of pages long and she was not going to read it, adding that the law would not specifically refer to the IUD, and that it would have only general statements applicable to all drugs.

I could not have possibly reviewed tens of thousands of pages on this prosecutor's disc myself with everything I had on my plate. All I could think of was that the moment I went to prison, my monthly income would drop down to $1,500 a month (revenue from a rental property), income that would not be sufficient to pay the mortgage and healthcare, and to raise my disabled son, another teenager and a baby. And we did not have more than two months of emergency funds in the bank. We were about to lose everything we had. I was in a state of agony. The banks, credit cards, and my retirement account's custodian, Charles Schwab, had already started to block me from doing any business with them, and our accounts were being closed, including backing out of an already-approved home equity loan by Wells Fargo. I have learned that this was all a result of the DOJ's Operation Choke Point, an unconstitutional and illegal program to financially choke every criminal to death, as though incarceration was not punishment enough. DOJ has devised many such programs that violate our domestic laws, peoples' civil rights and the Constitution of the United States.

I softened my approach and asked Bowman if she would be kind enough to at least look for the essential documents that could be exculpatory, for example, to see if there were any FDA's memos or notes on the August 17, 2010, interview, which Delahunty, had denied existed. Or an estimated 800-page deposition/testimony of Sandra Johnson that Bowman knew was conducted by two prosecutors in the presence of Gluck on May 29, 2015. I also asked her to see if she could find any FDA documentation regarding the FDA's interactions with me between August 17 and October 12, 2010. I requested that she thoroughly inspect the documents to see if she could find interview notes by a female Asian-American special agent of the FDA whose name had been deleted that might have accidentally slipped into this vast ocean of paperwork that the government had been creating against me and now released on a disc even though neither she, nor I, thought that the prosecutors would be stupid enough to put anything on the disc that they had denied existed, or concealed from the court. I was sure then and am sure today that criminals know how to commit a crime without leaving behind a trace of evidence. That would be even truer of people in government who were trained professionals.

I have no idea how much time Bowman spent searching for these things, but she informed me that she did not find Sandra Johnson's testimony on that disc nor the 2010 or 2012 missing FDA records, but she did find some handwritten notes by Pueschel dated August 17, 2010. She gave off an attitude as though she was overly accommodating by taking the time to look through this disc – as though she was not legally obligated to do so to best represent me. I know she was irritated and was doing it mainly because I was annoying her. My wife was reading my emails to Bowman behind my back and warned me that I would lose the only ally we had if I continued to be so impolite. I don't know what appropriate behavior is when one is falsely accused, but I suspect lying down in silence and just taking it, isn't likely to happen.

I could not wait to see those handwritten notes dated August 17, 2010, because Delahunty had denied they existed when he was asked repeatedly by my attorney. I was hoping a damning document would accidentally slip through the government's hands. Bowman sent me Pueschel's handwritten notes dated 8/17/10 (Exhibit 3), part of the *Brady* material that Delahunty denied existed or refused to hand over when Gluck made that request. Pueschel's notes prove that he knew on August 17, 2010, that the Cu-380A IUD I used was manufactured in Germany. This one fact alone would now contradict hundreds of documents Pueschel had created, referencing the German-made IUD as an unsafe, defective, and counterfeit IUD that was purchased on the Internet, something he told my patients repeatedly for five-years to induce false victim impact reports. In the five years he had been constructing his fraudulent case, he did not tell a single patient that the IUD I'd used was made in Germany by a reputable pharmaceutical company and researched and approved under the drug regulatory agency of Germany and by the CDC. Pueschel's handwritten notes contradicted many things in the memos that he wrote for the prosecutor to have me prosecuted. The handwritten notes also seemed to have been written with the same ink and the same handwriting style on DOJ's official legal notepad with pages numbered from 000225 to 000238. His notes have reference to events that did not exist till 2012 even though he wrote them on August 17,2010, which only proves that the notes are a forgery that was created at least two years after the fact. This further explains why the prosecutor did not want to reveal it when requested by the defense; because he knew these notes will raise more questions about the authenticity of the government's allegations and may incriminate the FDA and the prosecutor representing the FDA. Nowhere in these notes dated August 17, 2010 that describe events of the future in Pueschel's parallel universe does it say that I was "admonished" by two FDA agents on August 17, 2010, which was Delahunty and Pueschel's joint invention in collusion with each other to prosecute me when all allegations by Delahunty had failed to stick (Exhibit 4).

The handwritten notes are written in faint blue ink, sometimes hard to read, and have so many contradictory and out-of-context statements that it is hard to figure out where to begin. I have had Kinkos manually scan them to obtain the best possible photographs of these notes that I discovered in such poor condition on the electronic disc. Pueschel left several numbered pages in the government's legal pad blank. Without trying to read Pueschel's mind, I can only speculate that this is a clear indication that he deliberately left some blank pages so he could fill them with additional forgeries from time to time in the event this case went to trial, even though they had no intent of releasing this exculpatory but also incriminating document. Delahunty and Pueschel are ignorant to this day (until they read this book) that they accidentally leaked this document on their electronic disc after denying the existence of this handwritten document. I have made a few observational remarks on this (Exhibit 3). What a great criminal justice!

I emailed Bowman to ask her how we were going to proceed, given this latest turn of events. I wanted to hold Gluck to his word, which was that if Puecshel's handwritten notes were ever found, and Pueschel's supervisor didn't sign them, then Gluck would proceed with filing for the impeachment of the FDA agent. I told Bowman that we now had an opportunity to do what Gluck had promised since we found the desired evidence, an evidence that contradicted the prosecutor's story (Emails Exhibit 22). This document provided a basis for the reversal of my conviction, and a firm foundation for the criminal investigation of the FDA agent and the prosecutors in the Department of Justice. I reminded her that the law requires that Brady materials, when requested by the defense, must be released by the Department of Justice. Hiding them is a crime regardless of how and why such documents are exculpatory. Bowman responded that she was not aware of any impeachment promise made to me since she was not on the case at the time. She said she would speak with Gluck about it and get back to me. Then she went silent about this issue, without following up with me. I reminded her again that I needed the answer after she spoke to Gluck but still received no reply. My wife prevented me from pushing Bowman too hard, by belaboring the point that we could not afford to lose our only ally we had before being sentenced.

Perhaps a very wealthy defendant would have had the case reopened and fought until Pueschel and the prosecutors were impeached. What I had found could open the door to many more exculpatory documents the government was hiding. Perhaps it would have led to forcing the government to reveal other Brady materials if someone of the caliber and integrity of Judge Emmett Sullivan took over the case as he did in the case of a former U.S. Senator. I can say with confidence that if I were someone with enormous wealth, Pueschel would not be working for the FDA today, and the two prosecutor's careers would be in jeopardy for collaborating in criminal conspiracy with the FDA agent instead of appropriately censuring him for withholding critical information that could prevent great injustice from occurring.

I then read about other similar cases in which the prosecutors had accidentally released exculpatory materials (and materials that incriminated the prosecutors). One such example was in the Enron/Merrill Lynch case (see the highlighted exculpatory evidence on page 404 in the book, *Licensed to Lie: Exposing Corruption in the Department of the Justice,* by Sidney Powell). A piece of exculpatory evidence the government was hiding accidentally slipped into the hands of the defense on a disc in the Enron case, just as it had in my case, which reversed the conviction. In Senator Ted Steven's case, things went much farther in that the whistle blown by an FBI agent became part of the reason Judge Sullivan ordered a criminal investigation of the Department of Justice. The document accidentally released in my case showed that Pueschel and the prosecutors had the facts but continued to lie to patients and falsify and misrepresent this information in all court documents. And they said it repeatedly, something I tried to fight, but my voice was constantly muffled. Even the FDA scientists had confirmed that all Cu-380A IUDs given to the FDA by patients who had them removed for a variety of reasons, were T-Safe manufactured by EurimPharm of Germany — information that was systematically concealed throughout the criminal case except in the original documents presented to the Medical Board. These newly recovered notes confirmed that the FDA agent and prosecutors induced patients into writing false reports. No part of Pueschel's handwritten notes has any mention of what the government had repeatedly claimed as facts related to the August 17, 2010 event in all its fabrications and forgeries that became part of the government's discovery.

To say I was outraged is an understatement! I am not going to leave out a discussion about defense attorneys when I discuss the corruption in the criminal justice system in this book. The defense attorneys are very much an integral part of the criminal aspect of the criminal justice system, and I want to be sure to give credit where credit is due.

CHAPTER 4

MOVING FORWARD– INTO THE SINK OF DEBAUCHERY

"A lawyer who uses his/her legal education and skills to distort the law, to destroy the rule of law because he or she has adapted manipulative language when no judge, no adversary is watching is as blameworthy as his client."
—Stephen Gillers, America's leading professor of Legal Ethics, NYU

Fraudulent Alteration of My "Personal Statement"

DEALING WITH THE PROBATION DEPARTMENT WAS another sickening process, but not nearly as sickening as the requirement to write a Personal Statement by taking instructions from my defense attorney. Bowman asked me to be polite and to refrain from saying anything accusatory about the government in what she said would be my Personal Statement to the Probation department. I soon discovered that unlike my attorney, they called it an "Offense Statement."

I wrote a statement that was a page and a half long, signed it, scanned it, and emailed it to her. This statement was a very brief summary of what you have read in this book thus far. I focused on the history of my dealings with the FDA's agent Pueschel and other main events exposing Pueschel and Delahunty's fabrications and misrepresentations without the actual use of those words, as I was warned. I was supposed to be polite and unaccusatory. Bowman did not at all like my statement and asked me to rewrite it with emphasis on *taking responsibility*. She also told my wife and me that I should emphasize my son's disability and talk more about the stress in my life during the years the case was going on. Bowman had read my son's medical records, which she obtained from my wife, stating that my son's disability would be a mitigating factor in my avoiding jail so I could stay home and take care of my son. I revised the draft multiple times upon several requests from her, adding a sentence here and a sentence there, and sent her multiple revisions with minor changes made, by changing a word or a sentence here and there. My final revised statement was just about two pages long, an additional half a page added to my original version. To incorporate the idea of *taking responsibility*, Bowman suggested that I add that I should have doubly verified the Canadian distributor's claim that the German Cu-380A IUD was FDA-approved before purchasing it. She inserted these words on my Microsoft word document, which I agreed to be incorporated into the statement. What else I can do at this point, I thought to myself, I should let her do her job, after all she is only trying to help me stay home and not go to jail. I was willing to go this far in making the changes in my draft if it meant that it would help mitigate the case by *taking responsibility*. Bowman honed in on the words, "taking responsibility" that I have italicized everywhere so you could see how important those words were to Bowman to keep me out of jail. Bowman kept asking me to modify my Personal Statement further without saying what she wanted me to modify and why.

At this point, I was confused as to what Bowman was trying to tell me by reiterating the words, *taking responsibility* over and over, ad nauseum. Her mantra was that it was not about destroying government's credibility through my statement but *taking responsibility* if I wanted to stay home with my kids. (See emails in Exhibit 10). In my own final version, I emphasized the details of my interactions with the FDA for three months in the year 2010. I wrote in clear language that the FDA's designation of the August 17, 2010 interview as an "admonishment", was a false narrative. I also wrote about the predatory pricing of the ParaGard IUDs in my statement. Bowman was not happy with my final version and we were not getting anywhere and time was running out. The statement was due soon to be submitted to the probation officer. I got frustrated and told her to do whatever she wanted to do with my statement and edit or change it any way she wanted. She took over the editing process. She added volumes of information about my son's illness as a mitigating factor and asked me to approve the changes. I approved those changes as well thinking that this information couldn't hurt even though it was all irrelevant to my case. Although my family's unfortunate circumstances were true, they were irrelevant in that I did not need the government's mercy; I needed justice and I wanted the truth to be revealed. I was not there to oppose my attorney's every move, however, because I thought she was trying to help me and my family, which she claimed all along was her ultimate goal to help me stay home and not go to jail. She made so many additions that she essentially created a new statement, creating a much larger document with all kinds of true stories about my disabled child but mixed with false stories about me insinuating that I admit to having used poor Judgment in using FDA-unapproved IUDs and risking the lives of my patients.

But what bothered me about her draft was NOT that she added stories about my child's disability, but that every time she added a story, she also sneaked in to delete or alter the most important parts of my statements against the government for which I wanted to hold the government accountable. Her rationale was that this would mitigate my case in the eyes of the government. The result was that she submitted a fairytale to the Probation department. She kept telling me in her emails that what she would revise for me would be my story and not hers, but at the same time, she continued to write a story that was her own (emails: Exhibit 10). It is precisely for this reason I have included many emails in Exhibit 10 that shows the process I went through, with her making at least ten revisions and my continual objections to her revisions.

In a potential congressional investigation of this case in the future, I would like all the official and unofficial emails, phone records and interactions between my two defense attorneys and the FDA's Pueschel, and prosecutor Delahunty to see what they were up to while Bowman was busy altering my testimony. One of Bowman's emails to me suggests she was going back to Gluck after every revision to consult with him to make sure it fit their narrative and their "framework" (my attorneys' words) that they had devised to spin my case in a new direction, the idea was to make the case conform to the prosecutor's story. Bowman called it fitting their "framework," but it was not a framework, it was framing. The FDA and Delahunty had framed me, and now my defense attorneys were starting to frame me to custom-fit me into the prosecutor's frame. Bowman modified, altered, edited, shifted, underplayed, tone-changed, and manufactured my statement to make everything match the prosecutorial story, one piece at a time.

It was not until towards the end of her final draft of my statement that I understood what she was trying to tell me by *personal responsibility*. She was trying to get me to falsify the critical parts of my statement so it would completely conform with the government's narrative, that is what she meant by *taking responsibility*. But she did not have the guts to tell me that, both for ethical reasons and legal malpractice. I was shocked to see the changes made each time I received a new revision from Bowman, all filled with blue, yellow, and red lines, and passages altered, deleted or removed. She continued to remind me and my wife throughout her revision process that she was only trying to help me stay out of prison by *taking responsibility*. She removed all statements in which I attempted to gently expose the government and replaced them with vague comments supporting the prosecutor's claims.

I felt nauseated when I signed the final 6-page long document that she prepared for me. Her final version of the statement had two elements to it. It had a criminal component, in terms of altering, deleting and changing all the crucial parts of my testimony, and an ethical component which was Bowman putting new words in my mouth. I knew that if I refused to sign this Personal Statement, it would result in a much worse outcome for me. I felt worse in signing this than I had when I signed the actual guilty plea on July 28, 2015, because this time I felt betrayed by my defense attorneys. I wasn't willing to put my family through any more of the hell than they had already gone through, so I did what Bowman wanted me to do: I put ethics, morality, justice, and my soul and spirit on the back burner and complied. And as broken as I may have been at that point, I knew it would be temporary, because even the most corrupt government cannot hide from the truth for long.

The Probation Department's Showbiz - Cut-and-Paste Reports

A date was set for the Probation Department to review my case. I noted a provision in the last paragraph of the Guilty Plea Agreement that I had signed, which stated, "The defendant understands that the United States Department of Probation is not a party to this agreement and will conduct an independent investigation of defendant's activities and background. It will then prepare a presentence report which it will submit to the court as its independent sentencing recommendation" (Exhibit 11). To me, this was a confirmation that by law, the Probation Department was legally required to conduct its own independent inquiry before recommending an appropriate sentence to the judge. I saw this as an opportunity to present my case to the Probation officer. I knew I had to be polite, and I was as polite as I could be, under the circumstances. I also knew that bringing up the issue that the FDA agent lied, was no longer an option since my attorney had crafted my Personal Statement for the Probation department to match up with the prosecutor's claims — a statement that I had already signed. The Personal Statement was only one of many documents to be reviewed by the Probation department. Despite all of this, I was prepared to expose the FDA and the prosecutor to the Probation officer but would have to do so in a more covert manner.

Bowman accompanied me to the Probation department at the federal courthouse in Fresno Eastern District. As she started talking to the Probation officer, Mr. Michael Armistead, I took over the discussion as I had with the Administrative judge in my Medical Board case. I informed the Probation officer that the FDA Agent, Pueschel, had engaged in falsely inducing the patients into believing untrue information about the German-made brand of Copper 380A IUD thus leading them into writing accusatory victim impact reports. I informed him that the brand "T-Safe" copper IUD was manufactured in Germany by a reputable drug company, EurimPharm, and that FDA Agent Pueschel had known this since August 2010. I added that I could prove it, but the Probation officer did not bother to ask me how. If he had, the FDA's leaked document was in my pocket. I requested that he do his due diligence and get the facts about the IUD I used. I informed him that the FDA agent had misinformed patients that the IUD was dangerous, unsafe, and bought on the Internet. I refrained from saying that the prosecutor Delahunty conspired with the FDA on this because I knew that it would make my attorney mad and probably make my prospects for any justice much worse. Such an accusation would also contradict the Personal Statement she had already crafted and submitted to Probation with my signature on it. I informed Probation officer, Armistead that I could show him medical literature that I brought with me that would support the safety of the German T-Safe, based on research carried out by the World Health Organization and spearheaded by the U.S. Centers for Disease Control. As I spoke and tried to expose my case emphasizing this point, I saw Bowman becoming very uncomfortable with my approach. I felt her kick my foot from under the table as she tried to get me to shut up. I was not about to stop. I stood up, stepped away from her and continued to speak directly to the Probation officer. The only response I got from the Probation officer was something to the effect of, "Doctor, you can't be buying IUDs from Canada. As far as patient Impacts…that is not relevant. Those patients will settle by filing civil suits against you."

When we left the office, Bowman was furious, but she knew I was equally pissed at her and her senior colleague, Gluck. Later in the day, she called my wife and told her I almost botched the interview at the Probation office and that I was supposed to be interviewing while *taking responsibility* instead of accusing the government, which would only make matters worse for me. She made sure to add that the purpose of all of this was to get them to allow me to stay home with my family. When my wife told me this, it made me sick to my stomach all over again.

The Probation Department prepared its independent report, a pre-sentencing report, which consisted of text that appeared to be cut and pasted from the allegations written by the prosecutor. (Exhibit 11). It concluded that, because the IUD was not FDA approved, I consciously and recklessly put my patients at risk of death or serious bodily injury. In the end, the Probation officer recommended a reduced sentence to the judge of six months imprisonment followed by 1 year of house arrest, followed by an additional year of probation, instead of the Prosecutor's demand for a minimum 22 months of prison, followed by appropriate home confinement and probation periods. Perhaps the complaint I presented to Armistead did not hurt me as Bowman had thought. It's possible that my complaints to the Probation officer led to the suggested reduced sentence. The only thing I know for sure is that Michael Armistead was guilty of misconduct and dereliction of duty in failing to do the task he was charged with – doing an independent investigation without direct influence from the prosecutors. An independent investigation was specifically more important for him to do in my case because of the fact that I brought it to his attention that Pueschel fraudulently engaged in carrying out a disinformation campaign with my patients about the T-Safe Copper IUD, and that grave injustice had been done. The legal aspect of this misconduct by public officials working for the Probation Department is discussed at length in the legal section of this book.

Defense's Pretenses Personified – Complicity with Government Crimes

Prosecutor Delahunty informed Gluck that the sentence date was postponed because Judge Anthony Ishii had too many cases lined up. Sure enough, the sentencing date was pushed from November 6, 2015 to March 6, 2016. These postponements are indicative of the fact that Federal Judges are overwhelmed and cannot handle the workload. The government has too many people waiting to be sentenced in its mass incarceration program.

I am not sure if the postponement was good for my attorney, Bowman, but it was good for me. It gave me more time to dig a bit deeper into the thousands of pages of evidence that Delahunty had thrown at me in a very short time. Bowman informed me that Delahunty would be writing a pre-sentencing report of his own, and she would write one on my behalf from the viewpoint of the defense. I saw this as one more opportunity to provide the facts to the court, this time directly to the judge, but my hopes died when Bowman told me that the scope of our argument would be very narrow regarding what we were allowed to say to the judge. We could present only what the prosecutor would allow us to present. Many emails she wrote to me emphasizing this point can be found under Exhibit 24.

The more I delved into the evidence, the more I saw how problematic and flawed it was. There were victim impact reports with patient names redacted, and revealed to me only after convicting me. This wasn't a matter of confidentiality and HIPAA since the names of scores of patients were previously revealed to me by the FDA consistently for at least two years between 2013 and 2014 during the Medical Board case. So, there was no justification in hiding patients' names from me. I had asked Bowman before conviction to get the names from the prosecutor, which she said she requested, but I never received them. I was able to identify who they were, based on some clues in their stories, however, and provided their medical records to my attorney to show her how the victim impact reports were fabrications. In the case of one of the women, I wasn't even the doctor who implanted the copper IUD; it was done by another doctor (see that doctor's notes in Exhibit 13). The patient conceals this information in her report. This same patient, who later became the prosecutor's star witness talks about the pain and bleeding she was having without revealing the fact that her symptoms had to do with the ovarian mass she had, a solid-cystic tumor that was being ruled out for ovarian cancer, (although bleeding and pain are also normal side effects of copper IUDs.) The growing mass on her ovary had nothing to do with the IUD that she had in place for 18 months prior to the occurrence of this mass, an IUD that she had been very happy with all along. Her medical records contradict her story (see Exhibit 13 for medical records and her victim report.) The prosecutor claimed that her suffering was the result of what he called the unapproved IUD I had used on her, he completely ignored her medical file, which stated I was treating her for a large ovarian tumor that was causing her pain. When a patient is wearing an IUD and is going to experience bleeding or pain, it happens soon after the implant, not 18 months later.

In another preconviction victim impact report, that Delahunty submitted to my attention by redacting the patient's name is where the patient claimed her IUD led to her having a miscarriage. I had the opportunity to review her records from another Ob/Gyn who she received care from following a miscarriage. In reviewing the doctor's notes, I saw no mention at all that the IUD caused the miscarriage. In fact, the doctor found no evidence of an IUD in her uterus on an ultrasound examination. Bowman flatly refused to look at any of these medical records to prove that these patients were being fraudulently induced by the prosecutor in writing false reports. (see Exhibit 13 for details.)

It is imperative to understand that these victim impact reports are pre-printed forms provided to patients by the prosecutor. The form has a specific format with specific questions, including one that asks the patient to give an estimate of how much money the doctor owes her in restitution for the crime he committed. The form is designed to entice the patient to falsify stories in the hope of getting money because she is already made to believe that she is a victim whether she thinks she is or not. And the victim is encouraged to demand any amount based on manufactured stories of harm done to her health and safety. So even if the prosecutor were not to coach a patient to falsify her report, the form itself is an inducement for any impoverished person to lie in the hope of easing one's financial burdens in life. Some of these patients demanded up to $250,000 without saying a word about what harm they suffered from the IUD to warrant such restitution.

I again asked Bowman to acquire the names of these patients from the prosecutor since they had been redacted. She once again informed me that the prosecutor promised to give her the names of these women, but he never did until well after the conviction. I am not suggesting, however, that it would have made any difference if I managed to prove before my conviction that the prosecutor was falsifying information. Imagine living under Saddam Hussain and hoping to prove him wrong by telling him that he was breaking the law. Saddam Hussain is the law.

Patients picked up the terminology from their conversations with Pueschel and Delahunty and used it in their reports, such as the IUD they received was defective, dangerous, unsafe, unapproved and inferior etc. The victim impact reports might well have been completed by the prosecutor himself; you would not know the difference. Nearly all patients who filled out these reports claimed they deserved compensation because IUDs were defective, dangerous, and caused complications — echoing the government's accusations. I was able to compare many victim reports against their medical records whose initials were erroneously left unredacted and then later revealed after my conviction. Later, when I reviewed more patient files of some of the names revealed, it was clear that the government induced their claims of damage. I think even at that point, though I had pleaded guilty, the evidence would have been enough to reverse the case from indicting me to indicting those who had trumped up a false case against me, but my attorney wasn't interested in any of this. The evidence did not fit her new "framework."

The prosecutor had no choice but to ignore totally laughable claims, and there were many (more on this later), but he added dollar amounts from victim reports that he thought he could use before the judge without embarassing himself. When it did that, he had trouble adding his damages that would amount to his totals of $47,452, which is what the prosecutor was seeking from me in restitution. The prosecutor then approached the insurance providers to ask them how much money I had received from them for patients who had come to me for IUD's over the five-year period under investigation. About 90 percent of those insurance companies didn't bother to respond to him. A few responded only after Delahunty pursued them well after my conviction, so that he could continue to beef up the restitution amounts, without asking the insurance companies' opinion as to whether or not they considered it inappropriate billing or billing fraud. Per my conversations with the insurance companies, none of them regarded it as illegal billing. They personally assured me that I owed them nothing.

Defense Attorney's Pre-Sentence Report

I include this to make a significant point. No document generated by the prosecution or my defense attorneys or the FDA agent ever included a statement from me about my culpability or a response from me about the allegations being made. I was expected to stand in silence and watch my life be ruined. No one asked me, 'We'd like to hear what you have to say.' Ordinary people are unaware of this until they are faced with, or they know someone who is faced with, defending themselves in a court of law, and then they are surprised to find out the reality of how the system works.

The three months of written arguments filed between my defense attorney and the prosecutor illustrated how committed the prosecution was in finding me guilty. The more Bowman asked for evidence of the prosecutor's claims, the more innovative he became so he could continue justifying his accusations by deceiving the court. As the saying goes, "one lie leads to another."

Both the government and my defense attorney produced their pre-sentencing memos at about the same time and filed them with the court. I reviewed the prosecutor's memo first, which was filed with the court on February 12, 2016. Statements from the prosecutor that I've previously shared were all included, with claims of physical and emotional damages to more than ten victims. Delahunty was asking for restitution in the amount of $47,452, forfeiture, and imprisonment for crimes committed. Delahunty's report also included a new lie that claimed I received an average of $322 reimbursement per IUD device from insurance companies. This was no little lie – this was a whopper. This amount of $322 was an average for all IUD-related healthcare services provided to each IUD patient over a span of one year. It included not just the IUD device, but also the surgical supplies, initial ultrasound, and all IUD-related follow-up office visits, including, in some cases the initial contraceptive counseling and evaluation. It also included the cost of business overhead incurred by me, which among other expenses, also consisted of a $42,000 per year malpractice premium and the expected compensation one would expect to go toward a physician's salary for all services rendered. The amount of $322 represented a global payment for every IUD- related medical service provided, not just the price of the IUD, as Delahunty portrayed to the court.

Then I reviewed the pre-sentencing memo prepared on my behalf by Bowman. The 37-page report started with some history about my life and background information (irrelevant to the facts of the case), followed by a whole bunch of letters submitted by my patients testifying on my character as a person and as their physician. These patients had only good things to say about me, and while I thought that this information was also irrelevant to the case, I must admit that some of the things patients said about me were so kind that it brought tears to my eyes. Apart from these glowing testimonials, Bowman's memo was full of half-true and sometimes plain false statements that I never made to her, or any other attorney, or to the government at any time throughout this case. Comments such as "Dr. Singh had an apparent misunderstanding as to what Pueschel told him in 2010" (copied from the false Personal Statement that she prepared on my behalf to make it consistent with the prosecutor's allegation). And "Dr. Singh sought reimbursements for IUDs billing codes reserved for U.S. brand ParaGard," (copied from the prosecutor's reports). She also wrote, again in agreement with the prosecutor's accusation, "Dr. Singh never disputed that the amount he billed was consistent with the billable reimbursements for ParaGard," another big lie.

Bowman discarded the electronic billing records (the ones that Delahunty and Benjamin also had in their possession) I sent her to show that Delahunty was lying about me billing for the billable amounts for ParaGard. He was also lying that I billed between $475 and $625 for Cu-380A IUD. The billing amounts that my biller charged were between $450 and $475 for T-safe IUD and all related services (see Exhibit 18 for all details). The billed amount between $600 and $625 was for Mirena IUD, not Copper IUD. Mirena had a different billing code, was twice as expensive, and was manufactured only by a U.S. manufacturer, Bayer, a subsidiary of Shering Plough. On the very first day Gluck requested billing records, my biller explained this to him on the electronic billing sheets (Exhibit 18) so that he could easily understand everything. Later I forwarded and explained the same information to Bowman (Exhibit 18). I sent several emails to Bowman with attachments analyzing Delahunty's billing fraud accusations in his sentencing report. I pointed out his false allegations line by line, but Bowman ignored my emails just as she had hundreds of other emails that would have vindicated me and proven Delahunty's statements to be false. The billed amounts for Copper IUDs and all related healthcare services were, in many cases, far less than the price of the ParaGard device itself. It was tantamount to my total upfront cost for using the lower-priced T-Safe IUD and the related minimum necessary health services that I was required to provide at the time of IUD implant. The upfront cost of services such as ultrasound scan and surgical supplies were not separately reimbursable due to the bundled code for Cu-380A (Exhibit 18). Bowman wrote in her pre-sentence report, "Dr. Singh truly regrets the serious error in judgment that led him to violate the law, and that continues to impact those around him." These were all false statements, so they would echo the prosecutor's claims.

I was glad that she at least agreed to include a vague line or two from me stating that the government's pre-sentence report (PSR 19) claim that I received $322 on average in IUD reimbursements was not just for the IUD device but everything IUD-related. She also quoted from the Medical Board's decision, saying several times that pecuniary gain did not motivate me and that the government's claim that greed motivated me was false and that my only motivation was to provide healthcare to indigent patients, a service that was otherwise not available to the poor due to the exorbitant price of the ParaGard. She quoted the Medical Board case and referenced Centers for Disease Control and National Institute of Health (NIH) to show that the IUD I used on my patients was a safe product.

She did not provide the prosecutor the evidence I provided her that the billing codes for Cu-380A under Medicare guidelines were bundled services, inclusive of Copper IUD device cost and all related healthcare services (Exhibit 20). I provided her evidence that the billing code J7300 was not reserved for a particular brand of the drug such as ParaGard, as Delahunty had claimed (Exhibit 20). Instead of utilizing the evidence I provided, Bowman cut and pasted the prosecutor's accusations about billing, agreeing with the prosecutor that the billing code was reserved just for the U.S. brand, ParaGard, made by the U.S. manufacturer. Bowman ignored my emails to her that said that per my conversations with the insurance companies, the health insurers agreed with me and not the prosecutor. I had informed Bowman that the insurance companies I spoke with did not consider my billing for the Cu-380A I used as fraudulent billing. As discussed earlier, they did not audit me, or cancel my contracts, nor did they request any refund for overpayment after I asked them if I owed them any money because of the FDA's accusations. Bowman ignored it all and went along with the false statements made by Delahunty.

The prosecutor immediately wrote a reply to Bowman's pre-sentencing memo and filed it with the court. When I reviewed his response, I found that some of the lies were given a new spin in an attempt to make them a bit more believable. The prosecutor realized that the average $322 reimbursement figure he came up with initially was going to be an embarrassment for the government. How do you justify sending someone to jail who provided all IUD-related medical services for a total of $322 dollars, services that would cost up to a $1,000 or more in any Ob/Gyn office? So, now he used some creative accounting to come up with a new average reimbursement amount of $452 per IUD to show that I made more money than he had previously thought. Oops! He had made a mistake in his previous calculations. Delahunty's new list omitted the patients for whom I received no reimbursement or miniscule payment from their insurance companies. He referred to these deletions as "unknowns" that didn't need to be counted. He also deleted a few names of patients for whom I received an extremely low reimbursement such as less than $50 for hundreds of dollars' worth of services provided. Of course, Delahunty didn't want them counted; they didn't fit the narrative that greed motivated me, and including them would have reduced the average reimbursement significantly. He continued the lie that the $452 was for the IUD device only. He also pretended that some women who had received more than one IUD over the years, had only one device implanted to avoid reducing the averages to lower than $452. (Such accounting fraud works by dividing the total $47,452 by a lower denominator[lower number of IUDs] to keep the average higher.) In the end, he took the 149 patients who had received 152 IUDs between 2008 and 2012 and eliminated a number of names from the list, so only 105 were counted, thus increasing the 'average per patient' dollar amount with the hope that the accusation of being motivated by money and greed would stick with this new higher reimbursed dollar amount.

Delahunty also deceived the court by producing a 2006 ParaGard IUD invoice (Exhibit 14) that the FDA had taken from my office during the 2012 raid. Delahunty presented it to the judge saying that the price of ParaGard was $324 and argued that I still would have made a profit by continuing to buy it at that price, knowing full well that the IUD prices for ParaGard ranged from $372 to $754 during all the years I imported the cheaper IUDs from Canada. He concealed from the court the fact that I also used the ParaGard and Mirena IUDs, because if he had factored those in, it would have shown that it cost me many more hundreds of dollars from my own pocket to provide this healthcare to my indigent patients in exchange for an overall average reimbursement of $322.

Even though Bowman withheld many crucial pieces of evidence that I had provided her from the court, because of her "legal limitations of what evidence she was allowed to present or show the court", (Exhibit 24 emails), I believe that overall she provided adequate evidence to the extent that the Cu-380A IUD I used was deemed safe and recommended by the World Health Organization's comprehensive research, a study conducted under the leadership of the U.S. Centers for Disease Control (Exhibit 2). Despite the evidence Bowman presented, proving the IUDs I used to be safe and recommended in many countries (Exhibit 1 and 2). Delahunty, sardonically laid out a list of complications that he claimed patients suffered due to the Cu-380A IUD that I used. Delahunty backed off a bit in repeating himself that the IUDs I used were dangerous or causing death or severe bodily harm and now changed his lie to saying that my IUD was of 'inferior quality' and caused serious harm to my patients. My IUDs went from being dangerous to inferior. In every argument he made, he quoted and presented Teva, the drug manufacturer of the U.S. brand of IUD ParaGard, as the authority to support his arguments, as though no conflict of interest existed. He ignored the actual research and findings on the subject.

Most people working in the healthcare industry in the United States know that healthcare devices made in Germany are of superior quality. The quality of our healthcare system in the U.S. would be much lower without the advances of German technology, medical products and devices. Germany has been at the leading edge of medical advancements for decades. It was because of this that my overall statistics of side effects and complications from the German T-Safe were significantly less than those listed in literature as side effects from ParaGard, the U.S. product. The side effects listed on the drug inserts of these devices also showed that the German brand had fewer side effects. It was not without reason that nearly 100 percent of women of reproductive age in Western Europe used other brands of Cu-380A, other than ParaGard, and the most commonly used copper IUD in Europe was T-Safe, considered a gold standard.

I asked my attorney to write a full-scale response to Delahunty's reply to expose his lies, but she said she would not argue with the government or do anything that might generate hostility, adding that she just wanted this case to end. She hesitatingly agreed to write only a brief response stating if she wrote a longer reply, the prosecutor would keep coming back with more responses and the case would never end. Her response to Delahunty was only six pages long. It should have been 60 pages long in order to counteract every false statement from the prosecution. All of this was going on while waiting for the sentencing.

The sentencing date was now only a couple of days away, and the feeling of dread and desperation weighed heavily on me. I told Bowman that I had already provided her clear evidence that the prosecutor was falsifying information about everything. I had given her all the research papers, articles, news items, and government reports that I had compiled. Bowman wasn't willing to use any of it in my defense. She half-heartedly accepted the evidence that I provided her about Teva and price gouging. I gave her documentation that showed Teva sold a thousand ParaGard IUDs to the state of West Virginia in wholesale, a price that was greater than the average $200 price for German T-Safe. I even gave Bowman many posts found on the Internet in which female patients stated they had to spend $1,200 to $1,400 out-of-pocket to get ParaGard IUD from their Ob/Gyns because their insurance either did not cover it or only reimbursed a small portion. Bowman rejected all this, saying she wanted me to bring her proof of ParaGard prices from the ParaGard maker. I had tried for months to get ParaGard prices in writing from Teva but was unsuccessful.

In her reply to Delahunty's response, she reiterated that the prosecutor's claims, that I used unsafe IUDs on patients were untrue. She did not point out that the prosecutor's revised calculations of average insurance reimbursement of $452 per IUD were incorrect; instead she kept apologizing by saying that while the government's calculations of $452 dollars were correct, Dr. Singh also had overhead expenses which should have been considered, as though she was begging for mercy. Imagine being apologetic to a tyrant instead of telling him to his face that he is a liar and wrong about everything. She did point out again in her reply that the reimbursement was for all IUD-related services and not just the IUD device itself. Bowman continued to be apologetic on my behalf, repeatedly stating, how sorry I was while peppering in bits and pieces of the facts here and there to point to Delahunty's fabrications. I did not see a single clear statement in her response stating the reimbursement Delahunty conjured up represented only a fraction of what it cost me to provide IUD-related services or that I had contributed money from my pocket to provide this healthcare to my indigent patients. It was an important fact, and

I had informed Bowman that the general rule about ParaGard IUD reimbursement from insurance companies was that the insurance company paid one-third to half of the overall cost while the patient had to come up with the other half or two-thirds. In other words, a total cost of $1,200 meant insurance might pay plus/minus $400 and the patient would have to come up with $800 to cover the balance. And that was only if a private practitioner's charges for the service was reasonable. I provided Bowman, in face of dismissals from her, with literature from *Medical Economics* and Merritt Hawkins Associates research data (Exhibit 18) to prove to her that the average overhead of running a private Ob/Gyn practice in the United States was 55 percent of the total revenues of the practitioner. Bowman refused to mention these facts and figures in any of her arguments. In addition, she failed to point out that per my office statistics, the rate of complications and side effects from the generic Copper IUD I used was lower in each listed category of common side effects from a copper IUD, when compared to the side effects and complications noted in the ParaGard drug insert and literature (Exhibit 15.) In other words, patients would have had statistically more complications had they exclusively used the ParaGard based on the complications described in ParaGard literature. I have gone back and reviewed all the emails in which I was barraging Bowman with new evidence every day by sending her attachement after attachement of different documents including most published in the Exhibits, but her lack of response suggests to me that she was tossing this documentary evidence straight in the trash bin and responding to me once in while by email, stating she could not use this evidence because I had already pled guitly.

Bowman told me the judge was too busy to read all the evidence. There was no doubt in my mind that behind the scenes her law firm did not want her to spend any more time on my case because it was not producing additional revenue. It would not surprise me if they were even pushing her to end this case as soon as possible. It indeed seemed this way based on her attitude toward me. That also explains why she wanted to limit her response to Delahunty's reply to only six pages.

Two days before the Court date for sentencing, it suddenly occurred to me that I had chatted on the phone with a manager from one of the branches of the ParaDirect distributor, an amiable guy who had talked with me for a while, but whose name I could not recall. It was years earlier when I was ordering ParaGard IUDs from ParaDirect in the years 2002 to 2008, a time when I exclusively used ParaGard IUDs before I even knew that a copper IUD manufactured in Germany available from Canada even existed. I wanted to try my luck one last time. As they say, a drowning man looks for a straw to hang on to, even though a straw will not save him. I looked and looked all night for his name in my Rolodex. I finally found a name under the letter P, although I was not sure if this was the friendly guy I remembered. It was already 3:00 am in the morning, and I decided I'd call him the first thing in the morning.

Bright and early, I made the call, chatting the guy up for a few minutes as he looked for my account in his system. I came up with some excuse about why I had not been ordering the ParaGard IUDs. I was still not certain if I was speaking with the person I wanted to speak with, but I was able to get him to confirm that the price of the ParaGard in 2008 and 2009 was $372. I did not need written proof of that since the prosecutor had a copy of the ParaGard invoice from early 2009 when it was sold for $372 by ParaGard Direct. Then I managed to have him agree to email me the ParaGard prices as they were listed in his system for 2010, 2011, and 2012, the years in question for my prosecution. I paced back and forth hoping he would send me Teva's IUD prices so I could prove the prosecutor had been lying to the court. It would be written proof exposing Delahunty's persistent misleading statements about the ParaGard prices to the judge. I was extremely nervous as this was my only chance to expose at least one of the prosecutor's lies with written testimony from the horse's mouth. The email came through within thirty minutes – a half an hour that felt like it was hours long. I forwarded this email to Bowman right away to show her that I was right all along that the prosecutor had been deceiving the judge about the U.S. ParaGard prices. She asked me to sign an affidavit and have it notarized certifying that the email was valid, which I did right away and scanned it back to Bowman. She submitted it to the judge 24-hours before my sentencing (Exhibit 16). I was optimistic that the judge would be upset to find out that the prosecutor had been misleading him about the ParaGard prices, also putting the rest of his prosecutorial claims in question. That was my hope – and my last hope prior to sentencing.

March 7, 2016: Prison Sentence

March 7, 2016, the day I was going to be sentenced, had finally arrived. I drove to Eastern District Federal Court in Fresno. I appeared before Judge Anthony Ishii. Bowman asked me to look at a statement that she had written for me, which was to be read before the judge. The statement went something like, "I have already stated my position in my Personal Statement, but I would like to apologize to the insurance companies and the patients for what I put them through". As time goes by, I seem to manage to suppress all the bad memories except the memory of having to read this statement out loud. I just cannot erase it from my mind. It is the only thing left in my psyche that still makes me sick to my stomach. It is one thing to commit perjury by signing a false document under coercion when a gun is pointed to your head, but it is another matter to have to make a false statement aloud, even if the end goal is a reduced sentence or staying out of jail. After reading the statement, I felt like I had stooped to the lowest of levels to save myself from imprisonment. It did not sting less to know that I was doing it more for my family than myself. If not for my loved ones, I would not have signed the guilty plea, and would have refused to sign a Personal Statement I didn't write. I would have held firm to my standards even if it meant going to prison for 20 years.

When I finished making my statement, which was only a few seconds long, Delahunty stood up and made his points. I waited for him to try to cover up his lies about the ParaGard price that I exposed with the email from the ParaGard Direct manager that was submitted to the judge the day before - a surprise for Delahunty just 24 hours before the sentencing hearing. I knew him well enough by now, to know that he would again perjure himself to cover up his previous lies and I was right. He told the judge that most of my cases were in 2008 and 2009 when the IUD price was $372, which meant that I still could have profited by purchasing the ParaGard instead of buying the IUD from Canada. He did not explain to the judge why he had deceptively noted $324 as the price of ParaGard from a 2006 invoice as his evidence in his pre-sentencing report. He did not explain why he lied and the judge apparently could not care less that Delahunty lied or how many times he lied.

Theoretically speaking, even if I were able to buy all IUDs at $372 a piece, Delahunty still had an obligation to explain his numbers.

How does one make a profit by providing all IUD related healthcare services, when the cost of the IUD alone ranged between $372 and $754, especially if the total reimbursement for the IUD device and related services was either $322 or $452 according to Delahunty himself? In either case, he had to explain his previous position. A creature of habit, he once again deceived the judge by using obfuscating language that implied reimbursement was strictly for the IUD and not the IUD plus all of the contraception related healthcare services that needed to be provided to the patient for an entire year.

Prosecutor Delahunty told the judge that I did not pass onto my patients the financial benefit of having bought a cheaper IUD, even though he knew I contributed from my pocket to make this service available to my patients (Exhibit 18). In my entire five years of implanting IUDs, I never took money from any patient who did not have insurance or could not afford the IUD. There were only two patients out of the total 149, who had opted to pay because they could afford it and the amount I charged from them was just for the cost – something you'll probably never see in another private medical practice. The reason I charged them just the cost was because I wanted to be consistent in my billing practice for IUDs, because If I charged most of my patients, the largest indigent population, just the basic cost, why should I charge someone more just because this person could afford to pay me more.

Delahunty tried to minimize the written evidence that I provided from the Teva representative 24 hours prior proving that the price of U.S ParaGard ranged from $496 to $754 between 2010 and 2012 (Exhibit 16), while the average insurance reimbursement I received was $322. My audited data from my office (Exhibit 18) showed that just my own average upfront cost of providing Cu-380A to patients between the years 2008 and 2012 was $440 and that I took $128 of loss per IUD service provided throughout those years. The upfront cost did not include additional free physician's office visits nor did I receive a salary for these visits. The audited data further showed that the cost of providing ParaGard IUDs in my office in those years ranged from $664 dollars to $994 dollars which means I experienced substantial financial losses whenever I provided a patient with a ParaGard IUD, which I did in about 10 percent of the cases (Exhibit 16). The loss was greatest when I used Mirena on a patient (Exhibits 16 and 18). The purchase price of Mirena during those years ranged between $750 and $1000. I provided services and I accepted whatever I got paid or not paid by insurance companies. Despite this, Delahunty urged the judge to give me a much harsher prison sentence to send a message to deter other ob/gyns from buying the IUDs from Canada. My defense attorney, completely useless when it came to my defense, did not raise an eyebrow, let alone an objection.

What I found most shocking about Bowman's behavior in the court was that while Delahunty kept quiet about his "admonishment" story because he knew that it was his criminal fabrication to create a novel foundation for his case to incarcerate me, Bowman started making some nonsensical arguments based on this "admonishment" business to try to help my case. Bowman had become aware by now based on her new knowledge of the leaked document on the electronic disc that I had brought to her attention that the government's admonishment narrative was a forgery and a fabrication.

To illustrate how criminal defense lawyers adopt the culture of blatant corruption, Bowman told me in multiple emails that I should have bought the expensive U. S.-made ParaGard and left the financial burden on the shoulders of my indigent patients for them to figure it all out. For Bowman, that would have been a better choice than to provide my patients a safe, affordable, well researched, high-quality product that they could afford even if it meant I contributed money from my pocket. I am still stunned by the ignorance that has one believing these women would be able to get an IUD at four times the price when they couldn't afford the IUD at the lower price.

When it was his turn to speak, Judge Anthony Ishii rambled on, repeating himself that I tried to assist my low-income patients in my practice. It was hard to tell what direction he was going with this. He did not make any comment about the questionable evidence provided by the prosecutor versus the strikingly robust and undeniable evidence provided to refute prosecutorial claims, no matter how limited and restrained it was, to address all the issues and facts of the case. It was as though none of it factored into his decision. After beating around the bush for a while, Ishii got to his point and said that he believed that the case was about false Medicaid billing, repeating Delahunty's accusations, but not explaining how my billing was a billing fraud. Neither Delahunty nor Ishii seemed to care if Teva, the drug company whose predatory price-fixing of IUDs they were both so enthusiastically defending, was the leading Drug giant in the world in having been repeatedly found to be engaged in Medicaid billing fraud and briberies to governments and public officials, for which the company settled lawsuits for billions and continues to settle for more in thousands of lawsuits filed against Teva around the globe with new lawsuits being filed almost on a weekly basis. Teva was an example for which there was no match to be found in the world of Big Pharma corruption and crime. Ishii did not use the word 'Mail Fraud' once in his entire speech, which was Delahunty's official accusation and criminal charge under 18 U.S.C § 1341 for which he wanted to send me to jail (Exhibit 23.)

How was my case a medical billing issue to the judge when it was not a billing fraud in the eyes of any of the private insurance companies that reimbursed me for my services? This is one thing I hold Bowman entirely responsible for, and I will never forgive her for that, regardless of what her intentions were, i.e., to help reduce my sentence by being apologetic to the prosecutor and the court. Even if she had a conversation with me today and said that I could have refused to sign off on her version of my Personal Statement, that excuse would not be enough for me to forgive her. Her job was to speak in my defense, to act on my behalf, be truthful, and not to just go along with what the prosecutor wanted. She was a colossal failure in doing her job, when it came to my case.

As stated above, the judge acknowledged I was trying to assist my low-income patients. He said that he did not want to characterize me as greedy, and then he suddenly turned around and repeated the prosecutor's lies in stating that I did not pass the savings from buying cheaper IUDs to my patients, contradicting the irrefutable evidence provided him to the contrary. Ishii ignored the Medical Board's findings that I had no personal financial gain or benefit from using the cheaper IUDs. He ignored the evidence in all the exhibits submitted to him as evidence disproving Delahunty's accusations; he kept hush hush about the WHO and CDC report that the IUD I used was safe and echoed Delahunty's words that I put my patients in jeopardy by using the T-Safe IUD. He also ignored the fact that the Medical Board's IUD expert, Shirley Wong did not find any difference in the side effects of T-Safe and U.S. ParaGard. He said nothing about the mail fraud, which I was waiting to hear from him, the sole count I pled guilty to, the actual basis of Delahunty's prosecution.

In his concluding remarks, Judge Anthony Ishii gave me a reduced sentence along the lines of what Probation officer Armistead had recommended, which was six months in prison followed by a year of house arrest to be monitored through an ankle bracelet, followed by yet another year of probation. Anthony Ishii sent me to jail for six months for providing care to my indigent patients by contributing part of the cost of their healthcare from my own pocket. He insinuated that I engaged in Medicaid fraud. He had no qualms about the fact that Teva, a drug giant, whose financial interests he was defending had just paid $35 million dollars in Medicaid fraud penalties, not to mention the billions it paid in bribing government officials in order to be able of price-fix its drugs at predatory levels, for false advertisement and to drive competitor drug manufacturers out of the market.

As soon as the Judge gave his verdict, Gluck, who had been sitting in the back of the courtroom, quickly came forward and asked the judge to have the Probation Department wait until the type of prison I was suited for was determined. Then he requested ninety days before I would need to surrender and start serving my sentence so I could prepare for it. The judge granted his request, giving me additional time with my family.

As I have had the opportunity to become more educated about such things, I have since learned that the convicted are often handcuffed and taken to prison straight from court, often at the sole discretion of the prosecutor. Sometimes people remain in county jails for months until the type of prison they're to go to is determined. Gluck's presence and willingness to make this request on my behalf, was invaluable. With Bowman's limited experience with the criminal justice system, I may have ended up in the county jail in a 23-hour a day solitary confinement while waiting for the official designation.

I was incredibly grateful for the additional time to prepare my family for my absence. One of my children is totally disabled requiring constant care as he's unable to move about and cannot even take a drink of water alone. We not only needed to plan for his care but I had to explain some things to my wife who had deferred so many decisions to me that she wasn't sure she would be able to make the right decision about things that may come up while I was imprisoned. We went over hundreds of various potential scenarios, as I explained how each should be handled if it were to arise. We were both concerned that it all might be too much for her. The logistics with the children was going to be challenging on its own, but to now be the sole breadwinner and decision-maker was going to be a significant change. She was also worried about me, due to my disability with little mobility in my right hand, a result of the spinal injury I referenced earlier.

I tell you this to give you an idea of why the additional time was so valuable and why I was so thankful to have it. I am not looking for pity. I know many people have it much harder, and they get up each day and do what they must do to keep moving forward. So, we are not unique or special in any way.

When we left the court, Gluck told me not to worry because I would be going to a prison that would be more like a dormitory and would not house hardened criminals. He knew I was mad as hell at him. He asked me if he could call my wife and I told him no. Once again he ignored anything I had to say and called her anyway to crow about how Bowman had managed to do such a good job that I received a reduced sentence. Only in their world would the reduced sentence of an innocent man be viewed as good news to share with the wife of the man going to prison.

Just over three months later, on June 20, 2015, a philosophy professor, a close friend of mine, also one of the editors for my books, drove me to Lompoc prison in Santa Barbara County. If I thought the previous years of my life exposed me to government abuse of power and injustice, they were nothing compared to what I witnessed while incarcerated. I expose it all in my next book, *Prison Torture in America* due to be published in January, 2019 along with this book.

Two Sets of Rules

Have you heard the expressions "preponderance of evidence" and "presumption of innocence"? The notion that a "preponderance of evidence" (overwhelming evidence that someone has committed a crime) and "presumption of innocence" (one is innocent until proven guilty through a due process of law) are the two basic tenents of the system in justice in the United States, are, in fact, the two biggest jokes in our justice system. I do not believe I can give a better example of how each can be ignored than the one I have described in this book. I've discovered there are two sets of rules. One for those in power, privilege, and money and one for everyone else. If the Department of Justice finds a target to dupe into committing a crime while telling them that what they're doing is legal, buying time to create a case against you – then that will happen. The government will find someone to make an example of, whose dire situation they will then point to in order to intimidate others. That's the kind of respect those in power have for we, the people. One thing one must understand is that if you, or anyone stands in the way of Big Pharma's profits or

Corporatocracy, they have soldiers recruited to do the job who will come and get you. And these soldiers are the government agencies such as the FDA and other public institutions that have a fiduciary duty towards us, the tax- paying citizens, and not the corporations who have bought them with cash by the wayside.

In conducting my own investigation after serving my prison sentence, an investigation that was intended to expose Delahunty, Judge Ishii and Teva Pharmaceuticals' claims that imported brands of Cu-380A were "inferior" (words of Delahunty in front of Judge Ishii at my sentencing hearing) to ParaGard, I discovered the following evidence:

The original long-term owner and manufacturer of the ParaGard IUD in the United States was a company called FEI Women's Health LLC, which sold the ParaGard business to Duramed Pharma, a subsidiary of Barr Pharmaceuticals in 2005. At the time of the sale, FEI and Duramed released independent and joint press releases in which they stated that the ParaGard IUD was the same drug that was known as Copper T Model Cu-380A outside the United States. Duramed turned around and sold the ParaGard business to Teva in 2008. I have included copies of these press releases by FEI and Duramed (Barr) Pharma under Exhibit 9, which clearly states that "ParaGard is the same drug that is known as Copper T Model, drug name TCu-380A, outside the United States." T Model Cu-380A is the T-Safe IUD, which is what I used on my patients. Pueschel and Delahunty had this information in 2010, and they concealed this fact from the court for five years while they were busy forging court documents to prove otherwise. This one document alone, the press release, proves that Delahunty in collusion with Pueschel and Teva concocted a story that the German made Cu-380A, (i.e.T-Safe) is some unknown IUD, therefore, unsafe and inferior to ParaGard, that I bought from Canada, and therefore I should be sent to jail for putting my patients at risk of death and destruction.

Subsequently, I had the opportunity to have one- full- hour conversation with the CEO of EurimPharm in Germany who also confirmed with me the history of sales of ParaGard, the CU-380A IUD (called T Model Cu-380A in Europe, the main brand of this drug in Europe being the T-safe). Teva bought the ParaGard factory from Barr Pharmaceuticals (Duramed subsidiary) in 2008 and then sold it to Cooper Surgical in 2016. Teva inherited the business and technology from FEI through Duramed, owned it for 8 years during which time they filed a sham citizen petition with the FDA and falsely advertised to show that any other brands of Cu-380A were inferior to their brand, ParaGard, and therefore the FDA should refrain from approving it for the U.S. marketplace. Teva did this in collusion with the FDA's full awareness that they were talking about exactly the same drug. Apparently, anyone like me who used the German-made IUD must be sent to jail for interfering with Teva's profits. That is what Delahunty really meant by T-Safe being an "inferior" IUD.

When I came home after serving prison time and went into house arrest, it was time for the Medical Board to finally do the dirty work for the FDA, which was to revoke my license, Teva and the FDA's ultimate mission. I was advised by Spackman before the hearing that being convicted of a crime, by law, is supposed to be an automatic revocation of a physician's medical license even though one still has to go through the theatrics of administrative hearings. I appeared in the court with my attorney, Spackman, before Judge Ralph Dash for the Medical Board's administrative hearings. Regardless of the consequences for my medical license, my primary goal in the court was to have Judge Ralph Dash pubicly acknowledge that the German-made T-Safe copper IUD that I used was the same drug as its U.S. counterpart, the trade name, ParaGard, and was the same in terms of side effects. I managed to have the judge admit twice to that effect and put him on record admitting that. I also went over Pueschel's FDA summary memo of March 28, 2012 line by line to show Dash that every statement made by Pueschel in that summary memo was a lie.

This court transcript of my testimony is a public record and is the same information I provided Delahunty through my defense attorneys, but Delahunty concealed this information in order to incarcerate me. My own defense attorneys concealed much of this information, let alone the prosecutor. Delahunty created fraudulent court documents in which he described the side effects of ParaGard as the side effects and complications from the IUD I used, giving the court the impression that these side effects would not have occurred if I had used the U.S. brand, ParaGard. Delahunty learned about these side effects from the ParaGard drug insert and deceptively assigned these side effects to the German-made T-safe and pretended that these would not have been the side effects of ParaGard. He created innumerable court documents including a press release to the media that "unapproved IUD" caused side effects such as pelvic inflammatory disease, ectopic pregnancy, hysterectomy and other serious complications etc knowing full well that they were, in fact, the side effects of the "approved IUD", the U.S. brand ParaGard. He also created innumerable court documents claiming that I was an example of American greed, with full awareness that I had no financial interest, personal gain or motive in helping my patients. I unknowingly continued using an IUD that was illegal, because the FDA agent Pueschel told me it had been approved and was legal to use.

Some readers will side with the FDA and say that whether or not I knew, I put the patients at risk by using it. Their argument may be that to control the quality of medications being prescribed and used, the FDA must limit us to drugs that are manufactured in our country. They will say the FDA is responsible for protecting us.

Let me give you one example of how the FDA protects Americans when it comes to pharmaceuticals. Between 2007 and 2008, 103 people in the United States died from tainted heparin, a blood thinner. The FDA launched an investigation to find the source of the contamination and traced it to Changzhou SPL Company, Ltd. In China. You read that right; the company is in China. In 2008, China supplied 70% of the heparin used in blood thinners worldwide. The remaining heparin came from Europe, Canada, the United States and Brazil. The suppliers Changzhou SPL used for ingredients to make the drug from unregulated labs and rural farms. There was no quality control. China officials denied any responsibility for the deaths due to heparin, saying they wanted to investigate the American plant where the vials were made.

The FDA was tasked with investigating what had happened. Three years later, in February 2011, Rep. Fred Upton of Michigan chastised them for not having done anything about all those deaths. In a letter he had written he said the FDA had stated that the cause of contamination was overly sulfated chondroitin sulfate, which the FDA felt was *economically motivated.* Here is a case where a shoddy operation in China, a country which had sent us tainted dog food and baby formula the year before, made a business decision that would increase their profit, resulting in over 100 deaths in the U.S. alone, and three years later the FDA was being called out for having done nothing about it. I am speaking only of deaths in the U.S. The number of severe allergic reactions, including in children, did not even enter the discussion, even though those had been reported in the years before the deaths after the heparin formula had been altered. And we do not know how many people died or had adverse reactions to the tainted drug worldwide. Heparin was administered to about 12 million people in the United States annually. Deaths occurred in at least ten other countries.

In mid-April of 2008, Food and Drug Commissioner Andrew C. von Eschenbach told a Senate subcommittee that the contamination was done "by virtue of economic fraud," quickly withdrawing the remark, saying he had "probably gone too far." Too far for Big Pharma, no doubt.

According to the U.S. Government Accountability Office in 2011, 80% of all active pharmaceutical ingredients used in drugs sold in the United States came from overseas, with China being the number one supplier of those ingredients. India is also a supplier. This is all done under FDA regulations drafted by the Pharmaceutical industry for profits and nothing else and the Big Pharma does it with the full blessings of the FDA.

The FDA inspects drug manufacturing plants that are located in America every two years. One would think they would have a similar inspection timetable for inspections of plants outside of our country, but in 2009 the FDA inspected just 52 of the 1000 drug manufacturing plants in China. China officials also denied any responsibility for the deaths due to heparin, saying they wanted to investigate the American plant where the vials were made.

Just as they do today, in 2008 the FDA showed a blatant disregard for quality despite the fact that safety regulations in China and other countries are much lower than what the FDA claims to have in the

United States. Does this sound like an agency concerned about the safety of Americans?

Many drugs approved by the FDA for market have risks that outweigh their benefits. Others are found to have risks only after they are approved, not because the FDA did not know, but because approving members on the FDA's approval committees are complicit with the Big Pharma lobbyists in concealing dangerous drug- related research information while official approval is pending. For example, Bayer, another drug giant (another pharma involved in selling IUDs here in the U.S. and Europe,) sold HIV- infected blood products first to Americans and then sold the remaining stock to Latin American countries, with the FDA looking the other way. This is when Bayer had become fully aware that their drug was HIV infected, killing hundreds here in the U.S. and thousands around the world. This is called the FDA's tacit approval of commission of crimes by the Big Pharma.

Today many drugs are sold by Big Pharma at a cost of $300,000 to nearly $700,000 a year, sometimes just one pill costing $1,000 (for example drug giant Gilead Sciences). The FDA has no problem with seeing Big pharma committing financial crimes against hundreds of millions of Americans. The FDA has no excuse in stating that it does not have power over fixing drug prices. What the FDA does not tell you is that it does have enormous power over preventing fraud, deception and corporate crime by the drug and food industry, but the money coming from Big pharma is too sweet that the FDA would look the other way and watch hundreds, sometimes thousands of people die from criminal activity by drug companies who gave the FDA enough money to shut its mouth. The FDA's complicity with the drug industry does not stop there, it actively seeks the drug companies to draft FDA regulations, regulations that harbor provisions to allow the Big Pharma to legally commit unlimited numbers of crimes against entire populations here at home and especially abroad. The DOJ has especially allowed corporations and big pharma engaged in illegal bribery abroad to completely avoid prosecution, and dramatically reduce corporate penalties for bribery at home.

I am giving just a few examples of the FDA's complicity with the drug industry, although I could do an entire book on this topic. I hope this clears up the fantasy that the FDA was only acting out of concern when they targeted, framed, and incarcerated me for implanting the safest, most widely used IUD in the world because it wasn't manufactured in the United States, instead of using the ParaGard, which most likely also wasn't made in the United States. I called Teva's plant in Buffalo, New York to find out if they manufactured the ParaGard IUD there and if they did, where did they purchase the ingredients that went into making the IUD's, and what was the difference between the quality of their ingredients and the ones used by German manufacturers. They refused to talk with me, let alone answer my questions.

Final Thoughts

The outcome of a case is often decided and ensured before a defendant even gets to court. If someone is being framed, the crime they will be charged with is determined before those in power find their unassuming dupe. They ensure this happens with falsified records, missing documents, and threats made in the front seat of a car.

I invite those of you who have your doubts to contact me for all the evidence which was too lengthy to include in this book or its companion book, *The Death of the Rule of Law*. I will gladly provide you with it at no charge beyond shipping and handling. Requests can be sent to Paul@ScienceLiteracyBooks.com. But you must prove your authenticity as an investigator who cares about the rule of law, so please include your credentials and the reason you are requesting the evidence.

I moved to this country filled with hope, admiration, and trust in the government. It has saddened and forever changed me to learn that the phrase *Criminal Justice System* does not refer to a system that ensures justice for those who have engaged in criminal behavior, but a system of selective justice run *by* criminals.

****

CHAPTER 5

APPLICABLE LAW — GOVERNMENT'S CRIMINAL MISCONDUCT

I SPENT FOUR MONTHS IN THE PRISON LAW LIBRARY learning about the criminal law which applies to public officials, government agents and prosecutors, who violated the law in their relentless pursuit to ensure my imprisonment. This section of the book should serve as a resource together with the companion book, *The Death of the Rule of Law*, which has all the documentary evidence and exhibits included in it, as they apply to different categories of the government's lawlessness in my criminal case. This section is written for law students and for activists who care about our constitution, equal justice and the rule of law for all citizens of the United States, and those who would like to hold public officials in positions of power accountable for their criminal misconduct carried out under the pretext of enforcing law and order. The discussion in this segment of the book is divided into various sections and groupings of applicable criminal violations as described in textbooks of criminal law and Black's Law Dictionary. I would like to introduce the following case law and statutory quotes before diving deeper into textual definitions.

> "A person subjects another to the deprivation of a constitutional right, within the meaning of §1983, if he does an affirmative act, participates in another's affirmative acts or omits to perform an act which he is legally required to do that causes the deprivation of which complaint is made." Johnson v Duffy, 588 F. 2d 740, 743 (9th Cir. 1978)

> "Every person who under the color of law…subjects or causes to be subjected any citizen of the United States to the deprivation of any rights, privileges, or immunities secured by the constitution…shall be liable to the party injured in an action at law, suit in equity or other proper proceeding for redress." (42 U.S.C.§ 1983).

With the above introductory quotes in place, I like to move forward with discussing criminal law violations by the government as they apply in my case.

Brady Violations: Withholding Exculpatory Evidence

The Supreme Court of the United States announced a constitutional requirement in 1963 known as the *Brady v Maryland* case which states that prosecutors must disclose to the defense any exculpatory evidence that it possesses that proves the innocence of the accused. Federal prosecutor, Delahunty, perjured himself in stating that the FDA agent Pueschel's handwritten notes of the August 2010 FDA interviews with me did not exist. Delahunty aided and abetted the FDA agent instead of disciplining him for a crime of concealment and forgery. Prosecutors Delahunty and Sherriff accidentally released the handwritten notes written by FDA agent, Pueschel, dated 8/17/10 [Exhibit 3] after denying their existence, notes which contradicted their evidence. Notes were involuntarily released to the defense attorney on a disc a week after convicting me of a crime. Delahunty and FDA agent Pueschel knew that these handwritten notes would destroy the credibility of hundreds of false documents that the two of them had helped create over the years to convict me of a crime that I did not commit. This was an analogous situation to the government concealing the government's notes in Senator Ted Stevens case and the Merrill Lynch/Enron case that prosecutors also accidentally released on discs, which contradicted the government's evidence. These events are described in detail in Sidney Powell's book, *Licensed to Lie*. This exculpatory evidence accidentally included on a disc would never have been released to me if I had not insisted that my defense attorney, Ashley Bowman, demand all records from my prosecutor, Delahunty. Bowman supposedly carefully searched the disc upon my insistence, specifically looking for any documents dated August 17,2010, and after. Frankly, if it were not for my consistent effort, Bowman did not give a damn what was on the disc, which only shows how defense attorneys also participate in this kind of corruption. After this one revelation, my defense lawyers failed to bring it up because she said she was "limited in what she could do" since I had already signed a plea agreement. Also, I followed up on a promise made to me by my attorney, Gluck who said that he would file for the impeachment of the FDA agent, Pueschel if we discovered that he had concealed any evidence of handwritten notes or written notes that were not approved or signed off by his supervisor at the FDA.

The evidence [Exhibit 3] proved the FDA had been aware for five years, that the Cu-380A IUD I used was a safe IUD manufactured in Germany. It was not counterfeit, dangerous or bought on the Internet. The government engaged in a disinformation compaign about the IUD for five years. It is clear that the FDA fraudulently and falsely induced and manipulated my patients to perjure themselves into writing false victim reports. Pueschel's handwritten document accidentally leaked by Delahunty also proved the forgery by Delahunty that I was "Admonished" on August 17 of 2010" [Exhibit 3 and 4]. The handwritten notes of Pueschel contradicted many statements that the FDA agent made in his official memos that he presented as evidence, memos that Judge Sullivan has described as government's frequent "opportunity for mischief and misinformation."

By hiding evidence that contradicted the government's case, in collusion with the FDA agent, the prosecutor Delahunty engaged in the first two common forms of prosecutorial misconduct as listed by the Center for Prosecutorial Integrity, a branch of the Department of Justice. The first violation was "withholding the release of exculpatory evidence" and the second was "deliberately mishandling and mistreating evidence."

This was obstruction of justice. In the words of Sidney Powell, "When anyone other than a prosecutor hides evidence or makes false statements in court or to a government agency, it is a federal crime or crimes: perjury, obstruction of justice, false statements to a federal agent, subornation of perjury, witness tampering, and so on." (pg. 397 line 4-7: *Licensed to Lie: Exposing Corruption in the Department of Justice*). It is ironic that when our government agents or prosecutors engage in similar criminal activity, they are above criticism, let alone conviction or prison time.

Federal prosecutors were found to have concealed exculpatory evidence in Senator Ted Stevens case, which helped reverse the Senators conviction. In his case, it was not just because of the accidental release of concealed information, but because an honest FBI agent broke ranks with the FBI and blew the whistle on the corrupt prosecutors. In my case, the existence of one of the two FDA agents who interviewed me on August 17, 2010 was eliminated from all discovery documents generated by the FDA and the prosecutor [Exhibit 5]. For these and many other reasons, the violations in my case were more egregious than those in Ted Stevens's case. Judge Emmett Sullivan, who presided over the case of Senator Ted Stevens and ordered the criminal investigation of the prosecutors from the Department of Justice, said, "Government was caught again and again in making false representations." If it were not for an honest FBI agent, Chad Joy, who exposed the DOJ by disclosing the government's willful Brady violations, the Senator would have still been incarcerated ten years later. Those who believe that the Senator was blown out of the sky in a plane crash wonder if the Senator would have been better off in prison. He might still be alive if he had not stated he was determined to fight the corruption in the Department of Justice as long as he was alive and in politics.

Referring to these Brady violations by the federal prosecutors, Chief Judge Alex Kosinski of the ninth circuit court has commented,

While no one openly disputes the validity of the Brady rule, many prosecutors see it as a thorn in their sides – an obstacle to overcome rather than a welcome responsibility to be scrupulously observed. Prosecutors want to win, for all the reasons mentioned by the Center for Prosecutorial Integrity, and they see Brady as an impediment to obtaining convictions. While there are certainly many honest and fair-minded prosecutors, a disturbing number fail to disclose exculpatory evidence to the defense. Some prosecutors affirmatively and knowingly conceal it.

Judge Emmett Sullivan who ordered the investigation of corrupt prosecutors in Senator Steven's case said: "The U.S. government has an obligation to pursue convictions fairly, and in accordance with the Constitution and when the government does not meet its obligations to turn over evidence, the system falters." The threat level to my family worsened every time I — even remotely suggested that the government divulge 2010 interview records, let alone accusing the government of wrongdoing. I was only able to vent with my defense attorneys, Gluck and Bowman that the FDA and prosecutors were lying to them. My attorney, Gluck was rebuffed by the prosecutor every time he tried to ask for Pueschel's handwritten notes of August 17, 2010, of my interview by the two FDA agents. Making such a demand from the government only resulted in receiving more threats of harsher punishment if I did not readily relent to Delahunty's demands to meet the fast approaching deadlines he had imposed on me.

A celebrated criminal defense attorney, Sidney Powell wrote, "The defense does not know what it does not know." She further says that "Judges almost always brush aside defective indictments, prosecutorial misconduct for witness intimidation and failure to disclose Brady materials, fabricated documents, and false evidence." I was not as fortunate to get a good judge as Senator Ted Stevens did. My case was heard by a corrupt judge, Anthony Ishii, eager to please the government. I wish Anthony Ishii had a fraction of the character and integrity of Emmett Sullivan. Powell states in her book that it is "close to impossible to prove that the government is hiding the evidence," and that is because "you don't know what you don't know." The judges won't order Brady materials upon defense's request, and if they do in a rare instance such as Steven's case, the government ignores it, and there is not a thing you can do about it.

One of the Department of Justice's own ethical rules (rule # 3.8) states, "The prosecutor in a criminal case shall make timely disclosure to the defense of all evidence or information known to the prosecutor that tends to negate the guilt of the accused, and in connection with sentencing, disclose to the defense and to the tribunal all unprivileged mitigating information known to the prosecutor." I was not only denied such information but was asked to plead guilty first before any discussion of any kind would even be considered. The reason given for this by prosecutor Delahunty was that he needed his conviction before he ran out of time, which he called his statute of limitations. The prosecutor's rationale was that if I didn't plead guilty right then and there, that it would ruin his deadline, a deadline that was fast approaching. The more I resisted pleading guilty, the more I was threatened with immediate arrest and public humiliation, and an imminent indictment.

After reversing Ted Steven's conviction and ordering the criminal investigation of the prosecutors, Judge Emmett Sullivan said,

> Whether you are a public official, a private citizen, or a Guantanamo Bay detainee, prosecutors, indeed the U.S. government, must produce exculpatory evidence so that justice shall be done. I therefore urge my judicial colleagues on every trial court everywhere, to be vigilant and to consider entering an exculpatory evidence order at the outset of every criminal case, whether requested to do so or not, and to require the exculpatory material be turned over in a usable format, because as we have seen in this case the memos and summaries is an opportunity for mischief and misinformation.

In my case, agent Pueschel and prosecutor Delahunty provided these mischievous forgeries of memos as evidence instead of providing the actual evidence in the agent's handwritten notes. Judge Sullivan has called such practice an abhorrent practice and further states that prosecutors should provide Brady materials regardless of whether they are requested to do so. FDA and government summaries and memos provided in lieu of hidden exculpatory evidence in my case were fabrications by the FDA agent. Judge Sullivan, while describing these "mischiefs" (memos) concerning Ted Stevens case went on to say, "… We must not forget the Supreme Court's Directive that a criminal trial is a search for truth, yet in several cases recently the court has seen troubling failure to produce exculpatory evidence in violation of the law and the court's orders." I quote the words of Schuelke, (the independent criminal investigator appointed by Sullivan to look into the prosecutorial misconduct) who said, "The government investigation and prosecution was permeated by systematic concealment of significant exculpatory evidence which would have independently corroborated the defense and seriously damaged the testimony and the credibility of the government's key witnesses." This statement precisely describes my case. This case and my own are like two parallel universes that split but carried the same genetic information.

Omissions and Concealments: Mishandling, Mistreating, and Destroying Evidence

Unless otherwise stated, most definitions of legal terminology in this book are taken from the ninth edition of Black's Law Dictionary as fully corroborated, doubly verified and supported by definitions used in case law and available statutes on the subject matter. Accordingly, a *concealment* is the "act of refraining from disclosure, especially an act by which one prevents or hinders the discovery of something." *Fraudulent concealment* on the other hand "is an affirmative suppression or hiding, with the intent to deceive or defraud a material fact or circumstance that one is legally (or sometimes morally) bound to reveal." Delahunty's concealment of 2010 FDA agent's notes meet the criteria of fraudulent concealment in the very legal sense of these words. Prosecutors were asked in my case to produce any notes of the August 2010 interview, but Delahunty flatly refused to give it to Gluck, my attorney by saying they don't exist. The prosecutors and FDA agent Pueschel thus perjured themselves which were grounds for their impeachment. Given that they had absolute immunity for commission of any number of crimes and could not be sent to jail regardless of the egregiousness of their crime, they certainly could have been impeached [Exhibit 22]. The government continually concealed this information from 2010 to 2016 up until my sentencing hearing; this is defined in law as an *Active and Continuous concealment of evidence used to undermine a witness's credibility* FEDR. EVD, 607-610 (Cases: witnesses West Key # 311-409).

Pueschel omitted the first 15 minutes - the most significant part of the FDA interview - in his memo labeled "3/28/12 FDA interview." The first 15 minutes of this FDA interview was an acknowledgment by the FDA agent, Pueschel reaffirming and maintaining the FDA's position of October 12, 2010 that the German made T-Safe Cu-380A IUD was FDA approved. This kind of "mischief" (in the words of Judge Sullivan) is defined as "a crime of omission" [exhibit 3]. Such omission refers to "intentional conduct that carries its material component, the failure to act" (18C). As benign as the word *omission* sounds, a crime of omission can be the most serious of all crimes depending on a circumstance. Imagine a hypothetical scenario where the government created thousands of pages of discovery in a criminal case in accusing someone of murder (and corrupt prosecutors frequently engage in such ridiculous piling of huge mounds of fraudulent discovery paperwork), but withheld, suppressed, or deleted just one sentence from the entire discovery, a sentence that stated, "John is in possession of a cell phone video which unequivocally shows that the prosecutor in the case is the actual murderer, not the person he is accusing of this crime." Those thousands of pages of the government's evidence, which appear to be so credible at surface, because of wonderfully corroborating DNA finger-prints, could lose all its credibility and turn the case on its head if this Brady material were ever allowed to be brought up as a piece of exculpatory evidence that contradicts the government's evidence. That is how serious a *crime of omission* of the deletion of a single sentence from the discovery can be. But good luck with that. No one has the guts to reveal that hypothetical video without taking a significant risk of reprisals for exposing the Department of Justice.

Criminal Conspiracy, Collusion, False Statements and Cover-ups

The documentation of the 2010 interview withheld by two FDA agents and the omission of the first 15 minutes of the interview notes from Pueschel's FDA memo dated 3/28/12 constituted prosecutorial "conspiracy" and "concerted action" with the FDA agent. The disclosure of the actual scripts of these interviews would have been detrimental to the government's fabricated claims that would have made all government's claims unlawful subject to immediate dismissal and vacation by the court. That explains why the FDA and the prosecutors hid this evidence from the courts.

Concerted action between an FDA agent and the federal prosecutors meet the legal definition of conspiracy because it was "planned, arranged and agreed on by parties acting together to further some scheme." *Conspiracy* - aka criminal conspiracy, is an "act, coupled with an intent to achieve the agreement's objective, and (in most states) action or conduct that furthers the agreement; a combination for an unlawful purpose" USC § 371.

A conspiracy is a separate offense from the crime that is the object of the conspiracy.

"A conspiracy ends when the unlawful act has been committed (or in some states) when the agreement has been abandoned. A conspiracy does not automatically end if the conspiracy's object is defeated." See Model Penal Code § 5.03 (7); United States v Jimenez, 537 U.S. 270, 123 S. Ct & 19 (2003). In my case, the conspiracy has not automatically ended with me going to prison because I can produce the evidence through the Exhibits in this book that prove a prosecutorial conspiracy. Thus, this case of a government conspiracy against me will remain forever alive until those who are adults in our government, who are supposed to provide supervision, deal with this problem head-on.

18 USC §241 refers to conspiracy against citizens' rights:

> If two or more persons conspire to injure, oppress, threaten or intimidate any person in any state, territory, commonwealth, possession or district in free exercise or enjoyment of any right or privilege secured to him by the constitution or laws of the United States, or because of his having so exercised the same; they shall be fined under the title or imprisoned not more than ten years, or both.

18 USC §1001 called Statements or entries generally

> A) Except as otherwise provided in this section, wherever, in any matter within the jurisdiction of the executive, legislative or judicial branch of the government of the United States, knowingly and willingly…
>
> 1) Falsifies, concedes or covers up by any trick, scheme or device a material fact;
> 2) Makes any materially false, fictitious or fraudulent statement or representation; or
> 3) Makes or uses any false writing or document knowing the same to contain any materially false, fictitious or fraudulent statement or entry; shall be fined under the title, imprisoned not more than five years.

The preceding bullet points describe what was done to me by people who are exempt from prosecution for their crimes if they can prove under subsection B of 18 USC §1001 that what occurred was part of the judicial process (an exception to the rule). The government officials often use this exception by using various devices to prove that government crime occurred as part of the judicial process and was not deliberate. If they can cover up for the actual crime, they can easily claim they innocently made mistakes and errors. Remember, however, that the Department of Justice decides whether their prosecutor had malevolent intentions or not. Good luck with that. In *Licensed to Lie*, Sidney Powell gives examples of prosecutors who were reported to the DOJ's Integrity section for corruption during the Obama administration but rather than being disciplined, they were given high positions in Obama's administration.

The FDA agent and the two prosecutors engaged in cover-ups, and then cover-ups of previous cover-ups. The FDA agent, Pueschel first covered up initial interviews with me by two FDA agents on August 17, 2010, by denying that any documents existed about that event. Then the agent and the prosecutors together covered up the FDA records of two months of FDA's interactions with me between the dates of August 17 and October 12, 2010. After that, Pueschel omitted, edited, altered, and falsified substantial parts of the March 28, 2012, FDA interview memo to cover up all the facts related to the history of the case. He made only very short and casual references to events of the 2010 FDA Interview and the FDA's interactions with me, in one or two sentences deeply buried and interspersed here and there into the hundreds of pages of false discovery that he created while hiding parts of the story that spanned over three months of interactions between me and the FDA in 2010. Together, the agent and the prosecutors also covered up the testimony of the Medical Assistant I refer to as

Sandra Johnson in my first book, in a deposition taken on May 29, 2015, by prosecutors, Delahunty and Sheriff, and the FDA agent, Pueschel. Johnson's testimony corroborated my consistent claims that I strictly followed the FDA's order in continuing to use only the Cu-380A IUD and immediately discontinuing the use of Cu-375 when instructed to do so on October 12, 2010. Covering up my medical assistant's testimony was the third cover-up of two previous cover-ups in a chain of endless cover-ups [Exhibit 6]. It is called *continuous crime* in criminal law according to a 1907 crime Statute. Per this Statute, "continuous crime is a crime that continues after the initial illegal act has been consummated, a crime that involves on-going elements." To make matters worse, the prosecutors successfully and systematically covered up this entire history of a series of previous cover-ups masterminded by three people: Pueschel, Delahunty, and Sherriff.

Fabrication of Evidence, Perjury, Forgery, and Fraud

Fabrication of evidence, forgery, and perjury are different faces of the same multifaceted coin in many legal scenarios. They tend to occur together, and seldom happen independently depending on the circumstance and the nature of a case. Pueschel, the FDA agent, perjured himself by sneaking into the discovery documents a sentence or two giving the impression that he single-handedly conducted an FDA interview of me on August 17, 2010 in which he claims (with full support from Delahunty) that he "admonished me." Delahunty did not provide proof of such a meeting of Admonishment by Pueschel when asked. Pueschel and Delahunty conspired with each other, or co-conspired, to call August 17, a "Date of Admonishment"

[Exhibit 4] while hiding Pueschel's handwritten notes dated August 17, 2010. This referenced interview allegedly took place between Mr. Pueschel and me without anyone else present. Calling this imaginary interview, "the date of admonishment," was a new idea that Pueschel alone or Delahunty and Pueschel together conjured up when I successfully refuted the government's false accusations. It is my opinion that it was Delahunty's way to cover up Pueschel's bases for concealment of the actual contents of the interview of 2010 that took place between two FDA agents (not one) and me. Pueschel magically made the name and identity of the female Asian-American FDA agent who accompanied him (and also interviewed me) vanish from all the FDA's discovery documents, removing any trace of those records. It's as though she didn't exist. This misconduct meets the criteria for the legal definition of "a fabrication, fraud, and forgery." According to Black's Law Dictionary: "To fabricate, in Criminal law is to invent, forge or devise falsely a story to create a plausible version of events that are advantageous to the person relating those events." Well before I was coerced to sign the Guilty Plea agreement, there was a strong indication based on the conversations between my defense attorney, Gluck and Delahunty that Delahunty was aware of this fabrication, but he chose to cooperate with the FDA agent, and worse yet, collude with the agent on this, instead of legally censuring Pueschel for obstruction of justice, and hiding brady and exculpatory materials. That is why I would like to see records of all the phone conversations and email exchanges among the two prosecutors, my defense attorney and the FDA agent, Pueschel, in a potential future investigation of the Department of Justice and that of the officials and supervisors at the FDA agency involved in this case behind the scenes, in addition to Delahunty's communications with Teva. I learned during my case that even defense attorneys make deals with prosecutors behind the scenes without revealing it to their clients to protect themselves from being accused of illegal acts. One expects that defense attorneys keep no secrets from their clients, but that is apparently not always true. This was a fabrication by federal public officials who were entrusted by the American people with the task of ethically enforcing law and order and to uphold and preserve the Constitution of the United States.

A *concerted action* is an action that has been planned, arranged, and agreed upon by parties acting together to further some scheme or cause." There is also much circumstantial evidence, as noted in the FDA's discovery documents and the Guilty Plea Document drafted by the prosecutor, that TEVA, the manufacturer of the U.S. brand Copper IUD ParaGard was part of this on-going scheme. The extent of TEVA's participation, in this case, cannot be established unless an ethical judge like Emmett Sullivan gets involved and calls for the release of all the government's hidden communication exchanged with TEVA between 2008 and 2016. A fabrication becomes a fact over time in the court documents if it is repeatedly quoted as evidence by the government, especially when the opposing evidence is suppressed or not allowed to surface by using coercive threats. Any document, once falsified and forged, is cut-and-pasted or copied onto hundreds of newly crafted documents over and over and it becomes impossible for judges or investigators to go back and find out who committed the original sin (lie). After a while, the prosecutors start talking to the court like this: "Your honor, the court documents show that Dr. Singh committed crimes x, y, and z" while concealing from the judge how these court documents came about in the first place, how they were created and who created them. Just a handful of false papers and forgeries by FDA agent, Pueschel was copied and pasted by everyone in the government thousands of times over until the false statements were carved in stone, making the narrative appear factual.

What is a forgery in law? Forgery is "an act of fraudulently making a false document or altering a real one to be used as if genuine." According to modern statutes, forgery is a felony and is no longer a misdemeanor. Under the Model Penal code, the "act of fraudulently altering, authenticating, issuing or transferring or writing by an agent *without appropriate authorization from his superiors* is called perjury" (Black Law Dictionary 9th edition.) In criminal law, this misconduct is referred to as "depravity" or "gross impropriety" as it relates to public officials. My attorney, Benjamin Gluck, told me that if any notes by the FDA agent were found *without appropriate authorization from his supervisor (superior)*, we would go file for the Impeachment of that FDA Agent, Richard Pueschel. Gluck said nothing when the prosecutors accidentally released a bunch of unauthorized handwritten notes, 12-page long, written in Pueschel's handwriting after condemning me to a prison sentence, previously having denied that such records existed. One thing I learned in my case is that a criminal defense lawyer promising to do something ethical is the equivalent of a dog making you a promise that he would no longer take a piss on the grass. What are the odds? What happened to that impeachment of government officials that was promised to me so enthusiastically? Should my conviction have been reversed and these prosecutors and agents impeached or prosecuted? (Exhibit 22).

Forgery and Fraud have been found to be species of each other by legal scholars of criminal law. It is also forgery when it is done by someone "other than an ostensible maker or drawer or an agent of the ostensible maker or drawer" 37 C.J.S Forgery § 2, @ 66 (1997). Jesse

Townsend, the Medical Board investigator, forged a portion of the Medical Board investigation report by copying, cutting, and pasting Pueschel's forged statements and pretending they were his own. To a naïve reader, his report makes it look as though he knew me in 2010 and had firsthand knowledge of 2010 events, when in fact he did not know that I even existed at that time. Such an act of framing a report in this manner was a forgery of a forgery and a co-conspiracy that he engaged in under direct instructions from Pueschel. In other words, the Medical Board investigator created a parallel universe in which he was present in all the 2010 events. This also makes the Medical Board a part of this collusion, conspiracy, and forgery. The way Townsend presented his Medical Board Investigation report is called the "framing effect." In framing effect psychology, framing is a concept which says that the way information is presented influences how the audience feels about the information and can affect the judgments the audience makes about the information. Lawyers and judges are no exception when it comes to the influence of this effect, which they are often subjected to by the corrupt government officials and prosecutors standing before them. Fortunately for me, this forgery by Jesse Townsend, the so-called "Medical Board investigator" did not negatively affect the outcome of my second Medical Board case in which the Board decided in my favor despite many false reports submitted to the Board by Pueschel and Delahunty, in addition to Townsend's fake investigation.

Criminal law textbooks make a slight distinction between fraud and forgery, in that forgery contains some elements that are not included in fraud in the sense that "forgeries are a species of fraud, in essence, the crime of forgery involves the making, altering or completing of an instrument by someone." I am making this subtle distinction for the law student readers for their legal acumen.

Misrepresentation: Fraudulent Inducement of Patients and Witnesses

Fraudulent inducement of potential witnesses has been termed *fraud in the inducement* in the book, *Criminal Law.* Misrepresentation is a strong element in such fraudulent inducements. m*isrepresentation* in law refers to "a misleading assertion about something, usually with the intent to deceive." FDA agent Pueschel was aware on August 17, 2010, following his interview with me, that I used T-Safe Cu-380A IUDs, manufactured in Germany, a drug and a device that was known as ParaGard in the United States. Prosecutors assisted and abetted Pueschel in hiding this information. Pueschel repeatedly told scores of my patients in his numerous FDA patient interviews, that the IUD I used on them was unsafe, dangerous, defective, inferior, counterfeit, and bought from some unknown and unreliable source on the internet that risked their health and caused them serious "complications." Pueschel falsely induced patients into believing that all the side effects and complications they experienced were the result of me using this dangerous IUD, not revealing to them that all the side effects and complications that my patietns talked about were, in fact the side effects of the ParaGard as listed in the Paragard Drug Insert [Exhibit 15]. In other words, they were the usual known side effects of both the U.S. and German-made copper IUDs, side effects of a drug called Cu-380A which had nothing to do with what brand I used or could have used.

All written and reliable information about the German-made IUD was furnished to the two FDA agents and was part of the initial FDA interviews conducted on August 17, by two agents, and not one as portrayed by the prosecution. The FDA agents took an actual sample of the German-made Copper IUD, T-safe with them when they left my office. I gave them these samples because they requested them. Nowhere is this noted in the government's discovery. Going into the detailed definition of the term, Black's Law Dictionary states that the word *misrepresentation* denotes "not just written or spoken words but also any other conduct that amounts to a false assertion." So, the conduct in this regard of FDA agent Pueschel and the two prosecutors, leading to disinformation about the German Copper IUD, constituted *misrepresentation* or *false representation.* Disinforming and then eliciting emotional responses from patients in this manner is called *fraud in the inducement.* The assertions deliberately and maliciously made to the patients by FDA agent Pueschel did not align with all the facts about the T-Safe Copper IUD. Pueschel and government prosecutors systematically fomented discontent among patients - a systematic fostering of feelings of discord or rebellion. According to The American Heritage Dictionary, "To instigate is to conceive and encourage the implementation of a plan, usually an evil or illegal one." I was not aware of the lurking danger in the 2012 interview when Pueschel refused to directly respond to my specific questions in the first 15 minutes of the FDA's meeting while there were witnesses around. That was a tacit admission of guilt as he continued to gaze on the floor instead of having any eye contact with me to answer my questions. I trusted the FDA agent's honesty, and I trusted our government like most of us citizens do, unaware that the government does not always play by the same rules that it imposes on citizens with an iron fist. In fact, the government quite often does the opposite, with many people working for the government frequently breaking laws.

According to legal scholars, a misrepresenttion being a "false assertion of facts", commonly takes the form of spoken or written words. Whether a statement is false depends on the psychological meaning, syntax, context, and connotation of the words in all their circumstances, including what may be falsely inferred from them. And assertion may also be inferred from conduct other than words, which in my case were insinuations and innuendos to patients that I engaged in criminal conduct and serious wrongdoing. This had the overall effect of deliberate disinformation and misrepresentation manipulating the minds of many poorly informed patients. A 1979 case law states that an assertion may not even have to be explicitly fraudulent to be a *misrepresentation*; even a statement intended to be truthful may be a misrepresentation because of ignorance or carelessness, as when the word 'not' is inadvertently omitted or with inaccurate language. So, no matter how you cut it, the FDA agent's statements to patients met the criteria of "deliberate misrepresentation."

There was also a malicious component to this misrepresentation in that there was no element of excuse for ignorance, carelessness or inadvertence. The agent deliberately conveyed an inciteful message to arouse indignation in my patients while concealing from them information about all aspects of the Cu-380A IUD's made in Germany that he knew well. He had been aware of it since August 17, 2010, when I informed him that the IUD I used was a safe product made in Germany and was approved by CDC of the United States. The statements made to the patients by the agent were fraudulent because they were *material* and *intentional* with elements of "non-disclosure" with the malicious intent to harm me.

"A material misrepresentation is a false statement that is likely to induce a reasonable person to assent or the maker knows that that his/her statement is a statement to which a reasonable person would attach importance in deciding how to act in the transaction in question as to which the maker (the FDA agent, Pueschel in my case) knows and has reason to know that the recipient (a patient in my case) attaches importance." (Black's Law Dictionary). Agent Pueschel's malfeasance is clear. He told the patients that the IUD they received was unsafe while having full knowledge of the fact that the IUD they received from me was safe, well-tested, and manufactured by a reputable German pharmaceutical company and even researched by the CDC in the United States. "A false statement is a statement that is known to be false and is made recklessly without knowing or caring, and that is intended to induce a party to detrimentally rely on it." (Black's Law Dictionary)

According to the textbook, "A misrepresentation is also fraudulent if the maker (the FDA agent Pueschel, in my case) intends his assertion to induce a party to manifest his/her assent and the maker, (a) knows or believes that the assertion is not in accord with all the facts (of the German Copper IUD) (b) does not have the confidence that he states or implies in the truth of the assertion (c) knows he does not have the basis that he states or implies for the assertion." In the context of the above legal definitions, it is clear that the FDA agent's misrepresentations amounted to misleading my patients through instruction, insinuation, and deception calculated to be elusive, and misunderstood. This was a misrepresentation of the truth and concealment of material facts. The result was that my patients, previously my fans and admirers, turned against me due to a smear campaign attacking my reputation as a physician. It cost me financially, emotionally and physically, my family paid the price for these lies, as well and I suffered irreparable damage for life from which I will never recover.

All the previous information, according to a 1931 statute was *Fraud in the Inducement,* which is "the act or process of enticing or persuading another to take a certain course of action." Insinuating to indigent patients that their cooperation with the government might lead to financial compensation for them due to this perceived wrongdoing by me, the perception being falsely induced and programmed into their psyche by the FDA agent was a "Fraud in the Inducement" by both the FDA and prosecutor, Delahunty. Another statute from 1831 defines "Fraud in the Inducement" as follows: "Fraud in the inducement is a fraud occurring when a misrepresentation leads another to enter into a transaction with the false impression of the duties, risks, and obligations involved." My patients entered into a transaction with Pueschel and Delahunty based on this fraudulent inducement and the greed of monetary compensation and restitution promised by the prosecutors. They were misled. I am angry at the government for deliberately, maliciously and intentionally misleading my patients.

Fraud on the Court

Fraud on the Court in a judicial proceeding occurs when "a lawyer or a party's misconduct is so serious that it undermines or is intended to undermine the integrity of the proceeding. Some examples of this are the introduction of fabricated evidence and involvement of bribery." [Cases: Federal Civil Procedure West key number 2654; judgment west key number 372,340]. Prosecutor Delahunty was engaged in deceptively introducing fabricated documents to the court as evidence against me while submitting many other fabricated documents to provide evidence to support Teva's claims about the superiority of the U.S. brand Copper IUD manufactured by it. Whether there was any bribery involved or any form of incentivizing by Teva shall forever remain unknown unless a large-scale independent investigation by someone of the caliber, integrity, and character of Schuelke could uncover those facts. All I can tell you is that all claims made by Delahunty before the judge regarding CU-380A were as though a lobbyist paid by Teva was talking, not a prosecutor who is hired by the DOJ to fairly and squarely implement law and order. Prosecutors are held to higher ethical standards than the rest of the population and they should not be allowed to be prosecutors if their ethics are worse than those observed in the general population, or sometimes worse, equivalent to those of swine, a different species. Only a Teva lobbyist or salesperson could have been expected to make such false claims to promote Teva's drugs and products in constantly falsifying to the court information about Teva's IUD prices and the assumed superiority of its IUDs.

This was nothing new for Teva. Those who follow the news know that Teva, also the maker of opioid painkillers, was among the five painkiller manufacturers who had been routinely named in many class-action lawsuits for false advertisement, bribing people, agencies, government employees, physicians and healthcare workers to push its products and eliminate competition, price-fixing its drugs and devices, and false propaganda about the "safety" for "chronic use" of its opioids. This false advertisement about the "safety" for "chronic use" had been responsible for 180,000 deaths of Americans and millions of others around the world since 2001 [Exhibit 8]. The FDA knew it and looked the other way and let it happen. The FDA is continuing to allow this to happen despite lawsuits by 25 U.S.

States and many counties around the nation against this organized crime syndicate of Teva and four other Big Pharma makers of opioids.

In looking at the facts, it is clear that the prosecutor Delahunty continually worked with Teva behind the scenes throughout the five years of my case. This is evident from his unilaterally drafted "Guilty Plea" document in which he frequently and unashamedly takes instructions from Teva as being the authority on the law that governs the use/ non-use of Copper IUDs in the United States. Delahunty's interpretation of the law was that people must buy Copper IUDs directly from ParaDirect, Teva's distributors, regardless of Teva's out-of-reach prices. Teva was the prosecutor's guiding light for his legal decisions and his knowledge of the law and in the process of accusing me of many crimes. Scores of evidence exist that show that the prosecutor knew about the predatory pricing of the U.S. manufactured IUD by Teva even before I submitted the hard evidence to the court, but Delahunty continued to lie to the court about the prices of Paragard IUD until he was exposed 24 hours before the day of my sentencing. He did not expect Teva to provide me with any documentation about the ParaGard IUD prices, which could support my case and expose him, so he continued to lie to the court about the ParaGard IUD prices for as long as he could get away with it, which was up until the very last moment while continuing to fabricate many false documents as his evidence to support his claims. This was despite the fact that I managed to bring a letter from a manager working for Teva's distributor ParaGard Direct, testifying in writing about the actual sale prices of this U.S. brand Copper IUD, an email that proved that all the prosecutors' prior statements about ParaGard prices were plain lies. Unfortunately, in our system of practice of law, our judges are not supposed to be upset at all when they find out that the government is making false statements. These judges would have no problem sending any citizen to jail for ten years for telling a lie to the court, which might be insignificant compared to the lies of a federal prosecutor, for example, those of Delahunty in my case.

Fraud is defined expansively and can include many forms of falsehood. Fraud is most clearly defined in Black's Law Dictionary, 6th Edition, pg. 660 as follows:

> A false representation of a matter of fact, whether by words or conduct, by false or misleading allegations, or by concealment of that which should have been disclosed, which deceives and is intended to deceive another so that he shall act upon it to his legal injury. Anything calculated to deceive, whether by single act or combination, or by the suppression of truth, or by suggestion of what is false, whether it be by direct falsehood or innuendo, or by speech or silence, word of mouth, or look, or gesture. (Delahanty v First Pennsylvania Bank, N.A.., 318 Pa Super. 90, 464 A 2nd 1243, 1251.)

> A generic term, embracing all multifarious means which human ingenuity can devise, and which are resorted to by one individual to get advantage over another by false suggestion or by suppression of truth, and includes all surprise, trick, cunning, dissembling and unfair way by which another is cheated." (Johnson v McDonald 180 Okl 117.39 P 2nd 150)

There are other words in law which are synonymous, for example, *bad faith* and *fraud* are synonymous, and sometimes synonymous with *dishonesty, infidelity, faithlessness, unfairness*, etc. Delahunty, my prosecutor, proved to be the embodied incarnation of all these.

Our Constitution is a Contract between the government and our great people. I am a beneficiary of this contract; I am one of these people. I am a citizen of the United States of America and a party to this contract. (Please refer to Bypass v United States 273 U.S. 28; and 16th American Jurisprudence 2nd, Section 97, which held the Constitution shall be liberally interpreted to include every word, every phrase, and syllable, in favor of the clearly intended and expressively designated "beneficiary" - the CITIZEN for the protection of Rights and Property.) FDA agent, Pueschel and prosecutors, Delahunty and Sherriff, perpetrated fraud against me in FACT and LAW, depriving me of clearly established substantive rights to life, liberty and property thus injuring me permanently causing irreparable damage. Because of their activities of disinformation, whose purpose was to misinform and disinform all parties of interest in real facts and lawful rights, fraud had been committed.

It's obvious that unlawful institutional bad faith occurred, and the government entities and officers/actors therein who had participated in such fraudulent activity, knowingly and willfully, are in breach of their obligation to protect against a violation of faith, public trust, and oath of office. It should, therefore, subject the offending party to many laws, statutes and civil suits.

The conduct of the prosecutors and that of the FDA agent meets both the definition of criminal and civil conspiracy and collusion because they, by concerted action, intended to accomplish some unlawful objectives to harm me which resulted in damage. My case shows self-evidently that the "parties" reached a unity of purpose on a common design and understanding or a meeting of the minds in an unlawful arrangement.

> To be liable, each participant in the conspiracy need not know the exact details of the plan, but each participant must at least be aware the common objective of the conspiracy…A conspirator's knowledge of and participation in a conspiracy may be inferred from circumstantial evidence and evidence of the defendant's actions. (Gilbrook v City of Westminster, 177 F 3d 839, 856-57 (9th Cir. 1999 (citations omitted)

Delahunty participated in a scheme to present false evidence after false evidence to the court in an unending series of fraudulent written and verbal presentations. He crafted a "Plead Guilty Document" knowing full well that his statements about the "safety profile" of the Copper IUD I used to be false and reflected only Teva's false propaganda to eliminate competition and preserve a financial monopoly for the drug giant. Delahunty then gave a false statement to the court and the media saying I engaged in an enrichment scheme by buying cheaper IUDs and making profits and led the court to believe that I would have made profits if I had chosen to buy Teva's brand [Exhibit 16]. As I have shown this numerous times, I wasn't making a profit even using the German-made IUDs [Exhibit 18]. I was operating at a loss in providing this service so switching to the ParaGard brand would have resulted in an even larger loss to me. He falsified the actual prices of the ParaGard to the judge and also falsely stated to the court that the IUD I used caused harm to patients when he was fully aware of all the medical research and literature that contradicted his false claims [Exhibit 1 and 2]. Delahunty committed a *crime of omission* by deliberately hiding from the court that the FDA had two months of communications with me between August and October of 2010, part of the history of the case omitted on purpose. He repeatedly deceived the court saying that the reimbursements that I received for IUD plus IUD related healthcare services such as sugical supplies, ultrasound and mandatory follow up office visits were just for the IUD device. He submitted to the judge a ParaGard invoice from 2006 to show a lower price per unit device, once again to deceive the court, despite his knowledge that I had neither ordered nor used any German Copper IUDs till May, 2008 for the first time when ParaGard IUD prices were already much higher [Exhibit 16]. Delahunty hid the exculpatory evidence in his possession (all bank of Sierra business banking records and invoices he subpoenaed from the bank) that confirmed that I bought German-made Copper IUDs from the Canadian pharmacy in May, 2008 for the first time. I did not even know that the Canadian Pharmacy or German made Copper IUD existed before May of 2008. The prosecutor altered his position about alleged facts of the case like a chameleon that changes color without prior notice and he did that several times during the course of my prosecution. He changed color every time he noted his lie was about to become exposed. He introduced new lies to preserve his cover-ups whenever he noted the lie he had told was about to unravel or had been unraveled. For example, after I exposed that his production of a 2006 IUD invoice was a sham, he shifted his position one more time and told the court I could have chosen to buy IUDs at $374 per unit from TEVA and still made a profit, knowing full well that the average total cost of obtaining a ParaGard IUD and related health services from an Ob/Gyn office was average $800 (2008-2009) and average $1200 (in 2010, 2011 and 2012). He also tried to deceive the judge about the price of the T safe Cu-380A IUD as cheaper than what it was by printing from the internet a price list for Cu-375 which had no relevance to his allegations. Delahunty knew the price of the T-Safe Cu-380A IUD had always been $200 ($199 to be precise) as documented throughout the FDA's discovery documents that he participated in preparing, also confirmed by Pueschel's statements in discovery including T Safe IUD invoices made available to the FDA. The average reimbursement of all IUD-related services that I received for this entire 5-year period (2008-2012) was $322 while the ParaGard IUD device's price alone ranged between $374 to $754, during those years. Delahunty stated I was an example of American greed, while it was the drug giant Teva who engaged in financial crimes against the female population by charging them obscene, high-way robbery prices for ParaGard. Many corrupt prosecutors "making false statements to the media that are designed to arouse public indignation" is listed as one of the concerns expressed by the Center for Prosecutorial Integrity of the Department of Justice.

One would think that the prosecutor would feel a bit embarrassed every time I exposed a lie, but I discovered to my surprise that the prosecutor was not embarrassed at all. He felt entitled to lie to the court at will and change the fabricated facts of the case, as the situation demanded on an ongoing basis. For example, when Delahunty's calculations showed that the average reimbursement for an IUD and all related health services was $322 per patient, it would have been embarrassing for him to convict me, a physician who paid the difference in the cost of IUD services from his pocket, therefore he immediately devised a new scheme to falsify the numbers. He removed names from his Excel spreadsheet excluding 44 names from his calculations. He removed 44 patients to reduce the number of IUDs from 152 to 105 thus raising the average reimbursement to $452 from $322 by lowering the denominator in his revised calculations. He never said a word to the defense as to why and how these numbers changed dramatically. He buried everything under one statement in a *footnote* that he had found some unknown cases and decided not to count them in his calculations. He did not explain how they suddenly became "unknown cases" when the data available from insurance companies was all there and available just a phone call away. When a doctor is not paid for a service, it is called, "not paid". Not paid and unknown are not the same things. Then Delahunty deceptively counted multiple IUDs received by some patients as one count, hoping no one would notice. He compounded these lies by claiming that this his new, phony revised average reimbursement of $452 was for just the IUD device when he knew that the billing charge included all IUD-related health services not just the IUD device; it included three to five office visits, surgical supply tray, occasional ultrasound scans, and occasional unannounced emergency patient visits [Exhibit 18]. Delahunty knew from the bookkeeping and billing records made available to him (including full Bank of Sierra business records since 2005), that I paid $42,000 for the annual malpractice premium alone, not to mention employees' salaries, insurance, workers comp, rent and other expenses that are part of running a practice. The overhead for a gynecologist in private practice was reported to be 55 percent of total revenues in an Ob/Gyn practice as reported by Medical Economics and many other research journals [Exhibit 18]. Delahunty also falsified to the court that all IUDs I used I bought from Canada when he knew that at least 10 percent of them were U.S. ParaGard and Mirena IUDs which he knew I bought at much higher prices, never got reimbursed for, nor did I bill my patients.

Without sounding braggadocio, Delahunty could not have easily found an Ob/Gyn in the country who was as generous in providing care to so many patients at little or no charge to them. I say this because I know that is not the American way of doing business. I cannot deny the fact that not everyone in America is greedy, there are many generous Americans in all professions who do pro-bono work out of the goodness of their heart, including those in the profession of medicine, but that is not typical of American culture where money, profit and greed hold the highest value. India, where I grew up as a child, that was not the case. Money was important, of course, but people were just as important in the culture I grew up in.

Probation Department's Dereliction of Duty

The *criminal justice system* also termed as the "law-enforcement system" was defined in a 1929 statute as "collective institutions through which an accused offender passes until accusations have been disposed of or the assessed punishment concluded." The system has three components: law enforcement (police, sheriffs, marshals and the government agents in the FDA, DEA, and FBI), the judicial process (judges, prosecutors, defense lawyers), and corrections (prison officials, probation officers, parole officers, etc.). Criminal justice refers to the methods by which a society deals with those who are accused of having committed crimes in this context. The three components of the Criminal Justice System are required to do independent evaluations, assessments, and investigations of the seriousness of a crime committed by the accused.

The three branches of the criminal justice system are statutorily three independent branches under the Department of Justice, part of the Executive branch of the federal government. The Probation Department is supposed to do its own independent assessment of the gravity of a crime committed even if the accused has already pled guilty to specific charges. When I read the last paragraph of the memo of the Guilty Plea Delahunty crafted for me to sign, I noted the following statement: "Defendant understands that the United States Probation office is not a party to this Agreement (i.e. Guilty Plea Agreement) and will conduct an independent investigation of defendant's activities and his background. It will then prepare a Presentence Report of its own which it will submit to the Court as its independent sentencing recommendation." It was encouraging to learn that it was a statutory obligation of the Probation Department to evaluate my case independently. In addition to his mandatory and statutory obligation, the Probation Officer, Michael Armistead, should have been even more curious to investigate the facts of my case when I informed him that the FDA agent, Pueschel, had falsely induced my patients into believing that the German-made IUD device was "unsafe" and the "cause" for the side effects and "complications" that patients experienced, when the side effects and complications were, in fact, the complications listed in ParaGard's drug insert. I informed Armistead that the German-IUD was CDC approved, and I requested that he look independently into this matter (as he was required to do by law), but he completely ignored my request. He could have done a very basic investigation by simply calling patients and asking them a simple question, "Were you ever informed by the FDA agent that the IUD you received was made in Germany by a German Pharmaceutical company and approved by the CDC of the United States?" Rather than do his job and addressing my concerns, the Probation officer, Michael Armistead copied, cut-and-pasted the prosecutor and FDA agent's statements verbatim and made them his own in what he called the "Probation Department's own independent Presentencing report." [Exhibit 11]

Armistead followed in the footsteps of Delahunty. Just as Delahunty copied and pasted stuff from Pueschel, Armistead cut-and-pasted everything from Pueschel and Delahunty. Just like Delahunty, this was further aiding and abetting the prosecutors and the FDA in the pursuit of their criminal scheme against me. This was a dereliction of duty by the office of the Department of Probation.

The probation officer was duty bound and required by legal or moral obligation to consider the facts of the case when I informed him that the case was fabricated against me by the FDA agent, Pueschel. "The forsaking of a legal or moral obligation with no intent to reassume it; such abandonment is called Dereliction of Duty by a government official" (Black's law dictionary). Such abandonment of duty is a lot more serious when perpetrated by a government employee who has been made aware of the government's illegal actions. This is because the government is supposed to protect the public and enforce the law by ensuring equality for everyone before the law. Dereliction in the performance of his duties was a "willful or negligent failure to perform assigned duties; culpable inefficiency in performing assigned duties." The dereliction of duty statute mandates forfeiture of office if the holder (in this case the Probation Officer, Armistead) fails to perform official duties." [Legal ref: Cases: Officers and Public employees west key number 27]. The fact that the Probation officer suggested a reduced sentence for me to the judge (perhaps due to a guilty conscience that I might have induced in him) does not exonerate him in any way from aiding and abetting the prosecutors and FDA agent Pueschel in facilitating the perpetuation of a crime against a citizen. Finally, Armistead hit below the belt by directly seeking FDA agent Pueschel's opinion as to what he thought was appropriate in the way of fines and penalties for me so he could make it part of his sentencing recommendations and he did, based on Pueschel's recommendations.

This story with the Probation Department gets stranger. I informed my new probation officer, Alton Dural who was supervising my house arrest and checking the GPS devices hooked to my ankle, after I came out of six months of incarceration, that prosecutor Delahunty had created a false case against me through fabrications and forgeries. I made Dural aware that I had informed Michael Armistead of the Probation Department that I was framed by Pueschel during my interview with probation before being incarcerated. I wanted Dural to know that Armistead did not conduct an independent investigation. Instead of showing concern for what had been done, Dural was stunned by my boldness. He said that he hoped I didn't accuse the government in front of the Probation officer because it would have made matters worse for me. "You were supposed to take responsibility," he said. Then he went on to tell me that he did not know what the law meant as he looked at the legal excerpts from the plea agreement that I gave him to look at. He said that as a probation officer, all he knows is that he is supposed to do what the prosecutor had already decided. I showed him the law but he shrugged his shoulders. From this point on, I sent him many emails on a regular basis during my house arrest asking him to give me a half hour of his time so I could give him details about my case to see what he thought, but he avoided me and has yet to respond.

Prosecutorial and Judicial Misconduct

Nancy MacLean in her recent book, "Democracy in Chains" identifies a history of the federal judges. She states that 40 to 60 percent of federal judges have attended the Charles Koch funded judicial curriculum in the line of deceptive and immoral schemes devised by profiteers like Milton Friedman and James Buchanan. These judges are trained to serve the corporations and have no qualms about putting anyone in jail who stands in the way of corporate profits. I was the victim of the judicial misconduct that arose out of such educational tradition for these federal judges who only know how to serve their corporate masters who put them in those positions of power and authority with their corporate cash and political influence.

America's famous civil liberties lawyer Harvey L. Silverglate, the author of *Three Felonies a Day: How the Feds Target the Innocent* throws some light on yet another aspect of the corruption in our judiciary. He states "Over the years, the federal judiciary has acted too often as a handmaiden to federal prosecutors in their misguided effort to nail their targets." (*Three Felonies a Day: How the Feds Target the Innocent*, 2009, Page 257.) He further states that "we must foster the realization that the Justice Department's tactics too often are employed not to protect, but to attack law-abiding society." (Page 25).

Although all the information presented to the judge by the prosecutor in my case were fabrications, my defense attorney, Bowman, brought only some of it to the attention of the judge. Small parts that she presented in the politiest manner possible would have been enough to alert and alarm any judge, despite all the "restrictions" and the "limited scope of argument" imposed on the defense. There is a cliché that "you don't have to be a rocket scientist to figure this out." In my case, an idiot could have figured out that there was no substance to the accusations filed against me based on a very limited but irrefutable evidence that my attorney put forth in Ishii's face.

One can argue that Federal Judge Anthony Ishii was either an incompetent moron or merely corrupt. And the fact that he was most likely neither an idiot nor incompetent, one can draw only one logical conclusion which is that he was corrupt. He was another example of a judge in our judicial system that confirms that many judges have no problem participating in this corrupt corporate culture in which they are raised as children of lobbyists' laws. Bowman, despite innumerable restrictions, tried to bring important information to the attention of Anthony Ishii so he could decipher the truth and see through prosecutorial motivations behind the case, but he ignored them all, so much so that he did not bother or read the evidence provided to him or pretended he did not read it. There was no mention of any prosecutorial evidence presented in his entire speech at sentencing. Although an incomplete and meek version of the truth was presented by my attorney due to the fear of retaliation from the prosecutors to ruin me, with only bits and pieces peppered in a non-accusatory fashion, it had more than enough substance in it to show that the prosecutor's claims against me were false at the very least.

Bowman was right that this Judge would not read evidence if it were more than a certain number of pages. She discouraged me many times from scanning over more documentary evidence and papers that showed that the Copper IUD I used was a safe product or safer than its counterpart, the U.S. brand Paragard. *The Judge is too busy to read all this*, she told me. She limited the number of Exhibits to curtail the overall burden on the judge's shoulders to have to read it all. She also refrained from writing lengthy replies to the government and limited the number of Exhibits, and yet the judge failed to read this evidence. Or did he? He kept quiet about the overwhelming evidence provided to him and instead mimicked the prosecutor's false statement like a primate, in his written verdict: "Dr. Singh did not pass all the financial benefits of having bought cheaper generic Copper IUD to his patients." The judge knew from evidence furnished to him that I not only passed all the financial benefits of cheaper IUDs to my patients but added more financial benefits to my indigent patients that came out of my own hard-earned money. Ishii also repeated the false accusations of the prosecutor by saying, "this is a filing a false claims issue" without providing evidence to show the basis for this claim. What is the difference between a judge and a monkey on the bench if he is just going to repeat what the prosecutor said. Ishii had a legal duty to check and verify to see if Delahunty's assertions were backed up by any meaningful evidence, not to mention the fact that he had a legal obligation and moral duty to read the evidence that defense provided him.

I had been telling the Medical Board and my defense attorneys for three years that private insurance companies do not consider billing for any particular brand or generic of a drug as fraud. The Medicare codes were for the drugs and not for specific brands or generics. The billing code J7300 was for the drug code and not reserved for the U.S. brand, ParaGard. [Exhibit 20]. The insurance companies refused to audit me or cancel my insurance contracts despite many suggestions made to them by Delahunty. Insurance companies did not ask me for a refund of money despite the prosecutor trying to influence them in that direction. Anyone who is aware of how insurance companies operate knows that they love to deny claims and would never allow a claimant to keep an overpayment or put up with fraud on a claim even for a dollar, let alone tens of thousands of dollars. An insurance company will ask for an immediate refund of any money owed and will immediately cancel its provider agreement with a doctor who defrauded the insurance company. I asked all private insurance companies if I owed them money because of the prosecutor's claim of billing fraud and they all said that my billing code was legitimate as long as I provided my patients a Cu-380A IUD, they did not care about the brand, generic or the manufacturer of the drug. Majority of my business was with private insurances companies and none of them thought I did anything wrong in billing them for the IUD I used on my patients. I called every single company except Medi-Cal and Tricare for obvious reasons. I did not stand a chance of being able to reason with Medi-Cal, Tricare or KHS, government insurances that Delahunty was working with intimately to fabricate a criminal case against me. To the best of my knowledge, very few out of the nearly twenty-five private insurance companies that I had agreements with honored the prosecutor's repeated requests for an account summary of how much money they paid me in IUD reimbursements over the years so that he could show these dollar amounts as part of the "restitution" to be imposed on me. Make no mistake, all private Insurance companies would have taken me to court to recover their money even if there was a remote chance that I committed fraud in billing them. We all know that an insurance company will take a pound of flesh from you if you owe it any money, let alone overpay you for anything.

Delahunty used a previously disputed reimbursement issue I had with Kern Health Systems (KHS), a medi-cal provider in Kern county, that was unrelated to IUDs, and included phony dollar amounts in his restitution totals because he was having trouble beefing up numbers to help put me behind bars for a substantial amount of time (I learned that the length of incarceration depends on the amount of financial fraud; the greater the financial fraud, the longer the jail sentence.) Please allow me to say a word or two about Kern Health Systems (KHS). Kern Health Systems had illegally underpaid me thousands of dollars in reimbursements over the years and to many other physicians in Kern County, the poorest county in the State of California. Ironically, KHS owed me several thousand dollars in reimbursements that were held back after I had reported KHS to Kern County supervisors for corruption. Many physicians in the county sued KHS for underpayments, a lawsuit that I was not able to join due to lack of funds, but the plaintiffs (doctors) gave me access to all the inside paperwork that KHS was compelled to reveal during the lawsuit. I discovered that KHS spend $16,000 on ice cream for its staff working on two floors in one day using the Medi-caid funds that were given to it by California state to provide healthcare to the indigent of Kern County. I discovered that KHS had an account with Tiffany Jewelry store out of the Medi-caid funds which were meant to be reimbursed to the doctors providing care for the poor. KHS hoarded one hundred million dollars in its bank account that was meant to be passed on to the poor who needed healthcare. The CEO of KHS, Carol Sorrell, spent tens of thousands of dollars of Medi-caid funds on Monet's painting for her office. The CEO of KHS secretly and underhandedly settled millions in lawsuits for underpaying doctors and healthcare institutions such as the UCLA. When I made one of the Board members of KHS aware of this in my meeting in one of the Kern County supervisor's office, her jaw dropped, because she did not know about this even though she was one of the most prominent Board members of KHS. KHS employees openly admitted to financial fraud with public funds in television and newspaper interviews. When Kern County supervisors sent an auditor from the county to audit KHS books, they bribed the auditor and gave him a job with a very high salary and benefits he could not refuse, who then quit his job with the County and joined the mafia. KHS refused to reveal how much salary they paid the auditor when asked by investigative journalists. At the end of the day, CEO of KHS was fired, and most KHS Board members had to resign. The journalists who investigated KHS for three years got the highest award in investigative journalism given to anyone in the State of California. This is the KHS that Delahunty allied with to beef up the dollar amount of my restitution so he could justify me going to jail for long time. This is an ultra-short history of the criminal past of KHS in unfairly treating me and many other physicians and its history of financial fraud with tax-payer dollars. KHS frequently held Kangaroo court for physicians contracted with KHS, especially those who complained about underpayments or tried to point out to KHS its illegal use of public funds or unlawful withholding of reimbursements to cancel their healthcare provider contracts with KHS. I was one of those many victims of KHS. I will tell you that it is the same old story why criminal charges were not brought against KHS, because the government does not like to go after the corruption in its own agencies and affiliates. I have kept in my possession all the Bakersfield Californian headlines and articles about KHS as it was being investigated between 2008 and 2011 for anyone who would like to check the veracity of what I have told you about KHS thus far and much more.

Delahunty did not stop there. He went back to court after sending me to prison and presented more victim report claims to ask the judge to raise the amount of my restitution. The judge raised it to $90,000 from the original $37,000. I did not find out about this till two years later when I was in house-arrest after serving my prison sentence by insisting with my probation officer, Alton Dural, that he disclose to me how much government claimed I owed in restitution.

As I have stated earlier, Judge Ishii neither reviewed Exhibits for evidence nor asked any questions for clarification before convicting me. And he did not say a single word about one count of mail fraud that I had plead guilty to. You would rightfully be outraged if you went to a doctor who said to you, "I don't have the time to read your previous medical records or your medical history, but I am going to diagnose you anyway by looking at you and will treat you for whatever I think you have." It would be medical malpractice. Such uninformed diagnosis and treatment could kill you. I have been in the medical field for 25 years, and I can tell you that if I did that to a patient, not only would I lose my medical license but I could give the patient a wrong medication or treatment which might lead to injury or death. If such treatment from a physician is not acceptable to you, then why should the verdicts of judges who refuse to review the history of the case be acceptable to the American people? Every legal statute I consulted and studied while in prison confirmed to me that the definition of fraud had one essential element in its criteria to be considered a fraud: one must have stolen someone's money or property. How did I steal patients' money if I contributed thousands of dollars of my own hard-earned money to make IUD devices and related healthcare services available to my patients over a period of five years? And if my violation was that it was illegal to import Copper IUD from Europe or Canada, that it was mail fraud, then why didn't Ishii say so? I did not hear Ishii say anything about mail fraud, the one count I was charged with on my Guilty plea agreement. [Exhibit 23]. The judge's acceptance of lies from the prosecutor in the total absence of a single piece of evidence against me, and in the presence of more than sufficient, in fact, substantial evidence contradicting Delahunty's claims was a dereliction of duty and wanton and willful judicial misconduct based on "a statute that mandates forfeiture of office if the holder willfully neglects or fraudulently fails to perform official duties" (Cases: West Key #27).

I sat in his court and observed how he shipped people to jail left and right after spending two minutes on each case, 120 months here and 90 months there like he was distributing candy by blindly honoring the prosecutors' demands and recommendations without any review of the evidence. Cases were already negotiated before the criminals were brought before the judge, and Ishii was rubber stamping all these decisions privately negotiated by the prosecutors with the public defenders with utter disregard for the nature or the seriousness of their crimes.

Should Ishii be impeached for violating the public trust in him to enforce law and order? To impeach is to "charge with a crime or misconduct a public official with violation of public trust". An impeachable offense is an offense for which a public official may legally be impeached…for treason or bribery or other high crimes and misdemeanors." According to the Impeachable Offense statutes [Exhibit 22] the grounds on which an official can be removed do not have to be criminal in nature. They usually involve some type of abuse of power or breach of public trust." If we cared about and respected the rule of law and equality before the law in this country, then FDA agent Pueschel, the two prosecutors, Delahunty and Sheriff, and Judge Ishii all should be impeached based on their misconduct and dereliction of their official duties. These legal definitions that have scholarly consensus require that, not just the prosecutors in this case, but the judge should be impeached as well for being complicit. In a world where a government is conceivably above-board, they should all be serving a jail sentence for their crimes along with all the other characters in the corrupt Establishment [Exhibit 12]. Sadly, according to legal scholars, impeachment has become obsolete both in Britain and the United States because the governments do not like to investigate their own crimes. So, Gluck, my defense attorney, essentially bluffed me when he said he could have the FDA agent impeached for falsifying information; that was his way to keep me in the game, so he could continue to make money off me with the false hope of winning the case. I am glad I did not fall into that trap. I could have lost my house and made my kids homeless if I went for that option. Now I still stand a slight chance of survival.

What can we do and where do we go from here? The bottom line is that it is impossible for anyone to expose the corruption in the Department of Justice unless a messianic judge such as Emmett Sullivan comes once in a century to order the criminal investigation of corrupt prosecutors. Even someone with the integrity of Chad Joy couldn't accomplish it, since whistleblowers are met with punitive action and they are hounded for life by those who are powerful and corrupt.

Some great lawyers and legal scholars in our country - Harvey Silverglate, Sidney Powell, Gerry Spence, Glenn Greenwald, and Mike Papantonio, several renowned law professors of legal ethics, and many others in the field, all agree that Judges rarely get sanctions for corruption and prosecutors are almost never censured for criminal behavior. No examples exist of the DOJ disciplining their corrupt and unethical cabal of prosecutors, the ones who have been caught red-handed with their pants down in criminal misconduct and corrupt behaviors. The Center for Prosecutorial Integrity is for show only, intended for the purpose of giving the public the notion that we have some checks and balances in place to protect people against government corruption which, in fact, we do not.

I end this section with a quote from Harvey Silverglate in, *How the Feds Target the Innocent* which states:

> Since the 1980's the federal bench, too, has been undergoing a transformation that has seriously eroded the extent to which judges can be relied on in bogus federal prosecutions. Judges, many of whom are former prosecutors, not only buy into the bogus amorphous definitions of federal crimes favored by prosecutors, but they knowingly enable the tactics that allow prosecutors to present witnesses who bolster dubious prosecutions. (Harvey Silverglate, *How the Feds Target the Innocent*, Page 18)

Witness Tampering – Obstruction of Justice

The ninth court circuit Chief Judge, Alex Kozinsky in his foreword to *Licensed to Lie* states, "Prosecutors can, and often do, threaten to charge witnesses as accomplices or co-conspirators if they testify favorably to the defense."

The Center for Prosecutorial Integrity of the Department of Justice has listed "pressuring defense witnesses not to testify" as one of the most serious types of prosecutorial misconduct. A week after I had been convicted, on August 24 of 2015, I contacted my ex-employee, a Medical Assistant, a woman I refer to as Sandra Johnson (to protect her identity) to find out if she would be willing to share with me any details of what transpired at her eight-hour deposition. The interview was conducted by FDA agent Pueschel and the two prosecutors, Delahunty and Sheriff, with my two attorneys, Gluck and Spackman present, on May 29, 2015. I was not allowed to speak with her before my conviction but I could once the case was over. She surprised me with a lot of interesting details. She informed me that she was taken for a car ride by a former prosecutor, Stephen Jones [Exhibits and 12], who was hired by Gluck to represent her, about half an hour before her testimony was to begin. Jones intimidated her and threatened her with consequences and being dragged into court if she "tried to help Dr. Singh." This guy, according to my Medical Assistant, insinuated that she must follow the prosecutor's leads as to what the prosecutor wanted her to say or not say or else she might face prosecution. He was doing this to her despite the fact that she was given immunity by the prosecutor before her recorded testimony was to be taken.

As I discussed previously, she informed me that Stephen Jones first started talking with her by making some inappropriate comments, such as, and I paraphrase: "We know that you have had an affair with Dr. Singh." Then he warned her that she better not try to help Dr. Singh in her testimony. He added that he knew that Dr. Singh's wife was jealous of her. Johnson told me that she was terrified to hear him make those comments and she told him that her relationship with me had been strictly professional and an employee-employer relationship all the years she had worked for me. According to her, this revolving-door former prosecutor, Stephen Jones, now ironically defending my ex-employee against the government, resorted to threats such as being dragged into court if she did not cooperate with the prosecutors. She told me that she had never been so afraid in her life. Then she said that one of the prosecutors, the younger one, who interviewed her later that day "wanted you (meaning me) on the chopping block." She was referring to Delahunty, the younger of the two prosecutors, as I found out later.

Federal statutes make it a crime to bribe or threaten a witness. It is a felony to give or promise a witness "anything of value" in exchange for testimony. Since it is a crime for a defense lawyer or a defendant to promise a benefit to a witness, shouldn't it then be a crime for prosecutors to do the same? Isn't there equality before the law? Why should it not be a crime for a prosecutor to threaten, or offer money or other inducements such as immunity to witnesses to make them "cooperate" with the government? Shouldn't all untoward pressures and inducements be removed from witnesses, so that truth, and not just self-interest, governs their testimony?

The three-judge panel of the Tenth Circuit Court of Appeals has followed the seemingly precise wording of the witness bribery statute and found NO EXCEPTION for prosecutors who threaten and then reward government witnesses for their testimony. (Sonya Singleton case of 1998). Rewarding my ex-employee with no prosecution from the government in exchange for not helping me was a form of bribery, in my opinion. The DOJ panicked at the Tenth Circuit Court of Appeals' Sonia Singleton case report and sought and obtained further review by the full membership of the court. The full court reversed the upstart panel that had rocked the corrupt prosecutors. Only those prosecutors who have malicious intentions in prosecuting law-abiding citizens must worry about such a precedent becoming a reality. This case demonstrated that even where Congress seems to have spoken clearly on the definition of witness bribery, the DOJ's institutional imperative to obtain convictions at any cost has prevailed. Whenever any legislation to end the corruption in the Department of Justice has ever been introduced in Congress and supported by every single legal entity and institution in the country, there is always one entity, one exception opposing it, and that exception is the Department of Justice. Do you wonder why the DOJ is the only institution that is always opposed to legislation that will hold corrupt prosecutors accountable? Who can answer that question? I think we all can.

All acts described under witness tampering meet the criteria for "Obstruction of Public Justice" which is "Interference with the orderly administration of law and justice, as by giving false information to or withholding evidence or by harming or intimidating a witness or juror" (Black's Law Dictionary, ninth edition, page 1183). This is also termed as *obstructing justice, obstructing public justice or obstruction of justice.* (Cases: Obstructing Justice West key number one; Sentencing and Punishment West key number 761.)

> The goal – to proscribe every willful act of corruption, intimidation or force which tends in any way to distort or impede the administration of law either civil or criminal – has been very largely attained, partly by the aid of legislation. And any punishable misdeed of such a nature which is not recognized as a distinct crime is usually called 'obstruction of justice' or 'obstructing justice,' – a common law misdemeanor." Rollin M. Perkins and Ronald N. Boyce, *Criminal Law* 552 (3[d] ed. 1982).

I would like to end this section with a quote from page 270 of Harvey Silverglate's book, *Three Felonies a Day:*

> Judges play an important role in perpetuating a system that is becoming increasingly corrupt. They pretend to believe witnesses *whose testimonies they know have been forged* under enormous undue pressure … If judges continue to allow bought or coerced testimony; then pressure must be brought to bear on Congress to enact legislation outlawing this

> practice. Judges who go along with the system are undermining justice, not administering it, and they should be treated accordingly rather than honored for their public service. (Silverglate, p 270)

In my opinion, these judges are the real criminals, in Silverglate's sense of the word.

The "Due Process of Law" – "Justice" American Style

The American Heritage Dictionary defines *due process of law*, as "formal legal proceedings that are expected to be carried out regularly and in accordance with the law, for a fair treatment of a citizen's entitlement." Ordinary people not versed in law understand that it refers to a legal requirement to prevent an unfair, arbitrary, or unreasonable treatment of an individual.

A constitutional amendment, ratified with the Bill of Rights by the founding fathers in 1791, among four other provisions stated that "a person cannot be deprived of life, liberty or property without due process of law." The due process clause of 1890 is the constitutional provision that prohibits the government from unfairly or arbitrarily depriving a person of liberty or property. *Due process*, as defined in the 1930 statute, the rights to freedom and property, is so fundamentally important that it requires compliance with the standards of fairness and justice. I was deprived of life, liberty, and property through the DOJ's unlawful practices and violations of this due process of law to which I was entitled as an American citizen and as a human being.

The FDA and the prosecutors, Delahunty and Sherriff, violated the due process of law in the most violent manner. To begin with,

FDA agents who showed up with guns and ransacked my office without a warrant. I asked Gluck why I was not shown the warrant, he shrugged his shoulders as though it was the FDA's normal business practice with which he seemed to be very comfortable. It was quite shocking for me to know that such a violation was acceptable to my defense attorney who was supposed to help enforce due process of law. We also informed Gluck that the gunned federal agents blocked a member of my staff from entering the interview conference room to deliver the message from him (Gluck) advising me to stop talking with the FDA agents until my attorney arrived on the scene. To Gluck, it was business as usual and had no relevance to the case, dismissing it as something minor and irrelevant. Instead, he seemed to emphasize the fact that I needed to start thinking about planning my defense against the almighty government rather than focus on due process irregularities. I informed Gluck that FDA Agent Pueschel closed me off in a room by politely asking, "May I close the door?" Pueschel had carefully planned to cut me off from any communication with my staff during the so-called interview, as though I had hung a "do not disturb" sign outside the door. I also informed Gluck that the agents hung up on my wife when she told them that they needed to release me from the room, because I had engaged the services of a criminal defense attorney who was on his way to my office. Again, none of this surprised Gluck – this was just business as usual.

As time went by and a clearer picture emerged, it became evident that the entire case was staged from day one, with no intention of following any due process of law at any time then, or in the future. There was an "obstruction of process" from the very beginning, an offense that most jurisdictions have defined as "a crime." (Refer to *obstructing process* or *resisting process* [Cases: Obstructing Justice West Key #3].)

Substantive due process, as defined in 1933, "is the doctrine that the due process clauses of the 5th Amendment(federal) and the 14th Amendment (states) requires legislation to be fair and reasonable in content and to further a legitimate governmental objection" (Cases: Constitutional Law West Key #3892). A 1934 statute defines *procedural due process* "as the minimum requirements of notice and a hearing guaranteed by the due process." The FDA, and especially the Medical Board, with its established protocols under the laws of the State of California, were required to give notice and then interview me before accusing me of any wrongdoing. The Medical Board never gave me a notice of interview. Instead they worked underhandedly with the FDA and the federal prosecutors to engage in unlawful practices and violated the due process. The Medical Board instead secretly dispatched a hitman to bash me and break me down by taking direct instructions from the FDA.

One of the things that bothered me the most and continues to plague me to this day is that violations of the due process of law guaranteed by the 5th and the 14th amendments of the Constitution of the United States meant nothing to anyone involved in my case, including my defense attorneys. This showed me the extent of moral decadence that we face today in our legal system. Gluck, and later Bowman, fully cooperated with the prosecutors in propagating lies about the T-Safe copper IUD despite the plethora of evidence to the contrary. The prosecutor lied because he wanted to incarcerate me, but my defense attorney's rationale for telling lies was to conform and cooperate with the prosecutor to help mitigate (reduce) my sentence if I *took responsibility*. The basis for my defense was not a search for truth and justice, but an attempt to help me get my sentence reduced. That is all that mattered to them; they did not give a fig about anything else, least of all truth and justice. If that meant helping the prosecutors perpetuate their lies to help minimize the government's harsher punishment for me, so be it. What happened to the due process of law that we Americans always brag about to the rest of the world and portray on television shows like *Law and Order* or *The West Wing*?

My experience has shown me that the criminal justice system industrial complex is one entity in which everyone is supposed to be a "team player" going along with not just government agencies, prosecutors, and government agents but also defense attorneys and everyone else involved in it. This includes other profiteers such as doctors, psychologists, and self-proclaimed experts of all sort. Everyone was in it to make a big buck in as little time as possible. My case has been a scene of predatory vultures who had utter disregard for due process of the law, the constitutional rights of the defendant, and elementary human rights of the accused. They all swooped down on me to get a piece of the meat when it was their turn.

As per the procedural due process statute, "an elementary and fundamental requirement of due process in any proceeding which is to be accorded finality is notice reasonably calculated under all circumstances, to apprise interested parties of the pendency of the action and afford them an opportunity to present their objection." In other words, I was entitled to a notice of charges. When I continued to object to the prosecutor's unclear and undefined accusations, however, I was told that I needed to agree to a guilty plea first because the prosecutor Delahunty did not want to miss on the deadline of his statute of limitations, which was a couple of weeks away. We

Americans believe that the charge(s) in a criminal case come first followed by guilty or not guilty, not the other way around. It is incredible that Delahunty had five years to do his investigation and, after he failed to find any grounds to prosecute me, it all boiled down to agreeing to plead guilty first and then let him figure out my guilt later. Delahunty would not stop threatening me with consequences, such as putting my wife in prison as well, unless I agreed to plead guilty first without any flexibility from his side whatsoever to discuss merits of the case or the willingness to discuss if his incoherent and random accusations were true or false. Gluck begged for more time, but he was only granted more time subject to a verbal commitment from him that he would have me sign the guilty plea *no matter what.* This onset of my battle should have informed me of how much fairness I would be afforded. If Delahunty was immoral enough to refuse to discuss anything unless I first pled guilty, not knowing why I was guilty, then it is no surprise that he would conspire to trump up the rest of the case. I realize now that in almost 100 percent of the cases in which an innocent person has been convicted of something, the truth will never be revealed. The victim of the criminal justice system will waste away in prison without hope. What a tragic waste of human life caught in the grips of our corrupt system.

My legal research in the prison law library led me to find some other examples, where prosecutors frequently use this technique to coerce people to plead guilty – that is, for example, to threaten to incarcerate another member of the family, such as a spouse. I ran into a true example of this in Salinas, California, where I met a radio talk show host who had been imprisoned for two years and was now on his way out of the system through a halfway house. His radio show was critical of the government in many ways. He was charged with aiding and abetting an accounting firm for accounting fraud when he was a consultant for the firm. When he resisted pleading guilty, his defense lawyer called him and said, "please come and see me immediately, I would like to show you something very disturbing." When he arrived, his attorney showed him what he had received from the prosecutor. There were photographs of all his children and grandchildren with FBI numbers assigned to each one of them. His kids were grown up with children of their own. He knew right then and there that he was dealing with a Mafia-like organization and he must relent because he would never win, and so he pled guilty. He told me that it reminded him of a totalitarian government where disobedience of any kind was not tolerated. He said it reminded him of a store owner who refused to pay his dues to the Don. The Don sends his henchmen to beat him to a pulp. They break all his bones and give him a warning before leaving that he must pay his dues before dawn. The idea is to send a message to the rest of the store owners in the area that absolute compliance is in order.

Criminal procedure refers to the rules governing the mechanisms under which crimes are investigated, prosecuted, adjudicated, and punished, and it includes the accused person's constitutional rights. I was investigated for five years by the federal prosecutors and then given the rights of a "witch trial" days before the prosecutor reached his statute of limitations deadline. It was all about "admit to a crime or else, face my wrath." I resisted his demand because I did not know what my crime was. I was declared guilty by Delahunty before even *he* knew what the crime was. The only reason I signed the plea agreement was because Delahunty began to threaten me, saying that he had now decided to imprison my wife as well if I continued to resist pleading guilty. I could not let that happen. We had three children, two of them quite young, and one of them with severe disabilities. And how much time did I have to think about it? I was given a deadline of 5:00 pm.

The Burden of Proof – The "Evidence"

Let us say that in law the weight of evidence is rated on a scale of one to ten, number ten being the perfect, flawless, irrefutable, undeniable evidence and zero meaning no evidence at all. In this section I will use case laws, legal texts and definitions from law journals and legal scholarship to illustrate that the evidence I provided to the prosecutors in my case was ten on a scale of ten at all chronological stages, while the prosecutors showed zero evidence and, yet I ended up in prison. Ironically, the government's evidence, measuring zero on a scale of ten, was more acceptable to Judge Ishii than undeniably irrefutable evidence that measured ten on a scale of ten. "Evidence is any matter of fact that is furnished to a legal tribunal otherwise than by reasoning or a reference to what is noticed without proof as the basis of inference in ascertaining some other matter of fact." (James B. Thayer: Presumptive and the Law of Evidence, 3, Harv. L. Rev. 141-142 (1889).

A good example of zero evidence would be what was used as evidence in witch trials in Salem, Massachusetts. For example, David said that Joanna was a witch and his evidence was that he had a dream that Joana was a witch, and the judge and the jury hung Joanna from the tree using David's dream as the evidence. The evidence that the government provided in my case was tantamount to that furnished by David. I was treated as Joanna even though I provided evidence in my favor, something Joana could not have provided in her defense.

"Evidence broadly defined is the means from which an inference may logically be drawn as to the existence of a fact…evidence is the demonstration of a fact..." (31 A.C.J.S. Evidence § 3, at 67-68 (1996). So, what is the best evidence? What is material evidence? Substantial evidence? Corroborating evidence? What is primary, clear and convincing evidence? Demonstrative and conclusive evidence? What is scientific evidence? During five years of trials and tribulations with various government agencies and the federal prosecutors, I repeatedly provided evidence, which I discuss below, that meets all these definitions as found in law textbooks and the Black's Law Dictionary. Yet, not a single person in the entire criminal justice system that I met had enough integrity to say, 'Wait a minute, let us look at what Dr. Singh is giving us, maybe it is important or perhaps relevant.'

Physical Evidence: I opened packages of the German and the U.S. brand versions of the Cu-380A IUD along with the IUDs Drug Package Inserts in front of the two FDA agents on August 17, 2010. This "physical evidence," also called "material evidence" was physically handed over to the two FDA agents to be brought back to the FDA office for inspection and examination which the FDA scientists examined over a period of two months. FDA agent Richard Pueschel systematically deleted all references to this evidence from the discovery documents generated by him.

Scientific Evidence: I continually provided authoritative research literature on the Cu-380A Copper IUD, research-based in both Europe and the United States, to government agencies for three years on issues of the IUD's safety, and procurement procedures as described in a 145-page research report carried out by the World Health Organization under the auspices and leadership of the Centers for Disease Control of the United States. I also provided similar evidence on Copper IUDs from various authoritative national and international peer-reviewed medical journals. The medical research on the Copper IUD I provided was Scientific evidence. Scientific evidence in cases of this sort is defined as "indispensable evidence which is an evidence without which a particular fact cannot be proved" (West key – number 597). The Prosecutor, Delahunty, in collusion with the FDA agent, Pueschel, dismissed and unlawfully ignored this vital scientific evidence to deceive the court.

Best Evidence: The term "best evidence", also called the "specific evidence" in law, usually applies to writings and recordings which refer to evidence of the highest quality. In my case, I provided all legal evidence, both oral and documentary, to substantially prove the veracity of my claims. This evidence included Ob/Gyn Journals, such as *the Journal of Obstetrics and Gynecology* (also known as the Gray Journal), *OBG management*, and *Contemporary ob/gyn Medical Journal*, was the medical research journals including that of the CDC and NIH about the safety and quality of the Cu-380A IUD brands manufactured outside the United States. This literature referred to "that kind of proof which under any possible circumstances affords the greatest certainty of the fact in question or as evidence which carries on its face no indication that better remains behind" [32ACJ.S. Evidences 1054, at 417 (1996)]. The prosecutors and Judge Ishii and to some extent, my own defense lawyers ignored it and went along with false statements made by Delahunty.

Direct Evidence: The evidence I provided the FDA agents on August 17, 2010, was also by legal definition a d*irect evidence* which is "based on personal knowledge and experience which does not necessitate any further inference or question." The FDA agent's hand-written document dated August 17, 2010, which was accidentally released by the prosecutors after convicting me and after denying that the document existed, showed that FDA agents were aware that the Copper IUD I used was manufactured in Germany. Despite this, FDA agent Pueschel and prosecutor Delahunty continued to disseminate disinformation about this brand of IUD to my patients, the public, and the media before and after my conviction. They continued to lie even after the FDA scientists had confirmed that the Cu-380A IUD removed or recovered from my patients were all the German-made brand, called T-Safe.

Conclusive Evidence: *Conclusive evidence* in law is "so strong as to overbear any other evidence on the contrary" [(Cases: Criminal Law 549; Evidence 584(1)]. Every type of evidence I provided the government met the criteria of "Conclusive Evidence" as opposed to a government's imaginary narrative with nothing to back it up.

I, Paul Singh, the defendant stood there listening to the prosecutor, Delahunty in federal court on the day of my sentence, not allowed to utter a word, my life under serious threat of harsher punishment if I expressed any disagreement with him in any shape or form. I had asked my attorney if I could see the federal judge in his chamber privately for five minutes, just as I had with the Administrative Law Judge in my Medical Board case. I was informed by my defense attorney, Gluck, that I would never be allowed to speak privately with the judge or to anyone else because I had been accused of a crime. Judge Ishii accepted the witch trial evidence from Delahunty to hang me from the tree just like the example of Joanna, the witch in Salem, Massachusetts in 1692. I knew the prosecutors were going to throw me in the water to see if I sank or floated. If I sank, they would say I was not guilty, but it was too late for me because my sinking and death would do the job for the prosecutor. If I floated, the prosecutor's interpretation of this would be that I lied about not being a witch so he would hang me from the tree for lying. Either way, I would die. That was the medieval law and superstition. Today we know better and do better. Or do we?

False Statements to the Media to Arouse Public Indignation

One of the common unethical prosecutorial practices that the Department of Justice's Prosecutorial Integrity Section is concerned with is that some prosecutors make "false statements to the Media to arouse public indignation." Such actions help make these prosecutors popular in inner circles of the DOJ as cool guys who are tough on crime. This paves the path for them for future promotions, power, and money, even preparing a path for hire into the lucrative private legal corporate sector.

The release of a pre-drafted press release to the media by prosecutor, Delahunty within seconds of my pleading guilty was just such an attempt. It was unlawful, improper behavior and affirmative misconduct on the part of Delahunty. He knew that he had obtained the guilty plea from me through coercion and threats to my family and me, and he also knew that the statements in the plea document were lies which he now cut and pasted onto his Press Release. This kind of thing is referred to as an Affirmative Misconduct in Estoppel case law, in an 1897 statute defined as "An affirmative act of misrepresentation or concealment of a material fact; intentional wrongful behavior." The Guilty plea document drafted by Delahunty and the cut-and-pasted Press release from this forged Plea document was not an isolated act of disinformation but reflected an ongoing pattern of misrepresentation by Delahunty spanning over years of this case.

> With respect to a claim of Estoppel against the federal government, a misrepresentation or concealment of material fact by a government employee - beyond a merely innocent or negligent misrepresentation is affirmative misconduct." Estoppel West Key Number 62.2 (3,4)

Such official misconduct is defined as "a malfeasance…corruption in office or official corruption…political corruption" (CASE LAW: officers and Public Employees West key number 121.)

My defense attorney did not bother to call the press to make a statement in defense of me, or to tell my side of the story. So, I picked up the phone myself to talk to the news-channel to inform them that what they had telecast about my case was false. But they did not wish to speak with me. They did not want to discuss what had already been reported the day before, they said. I tried in vain to get my version of the story out there. One person took a message for someone else, but no one ever called me back. I was hung up on when I called the following day. I made this call even though my staff and I were told by Gluck not to discuss the case with anyone. I had previously succeeded in giving my side of the story to Tehachapi News after the conclusion of my medical case, which they published, giving the versions as told by both sides. I had hoped that I could do the same with the television station. I was told that my criticism of the FDA in the *Tehachapi News* soon after the Medical Board issued me a letter of reprimand in 2014 had probably hurt me in that it prompted the FDA agent to ramp up his case against me.

Our Constitution described the press as the "Fourth Estate" for a good reason: with the hope that the press would continue to robustly monitor and, thereby, keep check the power of those who govern us. The Constitution also established three branches of the federal government – legislative, executive and judicial – to divide power in the hope that each would provide checks and balances to one another. It is doubtful that the three branches of the government that are so dependent on the dark money-driven State corporate complex have ever performed that duty in any consequential manner to serve their electorate. Instead they serve the needs and demands of the ruling class that helped them get appointed to their coveted offices in the first place. That makes it even more important that the First Amendment protect the Press so it could keep an eye on potential government corruption. Our Constitution did protect the press when it described the Press as the Fourth Estate. The plutocrats who own the three branches of the government have now successfully bought nearly 98 percent of mainstream media, small and large either through outright ownership or through advertisement dollars. There goes your hope of freedom of the press because those who own the government now also own the press. We all know that a free press is essential to the cultivation of an informed citizenry, and thus the constitutional democracy itself. For a free press to function, reporters and the news organizations they work for should have access to the sources whose confidentiality they can promise, and therefore are bound to protect. Such things have now become hopes and dreams of the past; the reality of freedom of the press in the United States is a very different story than what one would expect as you could tell from what I went through myself. I am only one among innumerable people who are victims of the one-sidedness of the media that has now become an echo chamber for the government, corporations, and drug companies. Media serves the large corporations that own it and serves them both directly and indirectly through serving three branches of the government which have now become a vital segment of the business class.

In the words of Harvey A. Silverglate:

> Too often, the DOJ has successfully convinced the public and often all-too-gullible press that its prosecutors are acting to clean up some nest of corruption or a dire threat to the nation. In the kind of crusades to which we have become accustomed and far too comforting, the DOJ has often managed to enlist the press as a cheering section rather than as an appropriately skeptical Fourth Estate. Reporters are too willing to sit down with their prosecutorial sources to learn about the evil doers in the dock, without doing the hard work of understanding why and how the government claims their conduct broke the law, or even why and how they are supposedly bad people. (*Three Felonies a Day: How the Feds Target the Innocent*; pg. 268)

According to Silverglate, these reporters must begin to enlist the aid of the defense lawyers, as well as the few academics who understand these prosecutions, to offer sophisticated and critical reporting of federal prosecutors. Reporters who cover legal stories might also spend some time in law schools and as apprentices in legal practices, especially those that are devoted to public service. Silverglate further states that the criminal defense lawyers are not always helpful to reporters seeking to learn whether a prosecution is real or faux. A growing percentage of members of the criminal defense bar are alumni of the Department of Justice, and far too many, though hardly all, have imbibed the culture of the DOJ and carry it into their new careers

Silverglate writes that many lawyers are reluctant to talk publicly about the unfairness of the prosecutions against their clients, concerned about court rules restricting pre-trial publicity that might influence a future jury. Such rules when applied too broadly, are also unconstitutional. For example, I was forbidden from speaking to my patients during my case, so I could clear the disinformation campaign that had been launched by the FDA about the Copper IUDs that I implanted in my patients. All I wanted to do was to speak to all my patients directly and personally to show them the proof against the FDA's claim and make them aware that the government agent disinformed them. It would have taken five minutes to reveal the truth to each one of my patients and expose the government's mischief in the process. Again, if I were allowed to speak with the federal judge privately, it would have taken me minutes to expose the truth to him. I believe that no judge would have doubted me because the truth I had to tell him was so easily comprehensible and self-evident. You did not have to be a judge to understand all that I had to show in my defense. I did that in the court held in my medical board case and it was so easy for me to explain and easy enough for the judge to understand and it resolved all misunderstandings in no time.

I'd like to reiterate here what I have already referred to in my story earlier. After pleading guilty I asked Gluck a hypothetical question: "If we were to appear on C-SPAN television together with you regarding my case, what would you have to say to the American people?" His response was, "I would say I would have acquitted you if I were on the jury." I then asked, "What about the truth, what would you say about it?" He did not answer my question. Today I challenge him to appear on television with me before the American people to answer many questions related to my case that I have for him, and additional questions about the quality of his legal representation and ethics of his lawfirm, Bird and Mirella. I would like to expose the inner workings of the entire criminal defense industry, a money-making cartel, not just the Department of Justice. Hopefully, I will have an opportunity to do precisely that in the future. I am serving my prison sentence for now with my fingers crossed.

Silverglate makes an important observation in explaining, at least in part, why the media has become an echo chamber for the government. He lists fear of government tyranny as one among many reasons.

> To be involved in the news media today – whether print or electronic, "new" media or old – is to find ourselves in a precarious situation, operating at the whim of federal prosecutors and other bureaucrats. Possible sanctions, ranging from a prison sentence to crippling fines, loom over the press. The age-old tactic of sending a message in *terrorism* by randomly eliminating a few, to instill fear in many, has been used with increasing and alarming regularity by the Department of Justice. There are other criminal threats to the news media such as the Sedition Act and the Espionage Act.

When I read this in *Three Felonies a Day*, it reminded me of the case of a journalist who I met in prison. He informed me the DOJ put him in jail for 48 months for refusing to divulge the source of his information for an article he wrote to expose the government. He was imprisoned under the Terrorism and the Patriot acts. There goes the freedom of expression of the journalists in the United States. The U.S. Constitution has guaranteed journalists the right to keep their sources confidential, but the DOJ has no problem violating that constitutional right guaranteed to the press by our founding fathers.

Silverglate has listed fear of government tyranny as one among many reasons why journalists are terrified at the thought of exposing the government.

The Obama government seems to be specializing in this more than any other administration before in the history of our nation, i.e. using the Sedition Act, the Patriot Act, the Espionage Act, the Terrorism Act, and the NDAA (National Defense Authorization Act) to put all our most patriotic dissidents and whistle-blowers behind bars. The few gutsy non-conformists in the media who have the courage to speak up are also threatened with indictments on past publications, not just the one objectionable article they have published in exposing the government corruption. But this tyranny has also boomeranged on the government in many ways. People are angry at the mocking bird mainstream media and more and more whistleblowers are coming out for the first time leaking information about corruption in inner circles of the deep state.

I hope that one day someone out there in a position of power will help me hold these television channels accountable for calumny, slander, and defamation of my character that fueled permanent ostracization of me from human society and destroyed my medical career for good. The press can claim that the false statements in their newscast that injured me were without malicious intent because all they did was publish a government's press release, but that does not exonerate the press. The press is expected to do its due diligence in investigating a matter before announcing it to the American people. The press must interview all parties involved to find out the truth and to be objective in their reporting in giving both sides of the story. We the people own public airways; therefore, media is supposed to work for us and not be servile to the state-corporate complex and its coercive institutions. The media is not supposed to be the spokesperson for the government's official pronouncements without first verifying the veracity or validity of the government's assertions. That defeats the very purpose of the Press as the Fourth Estate expected to keep an eye on our government.

Fraudulently Induced "Restitution" and Civil Suits

The prosecutor claimed that I collected $47,452 from insurance companies in insurance reimbursements for IUDs over a period of five years, money that I now owe the insurance companies and to my patients in restitution. Ishii imposed an additional $25,000 penalty on top of that "to be paid immediately." Prosecutor Delahunty's claim was that these reimbursements from insurance companies were "reserved" for billing for only the U.S. brand of Copper IUD, the only Copper IUD brand approved by the FDA. I provided evidence that according to billing codes, the code J7300, code for Copper IUD was not reserved for a particular brand [Exhibit 20] but the evidence I provided was ignored. The insurance companies also assured me that my billing was not insurance fraud but my defense attorney ignored that fact.

But let us say the billing fraud claim by the prosecutor was correct in some remote legal sense of the word. In this section, I will first describe what "restitution" is to my readers, as it is noted in restitution related criminal case laws that I reviewed. This will help you to fully understand prosecutorial deceptive distortion of this law that I am about to throw light on in this section. I will spare you the pain of my own opinion on this and stick with legal scholarship on the subject. As I sit in prison, I have just read an opinion from Judge

Julio Fuentes of the U.S. Court of Appeals for the Third Circuit reported on October 19 of 2016 in the *Criminal Law Reporter*, which is published by the Bureau of National Affairs, (vol 100, no 3): Here is an excerpt:

> The Federal sentencing boost tied to the 'loss' a fraudster causes to victims must be based on a tangible harm and not the conceptual damage his lies cause to the integrity of the judicial process. The gravamen of loss calculation under Section 2131.1 of the U.S Sentencing Guidelines is a "concrete monetary harm to a real-world -victim. (Judge Fuentes ruling, U.S Court of Appeals for the Third Circuit, Oct 6, 2016 (United States v Fee, 2016 BL 334736, 3rd Circuit, No 15 – 2939, 10/6/16)

During my research at the law library in prison, I discovered another ruling, someone relevant to my case, by the sixth circuit appeals court which reversed a federal judge's ruling where an accused was told to pay a $25,000 penalty immediately, just as Judge Ishii ordered in my case. The ruling said that a judge could not order immediate payment of an amount without looking at the financial status of the accused. If a judge orders an accused to pay $25,000 immediately without even inquiring about their financial situation, he is showing massive ignorance.

At the time the court mandated that I make an immediate payment, I was seeking food stamps but was ineligible because I had two cars and more than $2,000 in my bank account. A worker at social services told me that I must lose my house before I could qualify for government help because owning a home disqualified me even though my bank account at that time did not have enough money for the next month's mortgage to clear. I argued that I should get help before losing my house, because if I got help after the fact, then it would defeat the purpose of seeking help. I was told, too bad, those were the rules. No one cared about the fact that I had contributed hundreds of thousands of dollars in paying taxes over the years and made great contributions to society in many ways including providing affordable and often free healthcare to many of my indigent patients, more specifically the IUD patients for which I was now serving a prison sentence. The Social Services Department that handles food stamps had me fill a form with the question, "Have you ever been convicted of a crime?" and I figured that saying yes would disqualify me for food stamps. The moment I saw that question, I shredded the questionnaire, dropped it in the trash bin and went home. If my wife hadn't immediately found employment, we were ready to hit the street with the kids and a carriage like the other homeless you have seen in the streets.

Some white-collar criminals I met in prison are amazingly knowledgeable people. One such man, an elderly Japanese-American, told me when he heard my story and I'm paraphrasing here, he thought, "If you were Japanese, born and living in Japan, the Japanese government would have endowed you with the highest honor for what you did for your patients. I do not know of a civilized country that sends one of its own to prison for helping the poor by providing medical care at his own expense, simply because it interfered with the profits of a pharmaceutical company." Then he laughed and said, "You were born in the wrong country, my friend." He thought I was born in America. I corrected him that I hadn't been born here, I had come here from India seeking a less corrupt government. How ironic.

I did extensive research in the prison law library about the meaning and definition of the word *restitution* as interpreted in case laws and textbooks on Criminal Law. The harshest, the most extreme legal interpretation by the government, that I came across was that an offender owes restitution even if he/she didn't personally financially benefit himself/herself but the victims lost money. Even if we were to accept this most stringent of all interpretations of restitution, a definition devised by some prosecutor for his self-aggrandizement, the federal government still has explaining to do for its prosecutorial actions against me. Here is why: Thoroughly audited estimates that I brought before Judge Ralph Dash in the Medical Board license revocation case in 2017 showed that my total estimated upfront hard cost of providing 152 IUDs to 149 patients over a period of five years was $440 per IUD case, a total of $67,760 for 152 IUDs. Hard cost refers to the upfront cost which came out of my pocket before I could offer this IUD and its health- related services to a patient. $440 dollars break down into $200 for the IUD device, $40 dollars for surgical tray for the surgical implant, the remaining $200 estimated for the upfront cost of necessary ultrasound for correct placement, and malpractice premium which I must pay upfront before I could offer such a service. This was just the upfront hard cost and did not include the soft cost of running overhead and salaries. I received a total of $47,452 from insurance companies in reimbursements. This means that these 149 patients owed me the difference, $20,308, a loss to my practice, upfront money that came out of my pocket [Exhibit 18]. The bundling code J7300 reimbursed for all these services as one global payment. In the billing CPT – ICD code book under Medicare's guidelines, a code is bundled when necessary services that go with the surgical procedure are not paid separately (Exhibit 20).

This is the audited summary that I submitted to Judge Dash, who did not dispute or contest the validity of that calculation.

If I were to include the soft costs such as employee's salaries, workers comp, rent, various insurance bills, utility bills and the rest of the overhead, patients would owe me additional $67,760 which would bring the total amount owed to me to $88,068. This is calculated based on the research data that shows that private practice Ob/Gyn's overhead cost is over 50 percent of all revenues collected before a physician could draw any salary for himself (Exhibit 18). I could have billed my patients for this over a period of five years but I did not because I made that choice. In other words, it would have cost my patients $135,520 ($67,760x2) if I were to charge them for all services that I had to perform to provide this contraceptive service, the amount they would have paid if they went to any other Ob/Gyn office in California. Now I will leave it to the American people to judge if I owe money in restitution to the government or the government owes me money in restitution. How could I have defrauded anyone, patients or insurance for receiving $47,452 on the one hand and spending $67,760 upfront from my pocket? How did I defraud my patients of money or property by having written off additional $67,760 which would have been my salary?

My salary and source of income in my practice came from billing insurance for my other patients (non-IUD patients) who were middle-aged federal employees, or officers at the Edwards Airforce base, and local businesses whose private insurances paid me well for my services. IUD service is one of the very few gynecological services in the United States for which insurance companies refuse to reimburse it all. They often do not reimburse and when they do, they reimburse it as a global payment and reimburse only a fraction of the total cost. The general rule is that about one third to half of the total cost is reimbursed by insurance companies, and patients pay the other half to two thirds, which translates into several hundred dollars for a patient. In other words, if an insurance company were to reimburse $400 to a physician for all IUD- related services, which is an actual average when an insurance policy does cover the service, one can multiply that number by a factor of two to roughly calculate the grand total cost to the patient to obtain such services from a private Ob/Gyn in practice. This translates into $800 from the patient's out-of-pocket cost. This is why American women do not opt for IUDs except for the wealthy few, unless they choose to go for some brand such as T Safe made in Europe, and the reason why thousands of Ob/Gyn's in the country are using the IUDs bought from England or Germany or their Canadian distributors, with the aim to lower the out-of-pocket cost for the patients.

The question arises, why was I so generous to my patients in not charging them their portion of the total cost? I made this exception for my indigent patients for an important health care service that they needed on this to prevent meth-addicted women from giving birth to meth addicted babies. The town Tehachapi, an indigent rural area where I practice is a very isolated place in the mountains of Kern County and is known as "Meth Mountain" because many poor who reside there are addicted to Methamphetamines. My attorney Spackman explained this to the judge in my Medical Board case. My generosity resulted in saving the taxpayer millions in Neonatal intensive care unit costs for the addicted newborns, and it was my way of paying back the community for their patronage. My family and I do not pay the church 10 percent every year; we believe that it serves a better purpose if our money goes where it belongs. We help the poor because my wife and I both come from poor families and we understand what it is like to be poor. You will never understand this unless you have experienced the humiliation that poverty can bring in your life on a daily basis. Theoretically, I am entitled to be paid for all services I have rendered for free as would any physician in a private practice. I am not suggesting, however, that these patients need to pay me because they owe me. Choosing not to bill these patients for the differences in cost was a conscious choice I made. In retrospect, I wish I knew when I did this that helping the poor was a recipe for going to prison in America, because the poor are treated like scum of the earth here, unlike any other country on the planet. So, I will leave it to the American people to decide after reading my story if I owe the government restitution or the government owes me. And more importantly, how Delahunty's definition of restitution fits the crime.

The prosecutors in my case misapplied and abused the definition of *restitution*. Not only did patients financially benefit from this, but the prosecutor probably benefitted on a personal level. As a result of my case, and others like it, he may have gotten a promotion, or an increase in salary because his record on convictions of white-collar criminals now looks better on his resume. What I am saying is not a strange notion; look at what happened to all the corrupt prosecutors who were caught red-handed in corruption in the Department of Justice under the Obama administration. They were promoted by the Obama administration. They were rewarded for their depravity and lack of basic morals. Corruption in the Obama administration's DOJ had reached its highest peak since the dawn of the Corporate welfare state in the early 1970s.

One does not have to study law when it is easy to rely on one's common sense to understand that a person who is convicted of a crime, one who owes financial restitution must have to have fraudulently stolen victims' money or property, not *given* them the money and property, as I did. So, you see government corruption can go as far as completely reversing the definitions from "I owe you" to "you owe me." This is the same as when our government calls its own terrorist acts against foreign enemies counter-terrorism when it wants to smash a foreign opponent who is not willing to give us free access to its natural resources, minerals and oil.

I would like to address the civil lawsuits filed against me by patients who were encouraged by Delahunty and Pueschel to do so. A patient can sue for a minimum of $250,000 for pain and suffering in the State of California. If all 149 patients were to sue me for $250,000 each, the amount of money I would owe them would be a minimum of $37,250,000. That figure could easily top 100 million dollars if judges chose to compensate patients for other damages that they could easily claim based on Delahunty's assertions against me with a felony attached to my name. Given the fact that I was told that I would have no defense against civil suits because I did not just plead guilty to a felony charge, but also used dangerous IUDs, there was no way for me out of this mess. My medical malpractice insurance covered me for a maximum of three million dollars, but I wasn't sure they would have covered me for this type of claim based on an alleged crime and even if they had, it would have left me with a balance that would be impossible to pay. Fortunately, only one patient out of the 149 sued me. Not too many patients out of the 149 provided the Patient Impact Reports to the prosecutors despite the prosecutor and the FDA's best efforts to manipulate them with lies and pursue them all around the country wherever they have moved to by spending millions of dollars of taxpayer's hard-earned money,

money which is yours and mine. I asked my attorney, Gluck, why the prosecutor was so determined to criminalize me when we had rendered all his accusations, step by step pointless and baseless, and he said something like, "Perhaps they want to justify all the money that they have already spent on the FDA investigation."

I believe that the patient who did sue me, and those who provided Patient Impact Reports, knew in their heart of hearts, that they were falsifying and exaggerating their symptoms beyond the usual side effects of the IUD, and did so because the prosecutor was pushing them to do so through psychology and criminal disinformation. They believed the lies and were angry that they had received a fake, unsafe, dangerous IUD that I had allegedly bought on the internet, or they were hoping for some cash to alleviate their everyday financial struggles.

I gave Bowman multiple female patients' consumer reports that were posted on Google by patients who complained about the total cost of ParaGard Copper IUD-services from their doctor's office, in some cases as much as $1,200 out-of-pocket. They also described the same side effects they experienced from ParaGard as listed in the ParaGard Drug insert as those my patients experienced from the German made IUD. Bowman conveniently looked the other way. I knew that I could not submit this information as an Exhibit of the proof of evidence because the source of such information was the internet, which would be debatable, but I wanted my attorney to see what female patients were saying about the cost and the complications from the ParaGard. Bowman did not even consider pursuing any of this as an argument in my defense because she said information from the internet is inadmissible evidence in the court.

I will briefly tell you the story of the one civil lawsuit, the only one brought against me. This suit was filed very shortly before I was ready to surrender to prison. My malpractice attorney, Michael Gonzalez, informed me that he would not be able to defend this case because I had pled guilty. I begged him to review this patients' medical records that she allegedly had with other physicians so I could show him why the suit was bogus. But he said it did not matter what the facts were, he simply did not know how to defend this case, because I had pled guilty which the patient was now using to show that harm was done to her. This was a terrifying experience for my wife, my children and I to think how many more such suits may come forth in the future that were indefensible. Gonzalez knew I was days away from going to prison and would be gone for a while, so he wanted me to sign an authorization form to settle with this patient while I was gone to prison. He said the case could not wait till I got out of prison. When I asked him for copies of the plaintiff's records from her new gynecologist who removed the IUD due to her reported "side effects", he simply ignored me because he felt it was irrelevant, there was no point, he could not defend the case and that he must settle on my behalf.

The long and short of this is that I signed the paperwork giving him authority to settle, just before I left for the prison, thinking that he would agree to pay $5,000 to this patient. I was familiar with his settlement style from a similar case a decade prior and trusted him to take care of it while I was gone. In August of 2016, when I called my wife from prison, she informed me that she received a phone call from Mr. Gonzalez, appointed by Norcal as my defense attorney for the civil malpractice case, who told her that the insurance company agreed to pay the plaintiff $250,000. I tried to contact Gonzalez through email, but prison officials who did not allow any contact with attorneys blocked my emails. The Bureau of Prisons does not allow prisoners to contact any attorneys when they request it, even when there is ongoing legal representation. I have discussed this prison policy in detail in my other book, *Prison Torture in AmericA: Shocking Tales from the Inside.* The prison officials had also blocked me from emailing my Medical Board attorney, Spackman.

This suit against me was another example to me, of our legal system, where all lawsuits, civil or criminal, are built not based on the discovery of truth but technicalities. The courts are not interested in facts, but fiction. Lose or win depends on who is better at playing the game. When I told my wife how upset I was that this patient got away with what amounted to a financial scam, my wife said something profound that I will never forget. She said, "She is poor and needs the money. The rich insurance company has lost nothing." Although I feel morally violated, I must agree with my wife that poor people in this country who are struggling to feed their children, will do whatever they can to ease their burden. We live in a world where fewer than 50 individuals own more than half of the wealth on this planet, and as far as our government keeping busy serving our corporations is concerned, the rest of us can starve.

"Mail Fraud Statute": Archaic Laws Vaguely and Corruptly Used

I have consulted the book *Corruption in America* by Law Professor, Zephyr Teachout from Fordham University that describes the history of the Mail Fraud Statute. Her goal is to show how the statute's original meaning has been turned on its head by the corrupt prosecutors and government in our country. The Statute was passed in 1862 primarily to criminalize state and federal officials who used U.S. mail to enrich themselves by receiving lavish gifts in the mail from their corporate sponsors and foreign powers. Today prosecutors frequently use the same statute through vague interpretations to prevent ordinary people from ordering lifesaving drugs from outside the U.S. In 1927, this Statute was interpreted to criminalize the theft of honest services. Over the next 60 years, the federal court of appeals made mail fraud the statute of choice for bribery of state officials.

In a series of cases, district after district expanded the application of the law to prohibit corporations against inducing public officials to use their public roles for personal gain. Public officials were required to disclose their ownership interest in a corporation or a pharmaceutical company when it was recommended that their city use the corporation's services. Prosecutors in federal jurisdictions were allowed to bring mail fraud cases to the jury when there was evidence of a public official's intent to defraud the public. Since the 1970's, corporations have learned to buy public officials, judges, and prosecutors who have now changed their interpretation of the statute so it applies only to the poor while they successfully sweep public officials' crimes under the rug. Money has been declared as free speech by the reactionary Supreme Court now, which means any corporation can give as much bribe money to government officials as it deems fit as long as it is not given in the form of a bagful of cash as quid pro quo in return for favors. Politicians now have no hesitation in telling their constituents what they want to hear to get their votes and then immediately dump them all, the moment they leave for Washington D.C. Any method of bribing except quid pro quo is now 100 percent legal. Corporations are allowed to buy all three branches of the government for cash, and they have, thanks to our Supreme Court made of 9 people who are eager to serve the oligarchs. The country is run by one political party, the business party with two factions, one Republican and the other the so-called Democrats. From now on, the only people that would be subject to this mail fraud statute and many other vague and corruptly passed statutes and regulations drafted in recent decades by corporate lobbyists and rubber-stamped by Congress under the direct fiat from corporations will be the poor of this country. The government can send a person to prison if they buy Marathon Pharmaceutical's lifesaving drug Enflaza for $1,000 from the United Kingdom, instead of having to pay $100,000 for it to buy it in the U.S. It is a crime to buy Marathon's own drug cheaper from Europe, now that the FDA has approved it for sale right here at home. 12,000 boys suffering from this terrible muscle wasting disease, called Duchenne Muscular Dystrophy, who desperately need the drug but whose families cannot afford to pay $100,000 a year will be unable to walk by the time they are 12 and on average will only live to be 26. The government would rather have these people die than to allow anyone to stand in the way of Marathon's profits by attempting to buy Marathon's drug from the United Kingdom. Marathon will only allow people in Europe to obtain its drug at one hundredth of the price that we have to pay here. There are hundreds of other drugs like this inaccessible to the U.S. population, some pills cost as much as $1,000 a tablet. Drugs that cost hundreds of thousands of dollars to a million dollars per year in the U.S., are available at a fraction of the cost in Europe and elsewhere, equivalent versions of the same drugs manufactured by the same U.S. pharmaceutical companies. Parents who are desperate to help their children cannot buy Marathon's drug from England, they must buy it here at a 10,000 percent markup.

When Delahunty charged me with mail fraud, I asked Bowman to review the mail fraud statute and explain to me how it applied to my case. I tried to read the drug importation law to the best of my ability and found nothing stating that a U.S. citizen could not buy a life saving drug from Europe in the event it was sold at a price unaffordable by most Americans with the exception of the super wealthy. I asked Bowman to read the statute from a lawyer's viewpoint and point out where it stated that buying an affordable Copper IUD manufactured in Germany that I shipped from Canada was against the law. Her response was that the statute is general and not specific to the IUD. Then I asked her to show me where it said it was illegal to order a safe drug from another country. She replied that the statute was thousands of pages long, too complicated and there was no way she was going to read it for me.

The drug companies have often made the argument that they have to sell their drugs at exorbitant prices because they need the money from profits for research and development. It is imperative for the American people to know that 80 percent of the research done in pharmaceuticals and biotechnology is publicly funded, research that is conducted at our universities with public funds. Once the discovery is made and a new drug discovered and tested, the results are handed over to Big Pharma on a silver platter so that it could now literally rob the consumers the second time around, the same tax-payers who already paid for the drug's research and development once. This research money is your money and my money, the tax payer's money which means we should benefit from this research, not drug companies. Unfortunately, our government officials work for the drug giants who paid to buy their elections, and not for us. The remaining 20 percent of the research by Big Pharma is not research per se, it is primarily product research to enhance profits, such as, for example, how to slightly modify a molecule in an existing drug and get a new patent to market it as a new drug under a different drug name to add a few more billion dollars of profit on top of the original. Thanks to our governmental institutions that have socialized the cost and risk of drug development on the shoulders of the poor of this country while it has privatized the profits from it once the research is completed. This is nothing short of criminal.

Violations of U.N. Charter, International Conventions, Human Rights & International Criminal Court

The international community that includes the United States has established a gold standard in terms of human rights. That standard has been named the Universal Declaration of Human Rights adopted in December of 1948 and agreed upon by all nations after experiencing the horror of the second world war. There is only one country today among those that signed on, that continues to violate nearly all provisions of the Universal Declaration of Human Rights. You guessed it right, that country is the United States of America.

When the fiftieth anniversary of the declaration was celebrated in 1998, newspapers wrote that the United States had been a beacon of human rights and democracy and had courageously upheld the human rights declaration as opposed to many countries that are frequent violators of these human rights. Not a single newspaper or media outlet in the U.S. reported that the United States is the only country on the planet that unilaterally exempted itself from being held accountable for any human right violations including committing genocides around the globe in violation of the Universal Declaration of human rights that it had taken a key role in establishing once upon a time. To this day, half a century later, the United States does not officially recognize two-thirds of the human rights listed in Article 25 of the Declaration, especially the ones that refer to social and economic justice and freedom from torture and genocides.

The Human Rights Watch and Amnesty International and many international leagues have repeatedly pointed out that the United States is in the lead in violating human rights at home and especially abroad. This is due to unilaterally declared assumption of American Exceptionalism, under which we are entitled to commit any number of human rights violations both at home and abroad. The rules of civilization that apply to the rest of the world do not apply to us, because we are an exception.

The research data available from the 31 wealthiest OECD (Organization of Economic Cooperation and Development) countries ranks the United States as number 31 on its list of human rights. Our media is forbidden from even thinking about it, let alone talking or writing about it. The United States routinely commits the same human rights violations around the world, the ones that it would invade another country for, and slaughter millions of its men, women, and children over. And the U.S. has done this over and over again since the second world war in nearly every country on the planet while making a mockery of its promises of commitment to the U.N. Declaration that it brags about being the author of.

The Universal Declaration of Rights lists three categories of human rights, political and civil rights, community and cultural rights, and social and economic rights. The United States is the only country in the world that openly brags about its ability, because of its military might, to thumb its nose at these human rights. For example, Jean Kirkpatrick of the State Department in the Reagan

Administration officially rejected the social and economic rights of the Universal Declaration as a "letter to Santa Claus." The United States has always made a mockery of article 25 of the Universal Declaration that calls for the fundamental rights of people to basic healthcare, employment, and the right to be free from hunger. The Bush administration called article 25 of the Declaration, a "dangerous provocation." As far as community and cultural rights are concerned, the United States considers it so ridiculous that it is not even worth discussing. The United States recognizes civil and political rights only in principle but not in practice.

It is ironic that the United States was the dominant player in giving birth to the United Nations and now it will choke any country to death if we can show that it has violated any human rights as listed in the United Nations charter. We take pride in being the number one rogue state and a terrorist nation in the world because of our military might as long as we can somehow manage to convince our population through the mass media that we are the good guys. There have been hundreds of Security Council and General Assembly resolutions in which the U.S is on one side and the rest of the world on the other. Whenever a weak country has been found to have violated a U.N. rule, ever since the formation of the UN. Charter, the United States has often taken punitive action and demanded other countries do the same. OECD Annual Reports on Social Justice repeatedly show the United States ranks the lowest in almost anything: human rights records, childhood poverty, infant mortality, education, life expectancy, healthcare, maternal and infant death, mortality and morbidity, life expectancy, workers' rights, public health, and public transportation. Available data confirms that the U.S. now ranks lower than many third world countries in many respects. Unfortunately, the media is not supposed to tell us any of that because that would be anti-American.

Recently Bloomberg reported something which I cannot believe my ears to this day when I think about it. The news item reported research findings of a study done to evaluate healthcare cost vs. outcomes in 200 countries, which is essentially the entire planet, and it was discovered that the United States, although the most expensive in healthcare ranks among the lowest among two hundred countries in terms of outcomes, which means that there are scores of poverty-ridden third world countries on the planet where you can get better healthcare free of cost than what you get in the United States as a U.S. citizen. You are much more likely to survive a health catastrophe in India without a dime in your pocket than you will in the United States with Obamacare. My readers will find this fact hard to swallow, but this is a fact. Famous professor of economics, Richard Wolff also reported this Bloomberg research on his radio show. After hearing about this Bloomberg research, the story of our government as told in this book about poor women being prevented from accessing cheaper contraceptive healthcare should not surprise you anymore. My IUD case now should pale in front of the news that tells us that our country is engaged in wholesale healthcare crimes against the entire U.S. population.

The United States of America is a party to the United Nations. Human Rights are described in the Preamble to the Universal Declaration of Human Rights of the United Nations. Americans who are not familiar with the true meaning of "American exceptionalism" should read the Preamble. The U.S. is not subject to the rules of most of the international organizations and conventions that America took the lead role in creating. I'm referring to organizations such as the United

Nations, International Criminal Court, World Bank, International Monetary Fund, International Human Rights organizations, Geneva and other international conventions, and the Nuremberg Principles for war crimes. Every country in the world is held accountable if it commits a war crime, violate human rights, genocide, aggression against another nation, or any violent crime of magnitude, but the United States can engage in all those violations, no questions asked. Because of all of this, please allow me to end this book by reviewing with you the relevant sections of the Preamble to the Universal Declaration of Human Rights of the United nations, which the United States took the leading role in writing and always took credit for.

> The PREAMBLE to the Universal Declaration of Human Rights of the United Nations states:
>
> Whereas recognition of the inherent dignity and of the equal and inalienable right of all members of the human family is the foundation of freedom, justice, and peace in the world.
>
> Whereas disregard and contempt for human rights have resulted in barbarous acts which have outraged the conscience of mankind, and the advent of a world in which human beings shall enjoy freedom of speech and belief and freedom from fear and want has been proclaimed as the highest aspiration of the common people.
>
> Whereas it is essential, if a man is not to be compelled to have recourse, as a last resort, to rebellion against tyranny and oppression, that human rights should be protected by the rule of law.
>
> Whereas member states have pledged themselves (and the U.S is a prominent member of the United Nations, in fact first

among equals) to achieve, in cooperation with the United Nations, the promotion of universal respect for an observance of human rights and fundamental freedoms.

Whereas a common understanding of these rights and freedoms is of the greatest importance for the full realization of the pledge.

Now, therefore, the General Assembly proclaims THIS UNIVERSAL DECLARATION OF HUMAN RIGHTS as a common standard of achievement for all peoples and all nations, to the end that every individual and every organ of the society, keeping this Declaration constantly in mind, shall strive by teaching and education to promote respect for those rights and freedoms and by progressive measures, national and international, to secure their universal and effective recognition and observances, both among the peoples of Member States themselves and among the peoples of territories under the jurisdiction.

(The above was primarily drafted by the United States which was at the helm of affairs at the time of its drafting. Little did the drafters, who spoke from their hearts, know that there were people sitting behind their backs, the men in charge would make a mockery of it all.)

Article 2: Everyone is entitled to all the rights and freedoms set forth in the Declaration, without distinction of any kind, such as race, color, sex, language, religion, political or other opinion, national or social origin, property, birth or other status. Furthermore, no distinction shall be made based on political, jurisdictional or international status of the country or territory to which a person belongs, whether it be independent, trust, non-self-governing or under any other limitation of sovereignty.

Article 5: No one shall be subjected to torture or a cruel, inhuman or degrading treatment or punishment. (The United States is the only country on the planet that does not recognize torture as torture, and subjects detainees and prisoners to inhuman treatment by using its own unique definitions of what torture is or is not, in violation of the international laws that it helped draft, then agreed to honor. For example, everyone else in the world recognizes solitary confinement as torture except the United States.)

Article 7: All are equal before the law and are entitled without any discrimination to equal protection of the law. All are entitled to equal protection against any discrimination in violation of this Declaration and against any incitement to such discrimination.

Article 8: Everyone has the right to an effective remedy by the competent national tribunals for acts violating the fundamental rights granted him by the Constitution or by law.

Article 9: No one will be subject to arbitrary arrest, detention or exile.

Article 10: Everyone is entitled in full equality to a fair and public hearing by an independent and impartial tribunal, in the determination of his rights and obligations and of any criminal charge against him.

Article 11: Everyone charged with a penal offense has the right to be presumed innocent until proven guilty according to law in a public trial at which he has had all the guarantees necessary for the defense.

ACKNOWLEDGEMENTS

MY SPECIAL THANKS TO MAUREEN BARBERIO AND SUE Kauffman who reviewed the original contents of *Guilty at Gunpoint* and The *Death of the Rule of Law* manuscripts and the evidence presented in Exhibits that I put together to support my claims of corruption in the government of the United States. Rhoda Feng, editor of Public Citizen deserves my gratitude for her assistance with reviewing the accuracy of the resource list at the end of the book, and proof-reading the manuscripts.

I also like to express my indebtedness to Noam Chomsky who made himself readily available to answer many complex questions and give me advice as appropriate as and when I asked for it, prior to the publication of these books. I am equally grateful to Mary Rasenberger, the CEO of Authors Guild of New York, Michael Gross of Authors Guild, David Snyder, the Executive Director of the First

Amendment Coalition of Lawyers, and its affiliated lawyers, Karl Olson, Duffy Carolan, and James Chadwick who freely consulted with me when I called them. I am thankful to ACLU affiliated first amendment and civil rights attorneys who advised me or tried their best to advise me or refer me to the right people who would address my civil, constitutional, and first amendment rights in writing these exposes. Finally, the credit of detailed review of my manuscripts from a legal perspective goes to Jonathan Kirsch, a copyright and first amendment attorney with 40 years of experience in legally reviewing pre-publication materials, also an author of two books on Publishing Law.

I would not have been able to accomplish these books in a timely manner without the emotional support and encouragement from various activist organizations and individuals, who gave me their time and expertise in explaining copyright and first amendment law, not only as it applied to Guilty at Gunpoint and its companion book, but also the other two books that I wrote about the prison conditions during my incarceration.

RESOURCE LIST

U.S. District Judge Emmet Sullivan

Alex Kozinski, Chief Judge, Ninth Circuit Appeals Court

American Free Press

David Rieff

Marcia Angell MD

In memory of Zahara Heckster

Senator Chuck Grassley

StopPharmagreed.com

Alexis Pleus, Executive Director of Truth Pharm

Times of Israel

Judge Betty Fletcher

Judge Sidney Thomas

Chad Joy, FBI's whistleblower

William Hodes

David Lat, editor at large of Above the Law

Sidney Powell

Zephyr Teachout

Gerry Spence

Ron Paul

Rand Paul

Martha Rosenberg

Mike Papantonio

EurimPharm, Germany generic IUD manufacturer

Harvey Silverglate, author of *Three Felonies a Day*

Michael S. Greco, former president of the American Bar Association

James Duane

Mark Godsey

Marianne Udo-Phillip, Executive Director of the Center for Healthcare Research & Transformation, University of Michigan.
AAUW
Margaret Flowers
Dorothy Rabinowitz
Susan R. Estrich
John Pfaff, Professor of Law at Fordham University
Professor Heather Johnson
Doctors Without Borders
Doug Casey
Robert Greenwald
Jennifer Reisch
Michael Marmot
John Porter
Canadian drugs .com
Gary Ruskin
WBAI
Lucy Flores
Ralph Nader
Larry Cohen
Justin Porter
Brandon Terry
Fight for the Future
Who runs Government
National Coalition Against Censorship
Lawfare
OpenSecrets.org
Equality Now
Women under Siege
Drug Truth Network
Students for Sensible Drug Policy
DrugSense
Corporate Crime Reporter
PR Watch
Corporate Crime
Top 10 Corporate Criminals of 2015
CorpWatch
Reclaim Democracy!
Physicians for a National Health Program
Inequality.org
People's World
Center for Popular Democracy
Resource Center of the Americas
World Health Organization
Physicians for Reproductive Health
Unite for Reproductive and Gender Equity
Union of Concerned Scientists
Working American
Center for American Progress
The New Civil Rights Movement
National Council of Negro Women
Native Americans Rights Fund
Freedom for All Americans
National Lawyers Guild
Advancement Project
Leadership Conference on Civil Rights
American Civil Liberties Union
NAACP
Black Lives Matter

National Women's Law Center
Free Speech Radio News
Free School
Jim Hightower
The Head on Radio Network
American Urban Radio Networks
People Tower
BackersofHate.org
Media Matters
Truth Out
Truthdig.com
ProPublica Investigations
Who What Why
Fairness and Accuracy in Reporting
Center for Public Integrity
MuckRock
SourceWatch
Fact Check
Crooks and Liars
Project Censored
Democratic Underground
Working Families Party
The Thistle, MIT
CovertAction Quarterly
League of Women Voters
Women's March Coalition
Women's Campaign Forum
Jezebel
Dissent Magazine
Nation of Change
Daily Beast
Talking Points Memo
Demand Progress
Democratic Socialists of America
Democracy Alliance
AlterNet
CREDO Action
Young Democrats of America
Linda McQuaig
Lawrence Lessig
Glenn Greenwald
Book TV
Judge Wallace Tashima
Michael Adams
Hugh Aynesworth
Victor Sperandeo
Mike Moses
James Davis
Steven Bernstein
Ira Lee Sorkin
Trial Lawyers for Justice
NAACP
ACLU
Stuart Namm
Lucas Walker
Steven Molo
Jeff Lamken
John Emshwiller and Rebecca Smith
Kurt Eichenwald
Huck Gutman
Newsmax TV
Howard Zinn
Lee Camp
Chris Hedges
Alex Winter
Amy Goodman
KGL Talk Radio

KFCF Free Speech Radio
Somerville Community Access Radio
Ellen Schrecker
The Hawks RT
George Galloway
Ramparts.com
Oliver Stone
Robert Corn Revere
AAUP
Bernie Sanders
Matt Taibbi
Revolutiontruth.org
Michael Moore
Crossing the Rubicon
CA PRA Public Records 1798
Websites of Marathon Pharmaceuticals, Teva Pharma, Jazz Pharma
CIA's Greatest Hits
Miriam Abu Sharkh
National Lawyers Guild
Z Magazine
Pacifica Radio Stations
Counterpunch
The Progressive
BlackCommentator.com
$ 516-29 Federal Statutes and Regulations (see Legal Section of the book for Legal references)
Stuart Taylor Jr.
Errol Morris
Bruce Fein
Steven Pinker
Adam Liptak
"Jailhouse Nation," *The Economist*
Three Days of the Condor by Robert Redford
Timothy Pilgrim, Australian film director/activist
Abby Martin
Reporters Without Borders
Medea Benjamin
Emily Ekins
Susan Harley
Susan Sarandon
Richard Belzer, Comedian
Jimmy Dore, Comedian
Tabetha Wallace
Jesse Ventura
Tyrel Ventura
Sean Stone
American justice Channel
Media Edge Channel
The Sanders Institute
Justine Bamberg
The Trial Lawyer Magazine
Shannon Jackson
Kyle Mercado (Our revolution)
Robert Weissman
Alternative Media Magazine
KGO Radio
The New York Review of Books
Larry Cohen
All the Plenary's Men
Craig Murray
Woody Harrelson
Project Veritas undercover videos

Cenk Uygur, Young Turks
Dr. Leana Sheyrle Wen
The Hart House
The Harvard Book Store
Peter Singer
John Nichols
Mollye Barros
Paul George
The Washington Spectator
Jordan Chariton
Radio WZBC Boston College
Marianne Williamson
Baz Dreisinger
Alternative Radio
Rob Mariani
Freedomain Radio
Annie Machon
Nina Turner
The Guardian
The Guerilla News Network
Democracy Now
Spare Change News
Catalina Velasquez
The New School
Sean Parker (Sean Parker Foundation)
Michael Sandel
Jen Senko
Thom Hartmann
Robert Reich
Dean Corn
Gary Johnson
Tamara Draut
Tim Canova
Russ Feingold
Jeff Merkley
Ameera David
Erin Bilbray
Dr. Kent Mesplay
Jill Stein
Melinda St. Louis
Steven Christian
Vincent Emanuele
Nick Davies
Donald Boström
Dana Priest
Thomas Tamm
Tom Devine
David Carr
Harvey Kaye
Katrina vanden Heuvel
Jonathan Tasini
Megan Markle
Jane Mayer
Bill Press
Ted Rall
Harold Pinter
John Pilger
Peter Joseph
Vivienne Westwood
Miguel Francis-Santiago
Lawrence Wilkerson
Virginia Held
Catherine Mackinnon (feminist)
Naomi Klein
Gary Null
Richard Eskow
Rama Rao

Henry Wallace
A Modest Proposal by Jonathan Swift
Manufacturing Consent by Noam Chomsky and Edward Herman
Profit Over People by Noam Chomsky
How the World Works by Noam Chomsky
Maryl Steeple
Lillian Crackel and Cindy Boiler
Joie Chen
Tad Devine
Rep. Pramila Jayapal
Jeff Weaver
Vinay Devnath
Deborah Parker
Shannon Jackson, Executive Director of Our Revolution
Andrew Kreig (author and founder of the Justice Integrity Project)
Judge Thelton Henderson
Thomas Wilner and Andy Worthington
Molly Crabapple
The Innocence Project
Michelle Alexander
Eugen Puryear
Heather Thomson
Jerry Allen Bailye (an innocent man in prison for 30 years)
MK Asante
Barret Brown
Kerry Kennedy
Ray McGovern
Jack Rice
John Kiriakou
John Irk
Angela Davis
Cato Institute (Prison Project)
Carol Anderson
Alexa Koenig (Human Rights Center, Berkeley School of Law)
Human Right Watch
Reporters without Borders
60 Days In
Kevin Zeese
Los Angeles Times: "Prison Faulted for Poor Healthcare"
USA Today: Kevin Johnson: "Nurses Assigned to Guard Prisoners"
USA Today: David Jolly: Journalist on Inmate Healthcare
Prisoner's Wives
Blogs for Prisoners
Jailhouse Lawyers handbook
Aid to Children for Imprisoned Mothers
American Friends Service Committee Criminal Justice Program
California Prison Focus
Center for Constitutional Rights
Criminal Justice Policy Coalition
Critical Justice
Federal Resource Center for Children of Prisoners

Friends and Families of Incarcerated Individuals
Legal Services for Prisoners with Children
Partnership for Safety and Justice – Prison Program
Peter Cicchino Youth Project of the Urban Justice Center
Prison Activist Resource Center
A Comprehensive Guide to Prison and Parole Law
Prison Self-help Legal clinic
Southern Center for Human Rights
Southern Poverty Law Center
Sylvia Rivera Law Project
TGI Justice Project San Francisco, CA
Transformative Justice Law Project of Illinois
Family and Corrections Network
Child Welfare League of America
Prison Legal News (Vermont)
Criminal Law Reporter
Dr. Darron Smith
Fund for Civic Rights
Tim Lynch
Benjamin Jealous
Pattie Brassard
Professor Leif Wenar of King's College, London
Greg Palast
California Guardian photojournalists
Edgar Cahn
Tavis Smiley
Lawrence B. Jones
In These Times
The New Press
Dollars and Sense magazine
Tulsi Gabbard (Sanders Institute Fellow)
Cape Codders for Peace and Justice
Human Rights watch Prison Project
Mark Hertsgaard
Thomas Drake
William Binny
John Crane
Daniel Ellsberg
Michael Isikoff
Michael DeKort
Seymour Hersh
Franz Gayl
Alex Poucher, Million Masks March
Shaker Aamer
Keith Best
American Friends Service Committee (Criminal Justice Program)
Alexander C. Lichtenstein, Professor of History, University of Pennsylvania
Michael A. Kroll
Rachael Kamel
Pennisula Peace and Justice Cente
Dreams publication
Michael Parenti

Senator Orrin Hatch
Law Schools, Social Justice Projects
Ralph Nader
Stephen Giller
William Hodes
Andrew Napolitno
GAP (Government Accountability Project)
1612 K. St. NW Suite 1100
Washington DC 20006
202-457-0034
Public Citizen
1600 20th St. NW
Washington DC 20009
202 -588-1000
Daily Post Silicon Valley for Ist Amendment
FDA Corruption and Scandals by Dr John Bergman
David Kaye UN Human Rights Council Official for Freedom of Expression
Lecture series at Stanford Continuing Education on Global Assault on Expression
Freedom of the Press Foundation (Freedom. Press)
Lannan Foundation
James Riser
CCS Criminal Capture System
Alexa Van Brunt (Blog)
Thomas W. Simon (Ranking on International Crimes)
Times of India
Hindustan Times
Common Dreams
Open Society Justice, Budapest
Amrit Singh
Michael Parenti
People for the American Way
Daily Kos
Karli Wallace Thomson
Genevieve Jones Wright
Noah Phillips
Pamela Price
Mother Jones Magazine
FirstAmendmentCoalition.org
First Amendment Project

CPSIA information can be obtained
at www.ICGtesting.com
Printed in the USA
FSHW020118070120
65337FS

9 780997 054187